Women, Gender, and Terrorism

STUDIES IN SECURITY AND INTERNATIONAL AFFAIRS

WOMEN,
GENDER, and
TERRORISM

Edited by

LAURA SJOBERG AND CARON E. GENTRY

The University of Georgia Press

Athens & London

© 2011 by the University of Georgia Press
Athens, Georgia 30602
www.ugapress.org
All rights reserved
Designed by Walton Harris
Set in 10/14 Adobe Caslon Pro

Most University of Georgia Press titles are
available from popular e-book vendors.

Printed digitally

Library of Congress Cataloging-in-Publication Data

Women, gender, and terrorism / edited by Laura Sjoberg and
Caron E. Gentry.
xv, 250 p. ; 24 cm. –– (Studies in security and international affairs)
Includes bibliographical references and index.
ISBN 978-0-8203-3583-4 (cloth : alk. paper) —
ISBN 978-0-8203-4038-8 (pbk. : alk. paper)
1. Violence in women. 2. Violence in women—Case studies.
3. Political violence. 4. Global politics. I. Sjoberg, Laura, 1979–
II. Gentry, Caron E.
HQ1233.W593 2011
303.6'25082—dc23   2011016411

British Library Cataloging-in-Publication Data available

To (and for) our colleagues, cohorts, and friends
without whom our careers would not be possible
and our lives would be less complete

CONTENTS

FOREWORD

Russell D. Howard

On December 13, 2009, a female suicide bomber attacked a police and CIA compound building in Peshawar, Pakistan, killing eleven people. She ran into a housing complex where officers lived and detonated a bomb attached to her body. Her attack was associated with attempts to thwart a Pakistani military attack on a Taliban mountain stronghold. The increased presence of women in the high-profile activities of al-Qaeda and other terrorist organizations across the world—in both kinetic and supporting roles—presents unique challenges for counterterrorism professionals, policy makers, and academic analysts.

Helping to work through these challenges is *Women, Gender, and Terrorism*, a timely and topical compilation of articles authored by an eclectic group of female terrorism experts. These selections were compiled by Jennie Stone, a recent recipient of a master's degree in law and diplomacy at the Fletcher School, Tufts University, and a lieutenant in the U.S. Naval Reserve who now works at the MITRE Corporation.

The genesis of this book was a grant from the Lynde and Harry Bradley Foundation to the Jebsen Center for Counter-Terrorism Studies, which culminated in an April 2007 conference at the Fletcher School entitled "Women and al-Qaeda." Several of this work's authors—Farhana Qazi, Alisa Stack, Caron Gentry, and Swati Parashar—presented papers at the conference. Stone planned and executed the conference with assistance from contributors Katherine Pattillo and Stacy Reiter Neal.

Both the conference and the scholarly work conducted by its participants were received with such enthusiasm that it made good sense to the conference organizers at the Jebsen Center and the Bradley Foundation to complete the enterprise with a published work.

Women, Gender, and Terrorism is not light fare. Instead, it is a comprehensive and factual recounting of the many varied — and often overlooked — aspects of women as terrorists, suicide bombers, supporters of terrorists, and even wives of terrorists. It also examines how women play an important role in counterterrorist activity. By examining the issue of gender in terrorism through women's involvement in terrorist activities, these articles make a valuable contribution to the expanding field of counterterrorism studies.

ACKNOWLEDGMENTS

This book originated at a conference hosted by the Jebsen Center for Counter-Terrorism Studies at Tufts University and has grown from there. Its completion would not have been possible without the hard and dedicated work of its contributors, General Howard, Jennie Stone, and others previously affiliated with the Jebsen Center. This book project has benefited from the financial, institutional, and creative support of the Boston Consortium for Gender, Security, and Human Rights; the Women and Public Policy Program at the Kennedy School of Government at Harvard University; the Feminist Theory and Gender Studies section of the International Studies Association; the Department of Political Science at the University of Florida; and the Department of Political Science at Virginia Polytechnic Institute and State University. This volume also would not exist if it hadn't been for the help and dedication of Nancy Grayson, our (totally amazing) editor at the University of Georgia Press or the press's excellent collection of work in security studies, of which we are honored to be a part. We are indebted to comments by anonymous reviewers that have made this manuscript stronger and more coherent. As we prepared this manuscript, the book's contributors' dialogues were interesting and exciting. We would like to thank two anonymous reviewers for the University of Georgia Press, who strengthened this manuscript substantially.

From Caron: Involvement in this project, from the conference hosted by the Jebsen Center to the various chapters I wrote for it to editing it, stems from various professional and personal relationships forged during my PhD to the current stage in my career. A special thanks to John Harrison for putting me in contact with Russell Howard, who then invited a young scholar to participate in a conference that opened many doors for her. As always, Laura has been a champion of mine and for all feminist work in international relations. Thank you for your effort in bringing this volume to completion. The interview with Leila Khaled was done while I was still a PhD candidate at the University of

St. Andrews. Financial support for that trip was made possible through the Department of International Relations and the Post-Graduate Student Travel Award Committee at St. Andrews. The interview never would have taken place if Anders Strindberg hadn't put me in touch with Leila—thank you for your trust. And I want to thank Leila for trusting me, being honest with me, and allowing me a glimpse into her life. I can only hope that I have represented your life faithfully. A special thanks goes to Dr. Kristina Campos who introduced me to the theorists I draw on in "The Neo-Orientalist Narratives of Women's Involvement in al-Qaeda"—what a great coach you were on this project! More importantly, I am fortunate to call you friend. And to the Kinzels, David, Peggy, and Jason, my home away from home for much of my life, thank you for letting me read to you early drafts of this essay and for your excellent suggestions. Finally, it would be remiss of me not to acknowledge the support that Abilene Christian University, my former academic home, gave to me. As an institution, it provided me with the means necessary to pursue this project. The Political Science department was also always a supportive and encouraging place to be and I want to specifically thank Drs. Mel Hailey and David Dillman for their confidence in me.

From Laura: First and foremost, I would like to express my gratitude to my coeditor Caron Gentry, whom I am *elated* to have had an opportunity to work with again. Caron has been such an inspiration to me as a friend and as a colleague, and I owe her a debt I will never be able to pay back. Personally, this book was edited at a transition time in my life, where I was going through a lot of changes, not the least of which was moving to the University of Florida, my new (and likely permanent) institutional home. Working with these brilliant authors' great empirical work helped me rediscover my motivation and my center. My center seems to be in Gainesville, Florida, among my Chihuahuas Max (who loves the space in Florida but hates the bugs), Gizmo (who dislikes the thunderstorms), and April (who, like me, is in love with the Florida sun). Personally and intellectually, my community at the University of Florida, including my mentor, Sammy Barkin, and my grad students (particularly those in "ABDs Anonymous"—Jessica, Joe, Ryan, Ty, Ingrid, and Ashley) have been sustaining forces.

Those of you who know my acknowledgments know that I often end with an example of why I think the work feminists do in international relations is so crucial. I recently received a review from a journal (anonymous of course), critiquing an article about women's violence (in that case, rape) "on meth-odological grounds" because it studied women who commit violence without comparing them to men who commit violence. While I won't argue that com-paring women to men can have some intellectual value, I remain floored that, in the twenty-first century, I have to justify studying *women* without compar-ing them to or using them as a foil for men. It's not even that, after centuries of political scientists studying (explicitly or implicitly) men and only men, I am arguing that we should study women and only women. Still, I do not under-stand how it could possibly be unreasonable to imagine that a journal article about women would be sufficient without a comparison to men. This book, and the chapters in it, are, unapologetically, *about women*, sometimes in comparison to each other, sometimes in comparison to men, sometimes not in comparison at all . . . but about women. We edit it, and present it, hoping there will come a day when that is no longer seen as a radical intellectual choice.

Women, Gender, and Terrorism

Introduction

WOMEN, GENDER, AND TERRORISM

Laura Sjoberg, Grace D. Cooke,
and Stacy Reiter Neal

A warning on the web page of the Israeli government published in 2003 notes that women's participation in terrorism in Palestine is increasing and that "the terrorist organizations behind the attacks want to exploit the advantages of dispatching females to perpetrate them . . . under the assumption that a female is thought of as soft, gentle, and innocent and therefore will arouse less suspicion than a man."[1] The website delineates the roles women have played in attacks, explaining that "the integration of females in terrorist activity can be divided among different levels, the highest being the *female suicide bomber* or one who intended to carry out a suicide attack but was thwarted. In addition, women have acted as *facilitators*, in both planning and perpetrating terrorist attacks."[2]

After mapping out the various kinds of women's involvement, the "warning" about women terrorists goes on to caution that "in each and every case, these women had a large amount of 'personal baggage.'"[3] Because of this, the Israeli government report concludes that "the *personal and social* motives appear to be the most dominant."[4] A number of reports from the scholarly and policy

1

worlds arrive at similar conclusions: women engage in terrorism largely for personal reasons.[5]

At the same time, recent academic work has questioned that conclusion. In 2007, Laura Sjoberg and Caron E. Gentry criticized the tendency to automatically explain women's violence as having different motivations from men's, arguing that, in many academic and policy discussions, "women who commit violence have been characterized as anything but regular criminals or regular soldiers or regular terrorists; they are captured in storied fantasies which deny women's agency and reify gender stereotypes and subordination."[6] Miranda Alison has noted in particular that women who engage in terrorism have been portrayed as unnatural, gender defiant, sexually deviant, psychologically unstable, or easily manipulated and has urged political scientists and policy makers to look seriously at the context of women's violence, which, she argues, would help to complicate and correct these portrayals.[7] An emerging literature looks to understand women's participation in terrorism in gender-sensitive ways—understanding that women terrorists (like all terrorists and all people) live in a gender-unequal world but also remaining open to understanding that individuals' personal and *political* choices are complicated and contingent.

Women have engaged in acts of terrorism in a number of capacities in modern history, including as part of such divergent organizations as the Ku Klux Klan in the American South and the Baader-Meinhof gang in Germany. Still, as the twenty-first century begins, women's terrorism—perhaps not unlike terrorism more generally—is changing. Women's participation in terrorism generally might be increasing, and women's engagement in suicide bombings has gone from virtually unheard of twenty years ago to somewhat commonplace in the current global political arena. Very recently, it was possible to somewhat reliably list women's involvement in suicide terrorist attacks in one book or even one book chapter, but such a project is increasingly unfeasible. Women's active involvement in militant and terrorist organizations—as support personnel; as logistics personnel; as kinetic resources; as attackers, kidnappers, and hijackers; and as "martyrs"—has grown substantially and become a matter of public attention and record across the globe. Whatever the actual changes in the level of women's participation in terrorism, media coverage and scholarly attention have both increased exponentially in the last five years.

While many questions remain about the frequency, importance, uniqueness, and meaning of women's terrorist activities, it is becoming clear that the relationships between women, gender, and terrorism cannot be ignored in academic work or policy analysis in the twenty-first century. Though a few books and scholarly articles look for explanations for individual attacks or the trend generally, there are few experts in this area and even fewer empirical studies. Questions about the motivations of the women who become active within terrorist organizations or the way women are represented in the media and/or in scholarly outlets remain seriously underexplored by scholars and counter-terrorism experts alike. Do women participate in al-Qaeda and other terrorist organizations for strictly religious or political reasons, or are personal motivations more important? Is increased, targeted recruitment of women by terrorist groups an influential variable? What are some of the additional motivating factors or explanations that have not yet been posited? Is women's involvement in al-Qaeda substantively different from women's involvement in other groups? Why does some scholarly work on women terrorists insist on finding separate, and often different, explanations for women's terrorism as opposed to men's? What are the dimensions of the relationships between women, gender, and terrorism in the twenty-first century? This volume sets out to address, if not answer, this group of questions.

After briefly exploring the ideas articulated in the title and theoretical framework of the book, this introduction provides an overview of the intersection of women and gender in terrorism. It concludes with a layout of the chapters in the book and their contributions to a better understanding of both their particular subject matter and contemporary terrorism more generally.

WOMEN (TERRORISTS)

The very statement that "women" can be terrorists or even violent seems to be a contradiction in terms. Most notions of what it means to be a "woman" emphasize peacefulness, mothering, care, and interdependence rather than violence. Though women have entered into many realms in the last hundred years previously reserved for men, women and femininity remain less powerful than men and masculinity in almost every area of global social and political life. Women remain underrepresented in the political and economic power structures of the world, which have not magically become gender neutral just because women have joined workforces or voting lists. Women in professions associated with masculinity are often identified by their sex — *women* soldiers, *women* political leaders, *women* CEOs, or even *women* terrorists. Conversely, women in professions associated with femininity are often identified only by the name of the profession—we do not hear *women* housekeepers, *women* teachers, or *women* nurses. Women in those professions are identified simply as housekeepers, teachers, and nurses, because women are assumed to belong in them rather than ones that remain at odds with ideal-typical notions of what it means to be "a woman" despite women's participation. We are now learning that gender equality is more than women being "added" as members of institutions; it is about changing the institutions such that standards of what it means to be "a man" or "a woman" do not dictate either participation or how such participation is received or interpreted.

One of the clear indicators that standards of what it means to be "a woman" still exist and are still subordinated to standards of what it means to be "a man" can be found in the subject matter of this book, terrorism and political violence. Norms associated with manliness (protection, bravery, and self-sacrifice) and womanliness (innocence and fragility) are as old as wars and war stories.[8] Women's violence, however, "falls outside of these ideal-typical understandings of what it means to be a woman."[9] Traditionally, women and warfare or violent death are not associated with one another, and the notion of women as militants, terrorists, or suicide bombers goes against the grain of many cultures' prevalent concepts of femininity. Often, the ideal-typical woman in many cultures is the backbone of the family structure, the defender of faith, and the giver of life. These stereotypes are replicated in Western media portrayals of female terrorists in (Islamic and other) cultures around the world. Particularly, "violent women, whether terrorists, suicide bombers, war criminals, or perpetrators of genocide, interrupt gender stereotypes about women, their role in war, and their role in society more generally: women who commit proscribed violence are not the peaceful, war-resistant, conservative, virtuous, and restrained women that just warriors protect from enemies. . . . Instead, these women are a security threat themselves."[10] A woman who engages in terrorism, then, interrupts stereotypical expectations of women as pure, innocent, and nonviolent. But, as the chapters in this book show, those stereotypes are applied in almost every aspect of the recruitment, coverage, and analysis of women terrorists and women involved in terrorist organizations. Portrayals of women terrorists rarely if ever characterize them as having individual agency in general or with respect to their violence specifically. This voiceless picture of women terrorists shows a lack of knowledge and understanding of the "subject" on the part of the media (and even on the part of the academy). Sensationalized media coverage of female terrorists follows a storyline that portrays women as capable of becoming bombers only if they are dominated by men instead of attributing their actions to similar factors as those seen to motivate men or even to other individual factors or choices.

These issues are particularly important given policy makers' unique concern with women's terrorist acts. The conventional wisdom among policy makers is that the consistent employment of female suicide bombers in terrorist groups is an ominous development, both because security forces and the public at large are less likely to recognize the capacity of women to be suicide bombers and because it indicates a degree of desperation among terrorist groups. The combination is seen to make women more dangerous than men because they have more access to sensitive areas and because their attacks carry significant shock value.[11]

The reasons laid out in most previous work for women's terrorism imply both that women's violence is fundamentally different from men's and that their motivations are intrinsically gendered. Scholars recount that women are often asked to play similar roles in terrorist groups as they are asked to play in societies more generally: to offer emotional and ideological support, often to husbands, sons, fathers, or brothers. These women, in short, are asked to be *mothers*, and it is often immaterial that they are mothering terrorists. These mothering roles then expanded to providing logistical support for the organization or its affiliates. Women might handle such administrative tasks as keeping the books, laundering money, opening bank accounts, and distributing messages.[12] But they might also provide services to terrorist organizations, whether at large or specifically within al-Qaeda, which are more difficult to understand as falling within the traditional confines of femininity, such as airplane hijacking or suicide bombing. As the chapters in this volume highlight, many portrayals link these kinds of activities to something bad that happened to the woman terrorist: she was abused, raped, or drugged and therefore turned to violence. Others understand women's terrorism as a pursuit of personal vengeance for the loss of loved ones. Still others have argued that women do violence in pursuit of women's liberation. Very few accounts link women's terrorism to political devotion to the cause, despite such devotion being a dominant feature in the literature's explanations of why men choose to commit terrorist acts. These very different interpretations of men's and women's participation in terrorism are difficult to disaggregate and understand without gender analysis, a key component of many of these chapters.

GENDER (AND TERRORISM)

Though they are frequently used as such, sex and gender are not synonyms. If biological maleness or femaleness is one's "sex," gender refers to characteristics that persons biologically classifiable as "male" or "female" are expected to have based on their sex.[13] In other words, genders are the characteristics associated with expectations of "being a man" or "being a woman." Gender, then, describes the socially constituted behavioral expectations, stereotypes, and rules that construct masculinity and femininity. These socially constituted differences are intersubjective and constantly evolve as they are intentionally manipulated or affected by changing social norms. Feminist scholars have argued that the social differences between masculinities and femininity are unnatural and reify gendered power.

Seeing gender as a social construction does not mean it is not real or not experienced in social and political life. Instead, gender as a social construction is a crucial element of how people go through their lives. Though there is not one "gendering" but rather multiple genderings, sets "of discourses which can set, change, enforce, and represent meaning" can nevertheless be found in almost every part of global politics.[14]

Gender analysis is interested, then, in identifying and discovering the implications of genderings in global politics. It is "neither just about women, nor about the addition of women to male-stream constructions, it is about transforming ways of being and knowing."[15] Looking through "gender lenses" is a way to filter knowledge; it is a way "to focus on gender as a particular kind of power relation, or to trace out the ways in which gender is central to understanding international processes. Gender lenses also focus on the everyday experiences of women *as women* and highlight the consequences of their own unequal social position."[16]

The stories about women and terrorism in this book are about women, but they are also about gender, and the two are often inseparable. Looking through gender lenses to study terrorism, scholars have examined where women are in terrorism and militancy, showing how they are terrorists or militants, supporters in terrorist or militant organizations, political allies or foes of terrorist organizations, victims of terrorism, and counterterrorism experts or operatives. They have asked how women "related to" terrorism in one way or another are portrayed in gendered terms.[17] Gender lenses have suggested that there are alternative voices out there who see, experience, and know terrorism differently—women, but not only women.

In particular, scholars studying gender and international relations have emphasized that gender relations are not power relations that just happen between men and women (or even between men and men or women and women). Instead, as the authors in this volume stress, gender relations happen among members of terrorist organizations, between terrorist organizations and their target audiences, between terrorist organizations and states, and between states. Many of these gendered relationships, including many of those described on the pages of this book, are ones in which "institutional hierarchies are *naturalized* by feminization and thus are effectively depoliticized," in which "feminization as devalorization" intersects race/ethnicity, class, gender, nationality, and other cleavages in global politics.[18] Since "gender is relational," "*privileging who and what is masculinized is inextricable from devaluing who and what is feminized*," one requires the other. Therefore, instead of looking at women in terrorism as if "women" were either a gender-neutral category or one separate from men or masculinity, the chapters in this book study those women as gendered actors, navigating gendered relationships and living in a gendered world.

TERRORISM (AND WOMEN AND GENDER)

In order to talk about terrorism, it is important to have both a general and a critical understanding of the word "terrorism" and its intellectual and political implications. Up to this point, we have been using the word "terrorism" as if it could be unproblematically or apolitically defined, but it is a term that has generated substantial controversy both in political science and in politics. There are a multitude of definitions for terrorism, and often these definitions are in tension with one another. For instance, the U.S. Department of Defense has defined terrorism as "the calculated use of unlawful violence or the threat of unlawful violence to inculcate fear; intended to coerce or intimidate in pursuit of goals that are generally religious, political, or ideological."[19] Yet, the U.S.

Federal Bureau of Investigations (FBI) defines it as "the unlawful use of force and violence against persons or property to intimidate or coerce a government, the civilian population, or any segment thereof, in furtherance of political or social objectives."[20]

These definitions are not in complete agreement (and indeed the FBI acknowledges that there is no single agreed-on definition). Terrorism studies scholar Bruce Hoffman has pointed out that definitions change from one agency to another and among international organizations, depending on jurisdiction.[21] For instance, Alex Schmid and A. J. Jongman surveyed academics and practitioners in the field of terrorism studies for a definition of terrorism and were presented with 109 different ones.[22] The definitions offered had commonalities: terrorism's goals are political, it is strategic in nature, it is directed at a wider audience, it has a psychological impact, and it is directed at civilians and/or noncombatants. But these are still only a few of the twenty characteristics found in most of those given definitions.[23] The definitions supplied by academics likewise had common elements yet also varied widely, and even when they agreed that a certain aspect was part of the definition, they sometimes interpreted that aspect differently. John Dugard sees these disagreements over the definition as stemming from divisions between the global south, which insists that most persons labeled terrorists are postcolonial fighters and therefore are viewed as legitimate by former colonies, and the global north, which tries to delegitimize their cause.[24] Dugard notes that these struggles were responsible for the United Nations' inability to come up with an agreed-on definition of terrorism in the latter part of the twentieth century. And there is still no one single, unopposed UN definition for terrorism.[25] Audrey Cronin further points out that what terrorism means and who counts as a terrorist change over time, as some people (like Nelson Mandela) who were once called terrorists are now seen as heroes.[26] Cultural context, political persuasion, and strategic interests also influence how terrorism is defined.

A number of scholars have argued that even agreed-on definitions are invoked selectively both by policy makers reacting to terrorism and by political scientists who study it. For example, feminist scholars have argued that

> there are several behaviors that fit the letter, if not the intent, of those definitions
> of terrorism which are normalized in everyday social life within the state. Many
> feminists in social work and psychology have demonstrated the parallels between

domestic violence and terrorism. These scholars point out that victims of domestic violence face violence or the threat of violence to inculcate fear and to coerce or intimidate them into compliance with a partner's objectionable demands for control, sex, or household labor — a pattern which is repeated, anxiety-inspiring and consistently aimed at a certain sector of the population . . . specifically on the basis of their gender. Feminist scholars have also identified wartime rape specifically and rape more generally as tools of terror.[27]

Even if broadening the definition of terrorism to include tactics with similar mechanisms and impacts as those that are considered "terrorism" in mainstream policy and media circles is not appealing, it is difficult to deny that, sometimes, similar tactics are considered "terrorist" or "counterterrorist," respectively, not based on the tactic but instead on the actor using the tactic, where nonstate actors (particularly Islamic ones) are considered "terrorist" and state actors employing similar tactics are seen to be fighting or countering the "terrorists."[28] A number of scholars have examined the propagandistic deployment of the word "terrorism" by states as diverse as the United States, the United Kingdom, India, and Russia.[29]

The ways that the word "terrorism" and "militancy" are variously used and interchanged also create confusion. One can see this confusion in the debate over the terms "guerrilla" and "terrorist" as well, "guerrilla" being understood as describing a somewhat more legitimate style of fighting that does not purposefully target noncombatants.[30] Jaitin Kumar Mohanty has laid out an argument that distinguishes between terrorism and militancy on a number of axes.[31] According to Mohanty, the word "terrorism" is often used to express intentionality, to describe a response to an external stimulus, to discuss a strategy of targeting defenseless targets, to connote sanctified goals, and/or to describe a process of bargaining based on "power to hurt" rather than conventional military power.[32] Factors that get taken into consideration in differentiating terrorism from militancy, in his account, include UN recognition of a state, the objective of the group and its means to achieving it, the magnitude of violence, the history of colonialism and decolonization in the state, whether a given act is morally justified, and the national and/or international impacts of the violence.[33]

Mohanty in particular intimates that militants fight for their (UN-endorsed) right to self-determination while terrorists attack sovereign, UN-recognized states; militants' actions are essentially domestic politics, while terrorists' actions are international in scope.[34] Terrorists fight for a list of demands, while militants look for independence by any means possible.[35] Terrorists' accomplishments are defined by their magnitude of violence, while violence is a means to an end for militants.[36] Additionally, Mohanty makes a distinction with respect to whom the fighters are fighting against, arguing that "to call a freedom fighter a terrorist is the brainchild of colonialism . . . but to consider a terrorist a freedom fighter in a liberated democratic country would mean political destabilization."[37] Along those lines, Mohanty argues that the basic idea of militancy (freedom) is morally good, while the basic idea of terrorism (rejection of civilized society) is morally bad.[38]

These distinctions are, to say the least, controversial, not least because there is probably no terrorist group in the world that would classify itself on the terrorist end of this spectrum in all respects. Also, many of these criteria are difficult to measure in any objective or certain fashion, and a number of them (like UN recognition or democracy and moral good) are themselves political and subjective. Still, that the distinction exists, is made, and has salience, both in the academic and policy worlds, is important to note for the purposes of this book's analyses given that it may be seen as substantive both by chapter authors and (especially) their research subjects.

Some of the chapters in this book use the word "terrorism" in a way consistent with the traditionally understood definitions coming from state departments, departments of defense, and international organizations, which combine some objective criteria with a sort of you-know-it-if-you-see-it sort of feel for terrorism as attacks on states (and more often, states' civilians) by nonstate actors, the aim of which is to cause fear in the interest of some religious or political cause. Other chapters in this book use the word "terrorism" in a representational way, assigning it only the meaning that it has already acquired in its frequent use (and some would say misuse) in scholarly and policy circles. Others criticize and interrogate both the labeling and representational use of the word "terrorism" on the grounds that it reifies both problematic preexisting assumptions in the international political arena and the unequal power relations that often accompany those assumptions.

It is not, in our minds, necessary that each of the chapters in this book interpret "terrorism" the same way in order for the book to present an interesting, and coherent, intellectual account of women, gender, and terrorism. Instead, we consider terrorism, in this volume and more generally, to be what W. B. Gallie identified as a contested concept "whose meaning is *inherently* a matter of dispute because no neutral definition is possible."[39] A contested concept, then, is "therefore a battleground in and of itself."[40] In this usage, then,

> the term essentially contested concepts gives a name to a problematic situation that many people recognize: that in certain kinds of talk there is a variety of meanings employed for key terms in an argument, and there is a feeling that dogmatism ("My answer is right and all orders are wrong"), skepticism ("All answers are equally true (or false); everyone has a right to his own truth"); and eclecticism ("Each meaning gives a partial view so the more meanings the better") are none of them the appropriate attitude towards a variety of meanings."[41]

The common approaches of either agreeing to disagree on what terrorism "is" or trying to win a definitional argument, this perspective contends, are both misguided, since the essence of the concept is in the argument rather than in its resolution. Instead of trying to establish a consensus among the authors in this volume specifically or among terrorism specialists generally as to what terrorism "is," this introduction and the essays in the volume focus on how it is "produced"; that is, instead of treating it as a product, we regard it as a process. Using what Hayward Alker has termed a "controversy-based path to knowledge cumulation," we stress that the "truth" about the meaning of terrorism is not to be found in the victory of one approach or the plurality of all approaches but in the dialogue between them.[42]

It is, however, important to note that this book reflects, criticizes, and sometimes reproduces the power relations between certain approaches used in the study of terrorism in the policy world, on the one hand and in the scholarly community, on the other. In particular, the volume focuses on meanings of the word "terrorism" that would be generally understood and accepted and devotes attention to a number of terrorist groups and terrorist/terrorizing conflicts that have been a priority for governments, governance, and those who study it so far in the twenty-first century. Grounding itself (though critically) in "terrorism" as colloquially used and traditionally understood allows this volume to sit at the intersection of theoretical inquiry and practical applicability and, perhaps, to provide ways of navigating a path between the two.

Contemporary Terrorism

The title of this book explicitly refers to "terrorism" rather than referring only to al-Qaeda or even privileging that organization as the "main story" of contemporary terrorism.[43] This is not to say that al-Qaeda has not been a large (perhaps even dominating) factor in contemporary terrorism and counterterrorism. In fact, much of the scholarly, media, and policy-making attention paid to terrorism in the twenty-first century has focused on al-Qaeda, both because of the scale of the 9/11 attacks and the fact that the organization has remained viable in the years following the attacks. Still, contemporary terrorism is much broader than al-Qaeda, with many lesser-known participants in many places across the world. While this volume gives due notice to al-Qaeda and the U.S. "war" against it, it also addresses women's presence in, support of, and complex relationships with different terrorist organizations and counterterrorist institutions across global politics.

Although contemporary terrorism is often identified with extreme Islamist religious causes, this too oversimplifies the phenomenon and has contributed an alarming trend of Orientalist treatments of terrorism (see the chapters in this volume by Gentry and Brown).[44] Many contemporary terrorist groups (such as the Liberation Tamil Tigers of Eelam, discussed in chapter 7) understand their mission as secularist and others as nationalist or territorial (like the People's Liberation Front of Palestine, discussed in chapter 6). Still others carry out terrorist acts on behalf of non-Islamic religions (such as the Irish Republican Army).

Still, there are many scholars who demarcate terrorism in the twenty-first century as a unique phenomenon with commonalities. For example, in his canonical *Inside Terrorism*, Bruce Hoffman argues that "the terrorist attacks on September 11, 2001, inevitably redefined 'terrorism.'"[45] One of the distinctive features of that redefinition is scale, according to Hoffman, who notes that before 9/11 very few terrorist attacks had killed more than one hundred people and none had killed more than five hundred.[46] Another distinctive feature of terrorism in the twenty-first century arose in response to 9/11: many of the world's largest states determined that terrorism as such—rather than just particular groups with particular political, religious, or ideological causes—could be fought against. According to strategist Michael Howard, both nationalist and global needs came to be seen as "at war with an abstract entity described . . . as 'Terror' [and] a specific adversary who embodies the spirit of evil."[47]

While most contemporary scholars of terror and terrorism agree that how the term is applied is subjective (and depends on the interest of the persons or groups doing the defining) and that the persons and groups to whom it may be applied is diverse, they nonetheless argue that the scale of and attention to these actors in international politics and the discipline of international relations means that it is essential to study and understand them. Certainly, a subdiscipline of terrorism studies has sprouted up that reflects the growing influence and presence of these groups in global politics. Journals like *Terrorism and Political Violence, Studies in Conflict and Terrorism,* and *Critical Studies on Terrorism* have been quickly gaining both in readership and reputation as the interest of theorists and practitioners of global politics in terrorism has exponentially expanded.

It is to this developing literature in terrorism studies that this book hopes to contribute. Scholars interested in gender have critiqued the kinds of stories commonly narrated about women in contemporary terrorism in the terrorism studies literature, which often attributes women participants' motivations to personal pathologies while considering men's terrorism as political. For example, in addressing the question of why women martyr themselves in suicide terrorism, Mia Bloom cites almost solely personal reasons, including "revenge for a personal loss, the desire to redeem the family name, to escape a life of sheltered monotony, to achieve fame, and to level the patriarchal societies in which they live." Bloom in particular stresses the role of sexual abuse in pushing women into terrorism: "What is incredibly compelling about delving into how and why women become suicide bombers is that so many of these women have been raped or sexually abused in the previous conflict either by the representatives of the state or by the insurgents themselves."[48]

Studying women's integration into and relationships with terrorist and/or militant groups in Bosnia, Chechnya, Kashmir, Palestine, and Sri Lanka, as well as al-Qaeda, the authors in this book seek to question, complicate, and critique these essentialist (and often culture-insensitive) understandings of women's participation in and relation to terrorism at the individual, group, and international levels.

Al-Qaeda

Though it is important to bear in mind that al-Qaeda is not the sum total of terrorism in the twenty-first century, it is equally important to note that, both in terms of influence exerted and attention garnered, the organization is a large part of the evolving story of contemporary terrorism. This is true specifically with respect to women's involvement in terrorism. If al-Qaeda has not led the way in incorporating women into terrorist groups and attacks, its joining the trend has led to increased interest in women's roles in terrorism on both the part of policy makers and scholars. So, while women had participated in terrorist activities before they were suicide bombers and had been self-martyrs for other organizations before they were employed by al-Qaeda, the prominence that the question of women in terrorism has achieved as a result of women's involvement in al-Qaeda is unprecedented.[49] As such, a brief discussion of al-Qaeda and women's roles therein is crucial to introducing the stories of women, gender, and terrorism that make up this volume.

Al-Qaeda is a particularly interesting case because some branches of the organization explicitly incorporate women into their operations, while others do not. This is because al-Qaeda is best described as "a networked transnational constituency rather than a monolithic, international terrorist organization with an identifiable command and control apparatus that it once was"[50] (see box on pages 16–17). Al-Qaeda's organizational and operational infrastructure is distinct from other guerilla and terrorist groups in both its global reach and decentralization.[51] Al-Qaeda is a transnational phenomenon and an organization that cannot be characterized as a single group or even a coalition of groups; instead, its far-flung nodules are held together by an appealing, broad-based ideology and diverse membership that cuts across ethnic, class, and national boundaries.[52] Al-Qaeda's structure is essentially flat and linear, and its organization consists of little more than a loose network, though some hierarchy does exist among top leadership.[53] This is in contrast to a number of other terrorist groups, which, historically, have used a hierarchical, pyramidal structure to organize and solidify themselves and their message, as well as to plan attacks.

Al-Qaeda has proven to be mobile and resilient thanks to its regional affiliates, which operate autonomously within a networked structure. Each regional group, while supporting the ultimate goal of al-Qaeda Central, is an independent entity engaged in its own regional conflict with its own set of rules. As Hoffman illustrates, a broad range of organizations can be said to reside under the al-Qaeda umbrella.

These discrete conflicts and constituents account for the diverse set of tactics employed by al-Qaeda, particularly when it comes to the women's participation in terrorist activities. For example, despite a general reluctance within al-Qaeda Central to engage women as frontline operatives, affiliated groups in Iraq and Chechnya have openly recruited women to their cause and have regularly employed female suicide bombers—perhaps taking a cue from the successful female suicide bombers historically used by organizations such as the Liberation Tigers of Tamil Eelam in Sri Lanka.

Al-Qaeda in Iraq and its leader at the time, Abu Musab al-Zarqawi, began employing women as suicide bombers in 2005; most observers suspect they adopted this tactic as a shrewd means of facilitating operational success through the element of surprise. Al-Qaeda in Iraq secured significant television coverage by using this tactic, and al-Zarqawi confirmed his power and influence by challenging cultural gender norms. Additionally, it is generally easier for women suicide bombers to get through checkpoints and enter targets. A byproduct of this designed-to-shock strategy was that al-Zarqawi doubled the size of his recruitment pool and effectively shamed male noncombatants into increased participation.

WOMEN, GENDER, AND TERRORISM

The chapters in this book explore contemporary terrorism conventionally and critically as it manifests itself in organizations like al-Qaeda and in the far corners of the earth from both scholarly perspectives and perspectives interested in policy implications. The book is organized into four sections that address different facets of women's involvement in and relation to terrorism.

Part 1, "Historical Perspectives on Women and Terrorism," begins with this introduction and continues with Farhana Qazi's "The *Mujahidaat*: Tracing the Early Female Warriors of Islam," which provides readers with a historical perspective on women's involvement specifically in Islamic terrorism. Qazi points out that, despite a present-day social taboo against women as violent actors, there are examples of female fighters dating to the Quran. Known as the *mu-*

HOFFMAN'S DESCRIPTION OF AL-QAEDA

Bruce Hoffman's description of the al-Qaeda movement as four distinct, but not exclusive, dimensions is instructive here.

Al-Qaeda Central still contains some remnants of the pre-9/11 al-Qaeda. Led initially by bin Laden and al-Zawahiri, the core group now includes new senior-level leaders who have advanced because of the death or capture of other al-Qaeda leaders. This core is essentially al-Qaeda's professional force: the dedicated, committed, and thoroughly reliable members "in charge of high-value, 'spectacular' attacks." Al-Qaeda Central has considerable logistical and coordination abilities that can be global in reach.

Al-Qaeda Affiliates and Associates consist of a variety of established terrorist groups that are the recipients of financial support, training, arms, spiritual guidance, and/or other assistance from al-Qaeda. Since the al-Qaeda movement began, it has provided support to groups in Uzbekistan, Indonesia, Chechnya, the Philippines, Bosnia, and Kashmir, as well as to "homegrown" terrorist cells in Western Europe. While these groups vocally support the global goals of al-Qaeda, their terrorist activities are generally confined to within their state or region. By supporting regional terrorist groups, al-Qaeda leadership is attempting to meld local agendas into a global jihad movement.

jahidaat, these early female warriors were committed to protecting the Prophet Muhammad at any physical cost. Their legacy can be traced to present-day women who are willing to "carry the bomb under the *abaya.*" Understanding the tradition of these early female Muslim fighters, Qazi argues, is essential to comprehending today's Islamic female suicide bombers. She examines why a growing number of Muslim women participate in terrorist activities and identifies in what areas their participation is greatest or most concerning. Qazi also scrutinizes the reactions of Muslim men to women taking part in jihad, the clerical divide over whether women can take part in jihad, the meaning

Al-Qaeda Locals are small terrorist cells that have had some direct contact with al-Qaeda, usually in a training camp. This category includes two sub-sets of terrorist groups. In the first instance the local cells have first been cultivated, and then, before becoming operational, its leadership reaches out to al-Qaeda leadership. Although some local groups may have experience in planning and leading terrorist attacks in their regions, they usually turn to al-Qaeda central owing to lack of training and resources. The local groups' connection with al-Qaeda is generally limited, if not dormant. The second subset includes groups that may be ready and willing to launch an attack but lack the necessary resources and professional training and look to al-Qaeda leadership for focus and development. Both subsets direct their attention to simple operations that will create fear and chaos.

Al-Qaeda Network is comprised of radicals from the Middle East, North Africa, South and Southeast Asia and converts in Europe, Africa, Latin America, and North America who do not have a direct connection with al-Qaeda or other terrorist groups but are sympathetic to its global aims and are willing to carry out terrorist attacks in support. In general, these individuals have adopted al-Qaeda's goals and ideology and hatred of the West, as their own but lack training, support, and a specified goal. While these individuals may not be part of an organized terror group and are relatively unknown to federal authorities, they are still able to successfully plan an attack; a case in point would be the March 2004 Madrid bombings.

of jihad, and the unchanging social status of women within Islamic societies despite their increased participation in jihadist causes.

While Qazi's piece provides essential background to the roles of women as historic and modern-day violent actors within varied Islamic traditions, "The Gendering of Women's Terrorism," by Caron E. Gentry and Laura Sjoberg, takes a broader look at women's violence and the reception thereof from a historical perspective, focusing in particular on the stylized narratives surrounding women's terrorism contemporary to it and on the preservation of these gender-stereotypical accounts across time, space, and cultures. Reading stories about women's terrorism from ancient times to the twenty-first century, the chapter recognizes consistency and change in women's complex relationships with "terrorism" and how women, gender, and terrorism are performed, received, and portrayed in scholarly and media accounts.

This chapter provides a bridge to Part 2 of the volume, "Women, Terrorism, and Contemporary Conflicts," which addresses women's roles in and gender relations surrounding terrorism in a number of contemporary conflicts. In "Zombies versus Black Widows: Women as Propaganda in the Chechen Conflict," Alisa Stack focuses on the unique propaganda value of acts of terrorism committed by women in the Russian-Chechen conflict. While mainstream terrorism studies often characterizes acts of terror as "propaganda of the deed," Stack notes that the content of the resulting propaganda is sex-specific. When a woman commits an act of terror, the resulting propaganda is more about her (and her womanhood) than the act that she has committed. Using the case of Chechen women involved in the conflict with Russia, Stack explores how the media went from seeing Chechen women as victims of the conflict to (after the Dubrovka Theater hostage situation in 2002) representing them as fighters. This chapter introduces two major portrayals of Chechen female terrorists, as "black widows" (who engage in terrorism to avenge the deaths of men in their lives) or as "zombies" (who are drugged or tricked into terrorism). In Chechnya and Russia, assumptions about women's motivations are central to the effectiveness of the propaganda that builds the conflict's narrative, but they do not necessarily reflect the true group or individual motives of the female operatives.

Though it addresses different women in different social, political, and religious contexts, Swati Parashar's "*Aatish-e-Chinar*: In Kashmir, Where Women Keep Resistance Alive," tells an eerily similar story about the disjoint between women militants' realities and the ways those realities are often related and portrayed. As part of her extensive research into the roles women play in terrorist organizations, Parashar visited Kashmir in March 2007, where she conducted interviews with, among others, Asiya Andrabi, the founder and head of Dukhtaran-e-Millat. Militancy and terror tactics are not new in the context of the conflict in Jammu and Kashmir in the Indian subcontinent. While popular support for the militancy seems to be waning, Parashar notes, radical women who advocate an Islamic way of life in Kashmir and nurture aspirations for a global Islamic community have become an increasingly vocal presence. Indeed, al-Qaeda recently declared Kashmir to be the "gateway of jihad" against India. While the voices of some female suicide bombers have found their way into the public eye, Kashmiri women who are perpetrators, planners, and patrons of militancy struggle to find a space within the religious and nationalist discourse. Parashar's piece provides rare insight into this community and its aims.

In "The Committed Revolutionary: Reflections on a Conversation with Leila Khaled," Caron E. Gentry looks at the relationship between women, gender, and terrorism in the Palestinian context through a record of an interview she conducted with Leila Khaled, one of the first and most famous female participants in the People's Liberation Front for Palestine (PFLP). In a careful exploration of the fault lines between social gender norms, gender norms among members of terrorist organizations, and gender norms among Palestinian militants, Gentry paints a picture of Khaled at once more complicated and more interesting than those often featured in media and scholarly portrayals of her life and her involvement with the People's Liberation Front. Noting that "the myths surrounding her actions" do not correspond with Khaled's self-portrayals, Gentry emphasizes the theoretical importance of her claim that "she made a commitment to the Palestinian cause that has guided her actions throughout her life" and argues that women terrorists (in Palestine and elsewhere) are not objects that are "used" by masculine organizations but (perhaps like all terrorists) are agents who make the decision to join terrorist groups for both personal and political reasons.

Part 2 concludes with Miranda Alison's "'In the war front we never think that we are women': Women, Gender, and the Liberation Tamil Tigers of Eelam." The Liberation Tamil Tigers of Eelam, a Sri Lankan rebel group, is one of few terrorist organizations that explicitly expresses a commitment to women's liberation as part of their national liberation agenda (the FARC in Colombia being another one). As Alison recounts, this explicit commitment and its backing by detailed and consistent policies has had a significant impact on women's experiences in and relationships with the organization, though a gender hierarchy still figures in both internal or external relationships. After exploring women's experiences in the organization and internal struggles within it to cater to its feminist and nationalist goals, Alison looks at the how internal (gendered) struggles relate to the group's (gendered) interactions within Sri Lanka and the international community.

Part 3, "Women, Gender, and al-Qaeda," pays attention to a number of dynamics related to women's participation in and support of al-Qaeda. Jennie Stone and Katherine Pattillo's "Al-Qaeda's Use of Female Suicide Bombers in Iraq" explores the reasons why al-Qaeda in Iraq began recruiting and employing female suicide bombers, focusing in particular on the question of whether al-Qaeda is likely to continue tolerating women's participation and if so, whether it will encourage them to participate even more. The authors note that al-Qaeda was one of the last Islamic terrorist groups to engage women in support operations or direct attacks. It was not until 2005, under al-Zarqawi's leadership, that al-Qaeda in Iraq began using women in its bombing campaigns. The degree to which senior al-Qaeda leadership sanctions the use of female suicide bombers is contested; thus far, al-Qaeda in Iraq remains the only al-Qaeda chapter mobilizing women in this role. This tactic has, the authors argue, expanded al-Qaeda in Iraq's recruitment pool and provided important tactical and strategic benefits to the insurgency, but it has had mixed results with respect to gender relations and gendered power structures.

In "The Neo-Orientalist Narratives of Women's Involvement in al-Qaeda," Caron E. Gentry explores gender bias and why the Western media has a difficult time accurately portraying the profiles and activities of female suicide bombers. She asks an important question: does the Western media cover Muslim women in a racialized manner? As much as women's liberation has changed Western culture, certain social norms and gendered expectations, Gentry argues, persist: women are nurturing wives and mothers and as such are not meant to be violent. Beholden to a neo-Orientalist lens, Western culture, as represented through the media, has found it particularly difficult to explain the existence and motivations of female al-Qaeda operatives and suicide bombers. In both media and family descriptions of female suicide bombers, Gentry finds, the women are portrayed as rebellious, infertile, or submissive wives, which has the effect of sensationalizing their violence within a highly gendered context. Through her analysis of media coverage of Iraqi terrorist incidents involving female operatives, Gentry discovered that women who have connections to the West receive more media coverage than women with no Western ties, suggesting a favoritism of the Western "us" over the Middle Eastern "other." As a result, the media has missed an important aspect: that these women are shattering cultural norms.

In "Blinded by the Explosion? Security and Resistance in Muslim Women's

Suicide Terrorism," Katherine E. Brown looks at women's suicide terrorism with reference to critical and postmodern feminist studies of the Middle East, Islam, and Muslim politics. By deploying "resistance" as its conceptual framework, the chapter makes visible female suicide bombing, reclaims the agency of female suicide terrorists, and explores the power of the symbolic in female suicide terrorism. The chapter proposes that rather than looking for a theoretical position that would explain "women's participation" in al-Qaeda and other terrorist organizations, which assumes that men's participation is explained by theories that cannot explain women's, it would make more sense to look for a new approach to individual political violence that accounts for men's terrorism, women's terrorism, and the gendered world in which individual violence is performed. Brown suggests that feminist and subaltern studies may supply the means of constructing such an approach.

Laura Sjoberg's conclusion to this volume, "The Study of Women, Gender, and Terrorism," contends that it is important to focus gendered lenses on a number of different issues in terrorism studies—including women's participation in terrorist organizations, gender dynamics among members, gendered relations between terrorist organizations and target states, and the gendered impacts of acts of terror. It not only argues that gender analysis is necessary to understanding terrorism(s) but also that thinking about terrorism can expand insights of gender theorizing. This chapter ties together key themes across the diverse chapters in the volume, paying special attention to their implications for the study of women, gender, and terrorism (and their intersections). It focuses on three issues: gender and agency in global politics, the interdependence of gender and discursive representations of terrorism, and potentially productive ways of theorizing terrorism and counterterrorism in gender-inclusive and gender-sensitive ways.

NOTES

1. Israeli Ministry of Foreign Affairs, "The Role of Palestinian Women in Suicide Terrorism," January 30, 2003, http://www.mfa.gov.il/MFA/MFAArchive /2000_2009/2003/1/The%20Role%20of%20Palestinian%20Women%20in%20 Suicide%20Terrorism (accessed December 24, 2010).

2. Ibid.

3. Ibid.

4. Ibid.

5. Mia Bloom, "Female Suicide Bombers: A Global Trend," *Daedalus* 136, no. 1 (2007): 94–103; Mia Bloom, *Dying to Kill: The Allure of Suicide Terror* (New York: Columbia University Press, 2005); Mia Bloom, "Mother, Daughter, Sister, Bomber," *Bulletin of the Atomic Scientists* 61, no. 6 (2005): 55–62; Mia Bloom, "Terror's Deadly New Stealth Weapon: Women," *Guelph (Ontario) Mercury*, December 2, 2005; Phyllis Chesler, "Feminism's Deafening Silence," *Frontpagemagazine.com*, July 26, 2004, www .frontpagemagazine.com (accessed July 26, 2006); Karla J. Cunningham, "Cross-regional Trends in Female Terrorism," *Studies in Conflict and Terrorism* 26, no. 3 (2003): 171–95; Robin Morgan, *The Demon Lover: The Roots of Terrorism* (New York: Washington Square Press, 1989); Barbara Victor, *An Army of Roses: Inside the World of Palestinian Women Suicide Bombers* (New York: Rodale, 2003).

6. Laura Sjoberg and Caron E. Gentry, *Mothers, Monsters, Whores: Women's Violence in Global Politics* (London: Zed, 2007), 4–5.

7. Miranda Alison, *Women and Political Violence: Female Combatants in Ethno-National Conflict* (London: Routledge, 2008).

8. On women in war, see Jean Bethke Elshtain, *Women and War* (New York: New York University Press, 1987); Jean Bethke Elshtain, "Reflections on War and Political Discourse: Realism, Just War, and Feminism in a Nuclear Age," *Political Theory* 13, no. 1 (1985): 39–57; Laura Sjoberg, "Gendered Realities of the Immunity Principle: Why Gender Analysis Needs Feminism," *International Studies Quarterly* 50, no. 4 (2006): 889–910; Laura Sjoberg, *Gender, Justice, and the Wars in Iraq* (New York: Lexington, 2006). On war stories, see Nancy Huston, "Tales of War and Tears of Women," in *Women and Men's Wars*, ed. Judith Stiehm (Oxford: Pergamon, 1983), 271–82.

9. Sjoberg and Gentry, *Mothers, Monsters, Whores*, 2.

10. Ibid., 14.

11. See Farhana Ali, "Muslim Female Fighters: An Emerging Trend," *Terrorism Monitor* 3, no. 21 (2005): 9–11.

12. Caron E. Gentry, "Women as Agents of Violence," in *The International Studies Encyclopedia*, ed. Robert Denemark (Hoboken, N.J.: Wiley-Blackwell, 2010), http://www.isacompendium.com/public/tocnode?query=Gentry&widen=1&result_number=1&from=search&fuzzy=0&type=std&id=g9781444336597_chunk_g978144433659721_ss1-7&slop=1.

13. There is also a portion of the population (estimates are around 1 percent) who are born neither biologically male nor biologically female. See Intersex Society of North America, www.isna.org/faq/hermaphrodite (accessed August 23, 2006). According to

the Survivor Project (www.survivorproject.org), intersex people naturally (that is, without any medical intervention) develop primary or secondary sex characteristics that do not fit neatly into society's definitions of male or female. Many visibly intersex people are mutilated in infancy and early childhood by doctors in an effort to make their sex characteristics conform to their idea of what normal bodies should look like. Intersex people are relatively common, although the society's denial of their existence has allowed very little room for intersexuality to be discussed publicly. Trans people break away from one or more of the society's expectations around sex and gender such as that everyone is either a man or a woman, that one's gender is fixed, that gender is rooted in one's physiological sex, and that our behaviors are linked to our gender. Survivor Project uses "trans" as a very broad umbrella term. Transsexual people perceive themselves as members of a gender or sex that is different from the one they were assigned at birth. Many transsexual people pursue hormone and/or surgical interventions to make it easier to live as members of the gender or sex they identify as. The term "transgender" is used in so many different ways that it is almost impossible to define it. Some use it to refer to people whose behavior and expressions do not match with their gender. Some use it to describe a gender outside of the man/woman binary. Some use it to describe the condition of having no gender or multiple genders. Other possibilities include people who perform genders or deliberately play with/on gender as well as those who are gender-deviant in other ways.

14. Laura Sjoberg, "Agency, Militarized Femininity, and Enemy Others," *International Feminist Journal of Politics* 9, no. 1 (2007): 82–101.

15. V. Spike Peterson, "Transgressing Boundaries: Theories of Knowledge, Gender and International Relations," *Millennium* 21, no. 2 (1992): 205.

16. Jill Steans, *Gender and International Relations: An Introduction* (New Brunswick, N.J.: Rutgers University Press, 1998), 5.

17. Laura Sjoberg, "Feminist Interrogations of Terrorism/Terrorism Studies," *International Relations* 23, no. 1 (2009): 69–74.

18. V. Spike Peterson, "Gendered Identities, Ideologies, and Practices in Contexts of War and Militarism," in *Gender, War, and Militarism: Feminist Perspectives*, ed. Laura Sjoberg and Sandra Via (Santa Barbara, Calif.: Praeger Security International, 2010).

19. Department of Defense, *Dictionary of Military Terms*, 2008, www.dtic.mil /doctrine/jel/doddict/data/t/05488.html (accessed July 1, 2008).

20. Federal Bureau of Investigation, *Terrorism in the United States, 2002–2005*, http:// www.fbi.gov/publications/terror/terrorism2002_2005.htm (accessed February 10, 2011).

21. Bruce Hoffman, *Inside Terrorism* (New York: Columbia University Press, 2006), 30–34.

22. Alex P. Schmid and A. J. Jongman, *Political Terrorism* (New Brunswick, N.J.: Transaction, 2005).

23. Ibid.

24. John Dugard, "International Terrorism: Problems of Definition," *International Affairs* 50, no. 1 (1974): 67–81.

25. David Cortright, George A. Lopez, Alistair Millar, and Linda Gerber-Stellingwerf, "Global Cooperation against Terrorism: Evaluating the United Nations Counter-Terrorism Committee," in *Uniting Against Terror*, ed. David Cortright and George A. Lopez (Cambridge, Mass.: MIT Press, 2007), 44–45.

26. Audrey Kurth Cronin, "Behind the Curve: Globalization and International Terrorism," *International Security* 27, no. 3 (2002–3): 30–58.

27. Sjoberg, "Feminist Interrogations," 71.

28. See, e.g., Noam Chomsky, *9-11* (New York: Open Media Press, 2001).

29. See, e.g., Fahed al Sumait, Colin Lingle, and David Domke, "Terrorism's Cause and Cure: The Rhetorical Regime of Democracy in the United States and United Kingdom," *Critical Studies on Terrorism* 2, no. 1 (2009): 7–25; Michael Ryan and Les Switzer, "Propaganda and the Subversion of Objectivity: Media Coverage of the War on Terrorism in Iraq," *Critical Studies on Terrorism* 2, no. 1 (2009): 45–64; Gillian Youngs, "Media and Mediation in the 'War on Terror': Issues and Challenges," *Critical Studies on Terrorism* 2, no. 1 (2009): 95–102.

30. Boaz Ganor, "Defining Terrorism: Is One Man's Terrorist Another Man's Freedom Fighter?" *Police Practice and Research* 3, no. 4 (2002): 287–304.

31. Jaitin Kumar Mohanty, *Terrorism and Militancy in Central Asia* (New Delhi: Gyan, 2006).

32. Ibid., 22–41.

33. Ibid., 41.

34. Ibid., 42.

35. Ibid.

36. Ibid., 43.

37. Ibid., 44.

38. Ibid., 43–44.

39. W. B. Gallie, "Essentially Contested Concepts," *Proceedings of the Aristotelian Society* 56 (1956): 167–98; Steve Smith, "The Contested Concept of Security," in *Critical Security Studies and World Politics*, ed. Ken Booth (Boulder, Colo.: Lynne Rienner, 2005), 17.

40. Ibid., 19.

41. Eugene Garver, "Rhetoric and Essentially Contested Arguments," *Philosophy and Rhetoric* 11, no. 3 (1978): 168.

42. Hayward Alker, *Rediscoveries and Reformulations* (Cambridge: Cambridge University Press, 1996), 53.

43. Audrey Kurth Cronin, "The Evolution of Counter-Terrorism: Will Tactics Trump Strategy?" *International Affairs* 86, no. 4 (2010): 837–56; Stewart Croft and Cerwyn Moore, "The Evolution of Threat Narratives in the Age of Terror: Understanding Terrorist Threats in Britain," *International Affairs* 86, no. 4 (2010): 821–35.

44. Islamism indicates a set of ideologies that holds Islam to be not only a religion but also a political system that radically rejects the separation of church and state. This term is used to distinguish those who practice Islamic religion from those who wish to integrate it into political systems.

45. Hoffman, *Inside Terrorism*, 18.

46. Ibid., 18–19.

47. Qtd. in Hoffman, *Inside Terrorism*, 20.

48. Bloom, *Dying to Kill*, 125.

49. See, e.g., chapters on the Chechen and Sri Lankan conflicts in this volume.

50. Hoffman, *Inside Terrorism*, 282.

51. Rohan Gunaratna, *Inside Al Qaeda: Global Network of Terror* (New York: Berkeley, 2003), 72.

52. Ibid.

53. Hoffman, *Inside Terrorism*, 285. While we have yet to see how the organization of al-Qaeda changes after the death/assassination of Osama bin Laden, the decentralized nature of the organization has led a number of experts to suggest that it will continue to be a formidable force in radical Islamist politics. See, e.g., Daniel Byman, "Bin Laden Is Dead, al-Qaeda Isn't," *Foreign Policy*, May 2, 2011, www.foreignpolicy.com/articles/2011/05/02/obl_is_dead_al_qaeda_isnt (accessed June 4, 2011).

Historical Perspectives on Women and Terrorism

PART ONE

Historical Perspectives on

Women and Terrorism

The *Mujahidaat*

TRACING THE EARLY
FEMALE WARRIORS OF ISLAM

Farhana Qazi

Almost a decade into the global war on terrorism, the academic and intelligence communities have yet to agree on whether psychological profiles of militant women are a useful paradigm. Few scholars are able to ascertain common patterns across various conflicts and countries from which female terrorists emerge. Others question the utility of trying to study female terrorists as distinct or unique from terrorists more generally.[1] Scholars scanning the literature of jihadi mythologies as well as statements, trial transcripts, and other communication nodes do reveal common themes expressed by many women—and men—engaged in violent action.[2] These themes largely reflect common grievances; for example, perceived injustice and the indiscriminate use of violence by states on distressed Muslim communities and individuals.

It is important to recognize that women who join militant groups find themselves in similar (and, often, gender-specific) social, cultural, and religious contexts that may motivate their participation or support of violence. Because of their gender, women are often viewed as more alluring, attractive, and agile by violent male-dominated groups. The perception that women can strap on a bomb and perpetrate successful terrorist attacks compels Muslim men to reconsider "hiring" women even when conservative members argue against a woman's involvement. At the same time, women's willingness to engage in such tactics has led to a revision of the assumption that women are pacifists, moderate, and nonviolent.

The reasons why women participate in violence will vary, even where common grievances are present, but what motivates women to engage in suicide terrorism is bound to be different for each *individual* woman. The study of female bombers as a category is limiting and likely to be based on generalizations and lead to gender-specific conclusions. Researchers should not foreclose the possibility that each woman has a strong personal incentive for terror.[3] Hence, no two female terrorists may be alike.

Another obvious, though sometimes overlooked, observation is that no two conflicts in which female suicide terrorists originate are alike and therefore that the motivations of female bombers will vary both individually and from country to country. For example, "Russians in Chechnya believed the female suicide attackers were widows of fighters seeking vengeance," while the drive to include Palestinian and Iraqi women in male-dominated terrorist groups may be a "tactical maneuver."[4] The use of women in al-Qaeda's insurgency in Iraq allowed the terrorist group to discredit, damage, and possibly derail the Iraqi government's efforts to democratize a fragile state. What women have to gain by participating in male-oriented groups is a separate though relevant question.

Given the complexity of conflict, each one must be viewed separately, and the social context must be taken into account if we are to understand why some women are permitted (or encouraged) to join terror groups while others are excluded. Of equal value is the cultural psychology of men. Female acceptance by male leaders is key to gaining access to terrorist organizations and perpetrating suicide attacks.

Women's roles on the battlefield in different regions of the world are well known but not always widely accepted. For centuries, women's participation in combat has contradicted the traditional domestic roles women have occupied in patriarchal (Muslim) societies.[5] But as more women join terrorist organizations, they appear to shed their image as nurturers of their children and communities for the more active, operational role of the female suicide bomber. As more women take part in suicide operations, they not only counter the perception that al-Qaeda and affiliated groups are "male-only" confederations but also prove they are partners and participants in jihad.[6] Whether women achieve equality or empowerment through their involvement in terrorist acts is not entirely clear, but since there is evidence of women's participation in earlier armed struggles and nationalist causes and yet women's social status within their respective societies has not significantly improved, it seems their involvement has not helped them on this front. If women historically have little to gain from committing terrorist attacks, then why are women eager and enthusiastic to join? No one answer is sufficient, and giving a thorough one would require more in-depth fieldwork. For example, one would want to interview women and to observe them in conflict in order to learn the various means by which they are persuaded to join and the positions they accept *before* joining.

The purpose of this chapter is to understand why a growing number of Muslim women engage in terrorism and to identify what types of activities they participate in the most and which are most alarming.[7] While public information, including interviews with would-be female bombers, is not readily available, it is possible, if difficult, to locate. This chapter includes interviews conducted by the author with women intending to become suicide bombers and/or women actively supporting their husbands, brothers, male cousins, and fathers in a cause they deem worth fighting for.

While the rise of female bombers garners much attention and curiosity, few researchers have been able to gain access to female terrorists for security reasons as well as owing to deeply rooted cultural, religious, and societal norms that prohibit outsiders from interacting with Muslim women. Therefore, a wealth of literature on female terrorists leans heavily on theory, secondhand data, or sources that cannot be verified. The lack of primary sources skews the research and leads to an oversimplification of the reasons why Muslim women kill.

The fact that, as a former Marine officer serving in Fallujah told the author, "searching women is difficult in a society where there are strict prohibitions against looking at another woman" and poses a security problem, as it makes it hard to determine who the female bombers are.[8] Cultural and religious norms in the Arab Muslim world present unique challenges to U.S. and Iraqi security forces fighting a myriad of insurgent and militia groups in Iraq. Given the inability of international forces to search women in a traditional, patriarchal Islamic society, more female jihadis are able to use the physical separation of men and women, as well as strict Islamic dress codes, to their advantage.

Adding to a woman's advantage is the widely held belief that Muslim women are victims of violence (and indeed they often are), which protects the would-be female bomber from being detected or discovered. Non-Muslim men exclude women as killers on the grounds that the traditional role of women is as caregivers and compassionate members of their households and families. A Muslim woman, they assume, safeguards her society and state in the same way that non-Muslim women in Europe and the West at large do in contributing to nationalist movements as "mothers of the nation."[9]

Throughout time, women have been represented as reflecting "the image of the pure nation," an idea echoed by a number of scholars who argue that national struggles and programs use women to "internalize the desirable national image of mother and wife, of desexualized members of the community."[10] In the Catholic community in Ireland, for example, women have "symbolically represented the purity and tradition of the country" and have been encouraged to embody the "ideal of Mary [the mother of Jesus] in their own 'essence.'"[11] Muslim women are likewise raised to emulate the actions, behaviors, and practices of the pure Muslim women of seventh-century Arabia. For example, in his book *Fatima Is Fatima*, the Iranian Shia political philosopher Ali Shariati glorifies the Prophet's daughter as the symbol of piety.[12]

An equally important point framed in this study is that there is no consensus among militant men about the role of women as suicide bombers. The debate among male terrorists about the *mujahidaat* (literally, female fighters) is part of an ongoing discourse among members of al-Qaeda and other terrorist or insurgent groups. Leading clerics and some Muslim scholars offer varying legal opinions, or fatwas, on the permissibility of female suicide bombers, but most agree that women have served in important supporting roles, and indeed there is ample evidence within classical Islamic scholarship that this is the case. For example, early Muslim women in seventh-century Arabia nursed the wounded, protected their homes when men left to fight in the early battles, and in a few well-documented cases, trained and fought valiantly alongside men to ensure the faith's survival. These early Muslim women behaved no differently from how women do when they care for wounded soldiers or protect their homes and nations in secular, nationalist struggles or other religions' wars. In most conflicts women have participated in, they have contributed to nationalist ideologies and helped forge new identities.

No literature to date rejects the heroism of early Muslim women, but the reaction to the modern-day female bomber is mixed and varies among the Muslim clerical establishment in different countries and communities in which Muslims live. Not all clerics agree as to whether suicide is *haram* (forbidden) or *halal* (permissible). Despite the powerful works of a few ideologues, whose work may inspire both men and women to join the violent jihadi movement, a majority of Muslim scholars reject the use of violence and particularly abhor suicide, arguing that the Prophet of Islam prohibited taking one's life. According to the Prophet, a believer who committed suicide could not enter paradise. And yet the literature of martyrdom by militant groups argues the opposite. Militants, recognizing that Islam strictly forbids suicide, reject the Western use of the word "suicide" and choose to label their attacks "martyrdom operations" (*'amaliyat istishhadiyaa*). By referring to their willingness to die as "martyrdom," religious radicals and elites and their followers justify "suicide" as legitimate, legal, and laudable. Martyrdom is commendable, since it connotes the sacrifice on the part of the perpetrator, who has chosen the rewards of the afterlife over the shortcomings of this life.[13] Thus, the risk taken by a woman in strapping on the bomb, even when there is no guarantee she will explode, is worth the possible reward of *jannah* (heaven).

WHO ARE THE *MUJAHIDAAT*?

The term *mujahidaat* was coined by the first historians of Islam to honor the women who protected the Prophet during the early Islamic battles in the seventh century. These women included members of the Prophet's family and new converts to Islam. The tales of these heroic women are not only recorded in Islamic literature but were also orally transmitted across the generations. One of the most glorified female fighters is Nusayba bint Ka'ab, also known as Umm Umarah, who during the Battle of Uhud (625 CE) lost one arm and suffered eleven wounds while defending Prophet Muhammad.[14] She fought in at least six battles during her lifetime and is one of the few female fighters mentioned in the Quran.[15] Umarah's sacrifice for the Prophet and the new faith has been recorded in Islamic textbooks, stories, and historical memory.[16] Islamic scholar Nimer Busool offers the following rendition of her participation in the Battle of Uhud:

> I went out early in the day to see what was happening.
> I carried with me a vessel full of water. I reached the
> Prophet and his companions while the Muslims were
> Winning . . . but when they [the men] were defeated,
> And they started to flee, only ten men, my two sons,
> My husband and I stayed with the Prophet to defend him.[17]

Busool concludes that women like Umara, who fought using the bow and arrow and the sword, were trained and skilled in warfare.[18]

Umm Sulaim and her sister Umm Haram bint Milhan from the tribe of Ansar in Medina also joined the Prophet in the Battle of Uhud. Carrying a dagger, Umm Sulaim is recorded as having said, "O Messenger of Allah! I carry the dagger, so if any disbeliever approaches me, I will split his stomach open!"[19] Umm Sulaim's martyrdom is recorded in a hadith, in which the Prophet says, "I entered paradise, and I heard somebody walking. I said, 'Who is this?' They said, 'This is al-Ghumaisa' bint Milhan (Umm Sulaim).'"[20]

In addition, the Prophet's own female relatives took part in jihad. His wife, Ayesha, led the Battle of the Camel, and his granddaughter Zaynab bint Ali fought in the Battle of Karbala. Safiya, the Prophet's aunt and sister of his beloved uncle Hamza, is "noted for killing a spy with a tent peg while her terrified male guard cringed nearby."[21] In the Battle of the Trench, Safiya killed a warrior and threw his severed head into the enemy camp.

Even after the Prophet's death, Muslim women continued to take part in warfare. The story of a bedouin woman, Khawlah bint al-Azwar al-Kindiyyah, is less known and documented, but she is regarded as one of the early female martyrs in Islam. Ali ibn Abu Talib (the Prophet's cousin and son-in-law) discovered Khawlah after the battle against Heraclius the Byzantine and his army. Dressed like a knight, she entered the battle with her female companions and "slashed the head of the Greek." This event was the turning point in the battle. Muslims fought until the Byzantines retreated, and then Khawlah made herself known to Ali. Impressed by her heroic deed, Ali married the "woman of rank and honor" shortly after he became the fourth rightly guided caliph (656 CE).[22]

Although these women participated in Islam's conquests and defense, most Muslim women served in a supporting role.[23] 'Aliyya Mustafa Mubarak has compiled a list of sixty-seven women who played a part in the defense of Islam, many of whom participated in battles in an offstage role.[24] A notable example is Hazrat Asmaa, who counseled her sons to pursue warfare. When the Syrians seized the Ka'aba in Mecca, her son Hazrat Abdullah sought his mother's advice: "My son! Degrading and disgraceful peace for fear of death is not better to being killed because to fight with sword in honor is better than to be beaten with a whip in dishonor."[25] In another account, she is recorded to have told her son that "if you are fighting for the cause of Allah and are siding with truth, then you must put a bold front. Go and fight as befits a brave man. . . . If you are martyred, it shall be my highest pleasure."[26] Like Asmaa, the mother of Sayed Ahmed Shaheed encouraged her son to fight in the name of the Islam: "My dear son! Go. But listen don't ever show cowardice. Fight valiantly. And if you run away from the battlefield, I shall never see your face."[27] Shaheed was eventually martyred, fulfilling his mother's wish.

In short, a woman's primary role in classical Islamic literature is that of mother, sister, daughter, and wife of Muslim men at war. However, over time, the meaning of the word *mujahidaat* has changed. Like their male counterparts, some women defenders of the faith have now accepted suicide as the preferred weapon of choice. In asymmetric warfare, women defenders likely perceive suicide attacks as garnering wider media attention as well as achieving greater operational and tactical success than alternate tactics. This chapter uses the term *mujahidaat* to specify female suicide bombers, reflecting the evolution of women's role in conflict from passive to active supporters of the violent jihadi movement.

WHY JIHAD?

The word "jihad" is sacred to many Muslims, but is often misinterpreted on all sides of the political spectrum.[28] Some extremists' focus on a particular vision of Islam has given rise to a battle of belief against unbelief and sparked a war of words in which various groups and individuals are now reasserting their right to claim the true meaning of jihad. Discoloring the original intent and purpose of jihad, extremists are fighting in the name of the unrelieved agony of the Muslim *ummah* (community)—an idea that has some credibility with even "moderate" Muslims—but choose to satisfy their anger with narratives driven by revolutionary change in the society in which they reside.

The message that Islam is anti-Western is reflected in the propaganda of religious extremists, insurgents, and terrorists, all of whom contribute greatly to distortions of Islam in Muslim and Western societies. Insurgents in Iraq, for example, are credited with spreading anti-American sentiments and targeting the coalition for rekindling the Shia-Sunni divide and failing to restore peace to a troubled land.[29] The insurgents' use of propaganda to garner support for political Islam (i.e., a theocratic state) is manifested in broadcasts in various media outlets, from television to the Internet, that draw on the language of violence. On the Abu al-Boukhair Islamic Network, an online forum, one author calls on women to defend their religion because "Islam is under attack from the Crusaders."[30] Other chat rooms devoted to female jihadis make similar statements.

Contrary to popular Western myth, jihad is not synonymous with a holy war. It has a broad semantic content and is different from *qittal* (fighting). Both terms, jihad and *qittal*, have "significantly different meanings and uses in the Qur'an."[31] *Qittal* refers to killing and bloodshed, whereas jihad's original meaning is to struggle to attain God's pleasure. Among the first quranic verses for fighting is number twenty-two:

> Leave is given to those who fought because they were wronged—
> surely God is able to help them—who were expelled from their
> habitations without right, except that they say "Our Lord is God."

To infer that jihad is synonymous with "holy war" is therefore wrong. For the larger Muslim world, jihad is simply an everyday concept: an act of Islamic worship, derived from the Arabic verb *jahada*, which means "effort and striving."[32] For believing Muslims, jihad is a living, breathing concept. Muslims strive to embrace good and reject evil. Even for secular, liberal (nonpracticing Muslims), jihad is a positive term that reflects the inner struggle of one's life.

While there are many forms of jihad, all of which are defined by a set of rules, jihad is best described as self-defense, a means of defending oneself against temptation, against Satan, against the unjust, and against religious persecution.[33] The legitimate notion of jihad as self-defense has, however, been misappropriated, generating an "uncompromisingly belligerent interpretation of jihad."[34]

In the past, Muslim legal theorists have given Muslim scholars the right to declare war against a *kuffar* (infidel) ruler or people. Indian scholar Maulavi Chiragh Ali asserts Muslims have an absolute right to fight in defense of Islam when it is attacked; similar arguments have been circulated and repackaged in the works of Abdallah Azzam, the former veteran mujahideen coordinator of the Afghan jihad, and the writings of Yousef al-Ayiri, a key ideologue of the al-Qaeda network in Saudi Arabia.

JIHAD AS A RELIGIOUS DUTY

Since the start of the Afghan war, Azzam and other theologians in Saudi Arabia have been advocating defensive jihad as a means of reviving the golden era of Islam. The mantle of jihad prevails throughout Azzam's writings, in texts by the early Egyptian revolutionaries, and in fatwas issued by Saudi-based clerics.

Jihad as *fard ayn*, or religious obligation, was first introduced in a fatwa written by Azzam: "Jihad becomes *fard ayn* on every Muslim male and female."[35] According to this fatwa, then, no permission is needed from parents, husband, or a male guardian for women to wage jihad against the infidel— a notion that is echoed in earlier and later works by Islamic reformists, theorists, and jihadis. In "Join the Caravan," Azzam draws on classical Muslim scholars, quoting Ibn 'Abidin from the Hanafi school of thought:

> Jihad is *fard ayn* when the enemy has attacked
> Any of the Islamic heartland, at which point it
> Becomes *fard ayn* on those close to the enemy.[36]

One of the leading proponents of jihad is Umm Mohammed, Azzam's wife. In an interview that appeared in *al-Sharq al-Awsat* in April 2006, Umm Mohammed said she became the "mother figure" of jihad for the wives of the mujahideen (male fighters) in Peshawar.[37] In a memoir from late 1990, Umm Mohammed writes, "I ask my Muslim sisters to encourage their husbands and sons to continue with the jihad."[38] During the Soviet-Afghan war, women did support their husbands, brothers, and male family members. In extremist Urdu-language magazines published in Pakistan from the late 1980s to the early 1990s, women appealed directly to other women to back their men. Magazines such as *al-Irshad* (*The Message*), *al-Ittehad* (*Unity*), and *Sada-e-*

Mujahid (*The Voice of the Fighter*) referred to the "active participation by women in the jihad movement, following the example of the *Suhabiat* [wives of the Prophet's Companions]."[39]

Like his wife, Azzam appeals to all Muslim women to support the mujahideen. In part 2 of "Join the Caravan," published in 1988, he provides sixteen reasons why Muslims ought to fight, both practical and ideological, addressing women in particular, who he views as the prime supporters of men.[40] "What is the matter with the mothers," he asks, "that one of them does not send forward one of hers sons in the Path of Allah that he might be a pride for her in this world and a treasure for her in the Hereafter through her intercession?"[41] By declaring jihad as *fard*, Azzam transformed jihad from a *kifayah* (collective duty) to an individual duty.[42]

Like Azzam and his wife, al-Qaeda's number two leader Ayman al-Zawahiri and his spouse, Umayma, support a woman's role in jihad. In a December 2009 document by Umayma entitled "Letter to My Muslim Sisters," she encourages Muslim women to observe Islam (i.e., raise children in the path of God) and to fight with courage, as women did in the time of their Prophet in the early battles of Islam.[43] While Umayma does not openly advocate female terrorism, she does state that "jihad [today] is an individual duty incumbent upon every Muslim man and woman, but the path of fighting is not easy for women, for it requires a male companion with whom it is lawful for a woman to be. . . . We put ourselves in the service of the jihadis, we carry out what they ask, whether in supporting them financially, serving their [practical] needs, supplying them with information, opinions, partaking in fighting or even [volunteering to carry out] a martyrdom operation. . . . Our principal role . . . is to protect the jihadis [through] bringing up their children, [managing] their homes, and [keeping] their secrets." Like Umayma, other women support female activism with a concept known as *jihad bil kalam* or *jihad bil ilm* (literally, striving for knowledge). Women who may support suicide terrorism but are not operational prefer to use the pen to spread Islam and promote ideals of struggle and sacrifice in the name of religion.

The Belgian widow of a suicide bomber in Afghanistan, Malika al-Aroud publicly stated to media acclaim that "I have a weapon. It's to write. It's to speak out. That's my jihad. You can do many things with words. Writing is also a bomb." Other women express pride over their husband's suicide missions. For example, Defne Bayrak, the wife of the Jordanian suicide bomber Humam al-Balawi, who killed U.S. government officers in Afghanistan in December 2009, said in an interview, "I'm very proud of my husband. He has made a great operation in this war. I hope Allah accepts his sacrifice and converts him into a martyr."[44]

MARTYRDOM VERSUS SUICIDE

Today, extremists justify new rules of warfare to defeat their enemies, including the use of what they call martyrdom operations. Martyrs are held in high esteem in Islam, but some Islamic theologians and contemporary jihadis distort several hadith to suggest that 1) women receive *fewer* rewards for martyrdom than their male counterparts; and 2) the male martyr is *entitled* to more rewards, though his entitlement to these rewards is mentioned neither in the Quran or popularly cited traditions of the imams Bukhari and Muslim. It may be that this idea is circulated to motivate, inspire, and activate the male bomber. For example, a well-known and widely transmitted hadith of the imam Ahmad al-Tirmidhi explicitly notes that male martyrs will enjoy the pleasure of seventy-two virgins in paradise:

> The Martyr has seven special favors from Allah:
> He [or she] is forgiven his sins with the first spurt of blood,
> He sees his place in paradise; he is clothed with the garment of faith.
> He is wed with seventy-two wives from the beautiful Maidens of paradise.
> He is saved from the Punishment of the Grave.
> He is protected from the Great Terror (Judgment Day).
> On his head is placed a Crown of Dignity, a Jewel better than
> The world and all it contains, and he is granted intercession
> For seventy people of his household to enter paradise.[45]

Of these seven favors, the most controversial but at the same time widely accepted among violent jihadis is the promise of seventy-two "maidens of paradise." The promise is even "reminiscent of the medieval Assassins' doctrine, involving the paradise that awaits the holy terrorists," but the concept is not recognized by all Muslim scholars.[46] The translation of the word "virgin" in the hadith has sexual connotations, but other scholars insist that the word *houri* is closer to "the most pure," a likely reference to the Prophet's pious companions.[47] Veteran mujahideen coordinators like Azzam, among others, have accepted Tirmidhi's hadith (though they do not consider other hadith that are deemed more authentic and less disputed), providing greater credibility to the idea that rewards await the male suicide bomber in paradise.[48]

The idea that male martyrs are guaranteed a harem of untouched women in heaven has sparked a debate within the Islamic community at large. Many Western scholars have accepted this concept, partly because it is part of contemporary jihadi literature, while some Muslim clerics debate the Arabic word *hour al-ayn*—translated by jihadis and some scholars as "virgins." For Islam to consider women as "heavenly rewards" for men would be to discount all the social rights granted to women by the Prophet, whom Muslim women call a feminist for his egalitarian principles. To consider women anything less than the equal partners of men would be to offend the earliest revelations by God to the Prophet that elevated woman's status in Islam.[49] Therefore, the "seventy-two virgins" concept has no basis in the quranic exegesis.

Moreover, assured of the rewards of martyrdom, women, like men, perceive they have nothing to lose. In February 2004, in a monthly publication called *al-Muslimah* published by HAMAS, Palestinian female operative Reem Rayishi said, "I am proud to be the first female HAMAS martyr. I have two children and love them very much. But my love to see God is stronger than my love for my children, and I'm sure that God will take care of them if I become a martyr." In 2004, an al-Qaeda magazine published a special section dedicated to the recruitment of women for terrorist attacks, highlighting the story of Umm Hamza, who was "very happy whenever she heard about a martyrdom operation carried out by a woman, whether it was in Palestine or Chechnya."[50] The article further states that Umm Hamza would cry as she waited to be assigned a martyrdom operation "against the Christians in the Arabian Peninsula," a reference to Saudi Arabia.

More recently, women have been calling on Muslim men and women to defend Islam and pursue martyrdom operations. Umm Muhammad, the wife of the late Abu Musab al-Zarqawi, published a letter on July 6, 2006, addressing her husband's martyrdom. In the letter, she writes, "Al-Zarqawi's death will not make the women of this Ummah barren and they will bear those who are even stronger than [he is] who will join the ranks of your army . . . for your path is the gate of Martyrdom that the Prophet urged you to [follow]." Like Umm Muhammad, other women in South Asia and Europe support the pursuit of jihad. Websites such as www.al-minbar.sos glorify the virtues of jihad and martyrdom.[51] Other articles written by women to promulgate jihad used to appear on www.mujahidaat.com, but this website has since been shut down.

GENDER EQUALITY

With more women expressing support for jihad, the question often raised by observers and terrorism experts is whether women are empowered through the use of force. If so, how? If in the early battles of Islam, women were afforded a higher position in society for contributing to the war effort, why are contemporary Muslim women not offered the same rewards? These questions are part of an ongoing discussion among experts as to what militant women hope to achieve by joining terrorist organizations.

The available information, derived mostly from interviews of failed Palestinian bombers, does not suggest that all women are easily manipulated. In many cases, female bombers are better educated than men, and statistics show that "between 30 to 40 percent" of Palestinian women who join terrorist organizations "have attended university."[52] According to Israeli scholar Anat Berko, "they are the smarter of these smart weapons."[53] But despite women's higher levels of education, many male terrorists continue to regard women as the weaker sex and show no indication that they respect women any more for their participation in suicide terrorism — a point made clear to many women, including the veteran female activist and notorious Palestinian hijacker Leila Khaled. Journalist Judith Miller concludes — based on expert opinion — that an increase in female suicide bombers "reflects neither a progressive attitude towards women nor gender equality in the religious, revolutionary, and national liberation movements that promote such terror."[54]

However, the media's reaction to female bombers in the Arab Muslim world can be positive and can help to elevate women to a higher position than they would ordinarily occupy within their own societies. According to Umm Usamah, al-Qaeda spokeswoman in Saudi Arabia, the success of attacks by Palestinian women improved the status of the Arab woman and ended the debate about equality between men and women. For example, the attack in Jerusalem in 2002 by the Palestinian female suicide bomber Wafa Idris generated a wide response from the Arab media. The London-based Arab newspaper *al-Quds* quoted the Fatah Revolutionary Council as saying that "the martyr's death of Wafa restored honor to the national role of the Palestinian woman, who has carried out the most remarkable exploits in the long struggle for national freedom. . . . [Sh]e stands at the side of the men in the struggle for freedom."[55] A Moroccan-Belgian woman is known to have said to members of her community that attacks by Belgian-born female bomber Myrium Goris portray the weakness of men and the strength of women: "It's a woman saying, 'Look what I, a woman, have done. And you, the men — are you capable of the same?'"[56] By shaming men into taking up jihad, women hope to convince more Muslim men to join their struggle.

Women may be driven toward suicide terrorism when pressures from *within* their familial units and social structures violate, weaken, or constrain their right to live: "The decision for martyrdom is rooted within the local struggle for freedom from the social and worldly responsibilities women have to bear within a weak civil society."[57] Miller claims that some women may have chosen terrorism when those they "had loved and trusted the most had abandoned her," though alienation alone is not a sufficient reason to justify participation in suicide terrorism.[58]

Other conflicts have seen a steady rise of female bombers, but their participation will not likely change the religious and societal restrictions placed on women. In Iraq, more women are being recruited by Sunni and Shia militia groups to conduct suicide attacks, including for the female unit called al-Zahra, which is named after the Prophet's daughter and wife of the fourth Muslim caliph, Ali ibn Abu Talib.[59] But while insurgents are using women to perpetrate attacks, they appear to have placed greater limitations on Iraqi women by imposing strict Islamic behavioral and dress codes. Women failing to abide by the new laws are subject to violence from extremists, street gangs, and "elements within the anti-occupation insurgency."[60] An Iraqi sheikh loyal to Shia militia leader Muqtada al-Sadr says he beats women "because we are authorized [by God] to do so, and that is our duty."[61] These attitudes suggest that men recruiting female bombers have no interest in seeing women's position within Iraqi society change. With the bomb under the *abaya*, women seem to serve one purpose: to strike the enemy and be killed in the process. Increased levels of violence, such as rape and kidnappings, by militia groups indicate that women will unlikely achieve more rights. An Iraqi official exiled to the United States told me that should insurgents seize power, women will probably be denigrated in the new Iraqi society.[62]

Finally, women's participation in earlier national liberation movements has not significantly improved the status of women. The Algerian women who formed underground networks and fought against the French colonizers (1958–64), including in the Battle of Algiers, once again assumed traditional gender roles after Algerian independence.[63] The same is true for Palestinian women, who were determined not to meet the fate of their Algerian sisters. In June 1989, Palestinian women formed a Women's Higher United Council, "drafted an Equal Rights for Women bill and placed it before the Unified Leadership." According to one woman, "we wanted the men to know that we have teeth too."[64]

In short, the unintentional debate that women in conflict arouse is plastic; there are no conflicts today that have elevated the status of the Muslim woman, nor are there any that address the societal and religious norms that solidify the role of the Muslim woman. While her participation in suicide attacks serves the overall group or social movement, her individual contribution is seldom recognized. What we do not know is to what extent women (and men) grieve the loss of a female suicide bomber. Can we assume a culture of "jihad" in Islamic conflicts? The public versus private face of the families of female militants is often not reflected in research of female terrorists. Although we cannot downplay the challenge that researchers face when *talking to terrorists*, it is nevertheless critical that we accumulate evidence from the context in which violence occurs in order to avoid informed guesswork and glib rhetoric about "why women kill"; failing to do so could lead to dangerous conclusions. Therefore, a careful mapping of the conditions under which women join terror groups is essential to any study of female terrorism—still a new and emerging area of study.

THE CLERICAL DIVIDE

What we do know is that women's participation in violent political struggles remains controversial in Islamic theology and doctrine. In the aftermath of the 9/11 attacks and the July 2005 attacks in London, several Islamic scholars denounced the use of suicide as *haram* (forbidden) through fatwas that have been signed in documents made publicly available. To further justify Islam's rejection of suicide, the former head of Egypt's al-Azhar Fatwa Committee, Shaykh 'Atiyyah Saqr, referred to a hadith to argue that the Prophet Muhammad said a believer would be forbidden from entering paradise if he committed suicide.[65] More recently, Abdel Mon'em Mustafa Abu Halima (also known as Abu Naseer al Tartus), a prominent Syrian cleric in London, issued a separate fatwa prohibiting suicide operations. Abu Halima noted that "whoever hurts a Muslim has no Jihad reward," which supports another hadith in which the Prophet of Islam is reported to have said that "whoever murders a non-Muslim enjoying protection under the Islamic state would never smell the scent of Paradise."[66]

Today, the debate among the *ulama* on the permissibility of suicide continues to divide the Muslim world; some view suicide as a legitimate tactic, while others reject it on the grounds that it was never employed by the Prophet of Islam, and therefore, it must be forbidden. Many scholars argue that suicide is one of the major sins in Islam that annuls one's faith, and those knowledgeable of religious texts often cite the quranic verse "al-Maeda," which clearly rebukes those who kill: "He who kills anyone not in retaliation for murder or to spread mischief in the land, it would be as if he killed all of mankind, and if anyone saved a life, it would be as if he saved the life of the whole people."[67]

The issue remains open to interpretation by various Muslim clerics and terrorist organizations, leaving the question unanswered. Most mainstream Islamic theologians reject the use of suicide as an appropriate response to state-sponsored or group-initiated violence. Other clerics are far more ambiguous about their position regarding suicide, but one point on which most clerics agree is the role of women in warfare. Several Islamic websites, including www.resalah.net, describe situations in which women could participate in jihad. According to these former websites, the different ways Muslim women can support jihad include raising children to love jihad; to assist male family members in matters relating to jihad; to engage in *da'wa* (proselytizing); to pray for the male fighters; and to provide general support, which would include facilitating jihad activities.[68] Nowhere in the preceding statement, though, is a woman encouraged to fight alongside men, although the fatwa center on www.islamweb.net states that "women can participate in [war] if there is a dire need for it and provided they would not be prisoners."[69]

Still, a few Muslim religious male leaders in recent years have issued fatwas encouraging women to support their men. Many conservative clerics consider women to be just as capable as men when it comes to taking on the perceived enemy; they probably recognize the tactical advantages of using a female bomber, such as her ability to mask her identity and hide weapons beneath conservative Islamic dress. Others argue women should be able to participate in jihad without a male guardian, suggesting that under exceptional circumstances, such as when an attack is launched against Muslims or in ongoing war, women ought to be able to operate independently. The growing debate over whether women should support the global jihad or local conflicts is ongoing, and various arguments are made for and against using Muslim women in warfare.

Muslim scholars on Islamic websites, such as IslamOnline.net, provide answers to questions about a woman's role in jihad. Islamic scholar Abdel Fattah Idrees, a professor at Cairo's al-Azhar University, has responded to a question posted on the website concerning a Muslim woman's role in jihad by noting that jihad is not imposed on women except in three cases: if the enemy invades the lands of Muslim, which means that jihad becomes the duty of everyone, male and female; if Muslim leaders call upon the whole Muslim community to perform jihad; and if Muslim leaders appoint certain women to perform specific tasks, such as collecting intelligence against the enemy.[70]

In answer to another question posted by a woman on the Fatwa Bank, Yusuf al-Qaradawi, a Doha-based Islamic scholar and head of the influential European Council on Fatwa and Research, states that a woman's participation in "martyr operations carried out in Palestine . . . is one of the most praised acts of worship."[71] Al-Qaradawi first issued a fatwa on the role of women in jihad following the suicide attack by Wafa Idris. First published on the HAMAS Internet site, www.palestine-info.info in January 2004, the fatwa explains that Muslim women could disregard certain codes of dress and Islamic law to participate in suicide operations: "When jihad becomes an individual duty, as when the enemy seizes the Muslim territory, a woman becomes entitled to take part in it alongside men . . . and she can do what is impossible for men to do," even if it means taking off her *hijab* to carry out an operation.[72]

By creating new rules for women, al-Qaradawi is suggesting that women "have their own role in jihad and [have the right] to attain martyrdom."[73] In support of al-Qaradawi, who is a Sunni cleric, Mohammed Hussein Fadlallah, a Shia Lebanese Muslim cleric and spiritual leader of Hezbollah, claims women can take part "if the necessities dictate that women should carry out regular military operations or suicide operations."[74] In his fatwa, Shaykh ibn Jibreen, a Saudi-based cleric, claims a Muslim woman can participate in jihad on certain conditions: if she is fighting in a *kufaar*, or foreign territory, and if the act will ease her pain and inflict damage on the enemy.

Arguably the first cleric to state that women can participate in jihad is the veteran Afghan *mujahid* coordinator Abdallah Azzam. In a fatwa published in 1984, Azzam said that "jihad was the action required (*fard ayn*) of every Muslim, regardless of gender."[75] Like Azzam, terrorist leaders such as Ayman Zawahiri proudly cite examples of female jihadis, probably to encourage other women to fight for the cause. In an interview with *al-Majallah*, Zawahiri stated, "A British Muslim woman called Umm Hafsah carried out another operation during which she killed two Americans."[76]

The world's most glorified terrorist leader, Osama bin Laden, also extolled the role of the Muslim woman in jihad in his 1996 fatwa: "Our women had set a tremendous example of generosity in the cause of Allah; they motivated and encouraged their sons, brothers and husbands to fight [for Allah]." Shortly after the 9/11 attacks, bin Laden told Pakistani journalist Hamid Mir that "I became a father of a girl after September 11. I named her Safia after Safia who killed a Jewish spy at the time of the Prophet. [My daughter] Safia will kill enemies of Islam like Safia of the Prophet's time."[77] This is the only such statement bin Laden made in support of female suicide terrorists, but he more often glorified the auxiliary roles of early Muslim women, specifically referencing Khadija, the Prophet's first wife and the first Muslim convert in pre-Islamic Arabia. Bin Laden honored Khadija for inciting men at the time of the Prophet to participate in jihad against the Quraysh, Islam's fiercest and first enemy. In his "Declaration of War against Americans," bin Laden declared that Muslim women have "set a tremendous example for generosity in the name of Allah. They motivate and encourage their sons, brothers, and husbands to fight for the cause of Allah in Afghanistan, Bosnia-Herzegovina, Chechnya, and in other countries. . . . Our women encourage jihad."[78]

Religious enablers of jihad also include key al-Qaeda ideologues such as Yousef al-Ayyiri, the head of operations for al-Qaeda in Saudi Arabia until he was killed by Saudi security forces in 2004. Ayyiri, a prolific writer, penned *The Role of Women in Jihad against the Enemies*, referring to the early Muslim female fighters, he stated, "behind every *Mujahid* stood a woman," which suggests that women were the primary instigators of jihad.

Like Ayirri, other male and female terrorists encourage women to join militant organizations, but many instead use the Internet to communicate their message. Umm Muhammad, for example, posted her July 2006 letter on the Mujahideen Shura Council website. Similarly, the women of *al-Khansaa* magazine, a propaganda tool managed by the Saudi-based al-Qaeda organization, provide Muslim women a platform in which to encourage one another to join jihad. Named after an Arabian poetess and convert to Islam, *al-Khansaa* published an article in August 2004 entitled "What Role Can Sisters Play in Jihad?" in which the writer outlines three roles for Muslim women in jihad: to participate in the actual fighting; support the male fighters on the war front; or act as a guard and protectorate of male jihadis.

More conservative terrorists view Muslim women as key to maintaining the family structure. The sixth edition of *al-Fursan*, the magazine for the Islamic Army in Iraq—one of several Sunni insurgent groups—provides an example of an exemplary Muslim woman who supported her husband in jihad until she died.[79] Arguably the job that gives a Muslim woman the most power is raising her son for jihad. Umm Nidal, the mother of a male suicide bomber belonging to HAMAS, notes in a television interview that "jihad is a [religious] commandment imposed upon us. We must instill this idea in our sons' souls, all the time. . . . [T]his is what encouraged me to sacrifice Muhammad [my son] for the sake of Allah."[80] Nidal and other women like her support the stance of traditional terrorist groups, who appear reluctant to change their attitude toward women and prefer women to offer ideological and moral backing to men rather than assume an operational role.

A younger generation of male jihadis may not be as cautious. The worldwide crackdown against militant men and their networks has led to these younger men to be more flexible when it comes to women, though seldom do female terrorists assume a leadership position. Terrorist organizations amenable to female suicide bombers include Palestinian groups and elements within the al-Qaeda organization, as well as an emerging group of homegrown terror networks that are smaller and transnational, such as militant organizations found throughout Europe. The men in these organizations are willing to accept women in operational roles so long as they contribute to the overall objectives of the terrorist, insurgent, or militia. These same men would unlikely promote women's equal rights should the conflict end.

In sum, whether the fatwas permitting women to engage in violent action will enable other women to legitimize the use of suicide terrorism is questionable. What clerics have done, however, is grant would-be bombers and women sympathetic to extremist causes a religious justification to participate actively in jihad.

WOMEN, GENDER, AND TERRORISM

Should suicide attacks become a trend among Muslim women, it would be the exception rather than the rule. First, the violent jihad movement is not homogenous, and there are only certain places where social mores are perhaps conducive to more "progressive" treatment of women's status. Even in those Muslim societies where female fighters *appear* to be the norm (i.e., Palestinian territories), it still remains unclear how long and with what frequency Muslim women will conduct suicide attacks. The available data of female activists and bombers in the Palestinian-Israeli conflict, for example, suggests that female bombers ebb and flow. Opportunities and options for women to perpetrate attacks are often at the behest of their men.

Second, the inclusion of women in terrorist organizations is unlikely to change the social status of women in Islamic societies. While conservative and ultraorthodox Muslim men value their women for their work in sustaining the family, these men accord female terrorists a different status as men who commit the same attacks. That is not to say that female bombers' operations are not extolled by men in jihadi websites and magazines; in fact, a woman may receive greater attention than a man who detonates, simply because of her gender. But, as terror expert Mia Bloom observes, women seeking equality by becoming human bombs "reinforce the inequalities of their societies, rather than confront them and explode the myths from within."[81]

There is no indication that these men would allow the *mujahidaat* to transcend authority and replace the male folk hero. There is also no evidence that Muslim female operatives ever have contact with senior male leaders, except to execute attacks, which leads to the question of why women matter. Does this mean that women are expendable? Terror attacks by women over the past ten years may represent nothing more than a riding on the wave of al-Qaeda's success rather than a lasting effort in the global jihad. This might not hold true if conflicts in the Muslim world worsen over time (for example, if Muslim land were occupied).

Third, conflicts offer militant men and women an opportunity to indulge in violence. The steady rise of female bombers in Iraq suggests that women will play a wider role in terrorist operations in situations where jihad is more akin to an insurgency; in a conflict in which men are able to mobilize an entire population against a clear aggressor whose forces occupy Muslim lands *and* who is seen as oppressing an entire population, women are more apt to join terror networks. Like men, women arguably hope to participate in the liberation of their countries, even though men will continue to lead terrorist (and nationalist) organizations. Prior research on women's roles in resistance movements, guerrilla warfare, and conflict suggests that terrorist organizations provide compelling reasons for women to conduct operations with personal, organizational, societal, and national benefits.

Finally, ongoing conflicts in the Muslim world or in countries with significant numbers of Muslims who feel disenfranchised, disenchanted, or discouraged by state policies toward Muslims will likely encourage and enable more women (and men) to join local or global jihad. In the near term, Iraq will be the litmus test of whether more women will be recruited for suicide operations. Chatter on female-only jihadi forums indicates a growing acceptance of women who pursue more aggressive, operational roles afforded to them by male jihadis in Iraq. So long as these discussions occur and the terrorist landscape remains unaffected, more women will choose to detonate for reasons that may not be entirely clear to the outside observer.

NOTES

1. The idea that a profile for terrorists can prove useful has sparked a growing debate among scholars. Most experts now disagree with profiling, given the diversity and anonymity of terrorists' groups and members. However, David Lester, Bijou Yang, and Mark Lindsay contend that extensive biographies of terrorists need to be collected and assessed before ruling out profiles as an ineffective measure of understanding the psychology of terrorists; see their article, "Suicide Bombers: Are Psychological Profiles Possible?" *Studies in Conflict and Terrorism* 27, no. 4 (2004): 283–95.

2. For a detailed account of jihadi martyrdom narratives in Iraq, see Mohammed M. Hafez, *Suicide Bombers in Iraq: The Strategy and Ideology of Martyrdom* (Washington, D.C.: U.S. Institute of Peace, 2007). Accounts of female suicide bombers come from a wide range of sources, which include online communications (e.g., female chat rooms accessed with a protected password), female martyr videos (mostly filmed by Palestinian

would-be bombers), women's propaganda (including articles, poems, and letters addressed to male jihadis or the larger Muslim world), as well as transcripts of Muslim women on trial in Europe, many of whom are accused of supporting martyrdom operations, possessing knowledge of terrorist activities, or providing support to their male family members and/or associates.

3. Above all other motives, researchers of female jihadis emphasize personal motivations, which include a woman's personal link to a male member of a terrorist organization as well as the need to forge a new identity and gain acceptance from her community. A number of scholarly works address the importance of personal/individual (rather than group) reasons for choosing to engage in suicide terror. For this literature, see Farhana Ali, "Rocking the Cradle to Rocking the World: The Role of Muslim Female Fighters," *Journal of International Women's Studies* 8, no. 1 (2006): 21–35; Farhana Ali, "Ready to Detonate: The Diverse Profiles of Female Bombers," in *National Memorial Institute for the Prevention of Terrorism Annual 2006* (Oklahoma City, Okla.: MIPT, 2006); Farhad Khosrokhavar, *Suicide Bombers: Allah's New Martyrs* (London: Pluto, 2005), 131–37; Randy Borum, *Psychology of Terrorism* (Gainesville: University of Florida Press, 2004), 13; Deborah M. Galvin, "The Female Terrorist: A Socio-Psychological Perspective," *Behavioral Science and the Law* 1, no. 2 (1983): 19–32; Joseph Margolin, "Psychological Perspectives in Terrorism," in *Terrorism: Interdisciplinary Perspectives*, ed. Yonah Alexander and Seymour Maxwell Finger (New York: John Jay, 1977), 273–74; Ariel Merari, "The Readiness to Kill and Die: Suicidal Terrorism in the Middle East," in *Origins of Terrorism: Psychologies, Ideologies, Theologies and States of Mind*, ed. Walter Reich (New York: Cambridge University Press, 1990), 206. While individual rationale is important, of the idea that jihad is a global phenomenon that transcends national boundaries cannot be discounted. For this viewpoint, see Faisal Devji, *Landscapes of the Jihad* (Ithaca, N.Y.: Cornell University Press, 2005).

4. David Cook, "Radical Female Muslims Redefining Islam," *Sallyport: The Magazine of Rice University*, 61, no. 2 (2004), www.rice.edu/sallyport/2004/winter2/sallyport/islam .html (accessed March 10, 2011). Critics of these approaches (e.g., Laura Sjoberg and Caron Gentry, *Mothers, Monsters, Whores: Women's Violence in Global Politics* [London: Zed, 2007), and Miranda Alison, *Women and Political Violence* [New York: Routledge, 2008]) express concern that these approaches rely on, reify, and replicate gender-essentialist notions of femininity.

5. According to Laleh Khalili, a professor of Middle East politics at the School of Oriental and African Studies in London, women taking part in frontline military operations can have a shaming effect on men, "impelling them to take part." See report from Neil Arun, "Women Bombers Break New Ground," *BBC News*, November 15, 2005, http://news.bbc.co.uk/2/hi/middle_east/4436368.stm (accessed March 10, 2011).

6. Ali, "Ready to Detonate: The Diverse Profiles of Female Bombers"; see also Ali, "Rocking the Cradle to Rocking the World."

7. This is not to say that women terrorists (or even suicide terrorists) are exclusively Muslim; rather it is to focus this chapter's inquiries on the ones who are.

8. Interview conducted in April 2007. The officer is now studying law at Harvard Law School.

9. This is a common concept and the title of several books written by female scholars who argue that women as mothers protect their communities and states, that in their role as mothers, women have contributed to nation building and/or nationalist movements. See Patrizia Albanese, *Mothers of the Nation* (Toronto: University of Toronto Press, 2006), and Raffael Scheck, *Mothers of the Nation* (New York: Berg, 2004).

10. For background, see Julie Mostov, "Sexing the Nation/Desexing the Body," in *Gender Ironies of Nationalism: Sexing the Nation*, ed. Tamar Mayer (New York: Routledge, 2000), 103.

11. Angela K. Martin, "Death of a Nation in Ireland," in *Gender Ironies of Nationalism*, 67–70.

12. Reza Aslan makes the argument that Fatima was used to defy the Western image of womanhood. He discounts Shariati's approach and states that the "traditional colonial image of the veiled Muslim woman as the sheltered, docile sexual property of her husband is just as misleading and simpleminded as the postmodernist image of the veil as the emblem of female freedom and empowerment from Western cultural hegemony" (*No God But God: The Origins, Evolution and Future of Islam* [London: Arrow, 2006], 73–74).

13. For a genre of literature on the benefits of martyrdom (*shahadat*), see essays by Shia scholars Ayatullah Mahmud Taleqani, Ayatullah Murtada Mutahhari, and Ali Shari'ati in *Jihad and Shahadat: Struggle and Martyrdom in Islam*, ed. Mehdi Abedi and Gary Legenhausen (Houston, Tex.: Institute for Research and Islamic Studies, 1986). Sunni scholarship offers more diverse writings on the subject, including those by both militant and moderate authors; for example, see Sayyid Qutb, "Jihad in the Cause of God," in *Milestones* (Cedar Rapids, Iowa: Mother Mosque Foundation, 1993), 53–76; Yusuf al-Qaradawi, "The Prophet Muhammad as a Jihad Model," MEMRI report no. 246, July 24, 2001, http://memri.org/bin/articles.cgi?Page=archives&Areasd&ID=SP24 601 (accessed March 10, 2011); Majid Khadduri, *The Law of War: The Jihad*, vol. 2 of *War and Peace in the Law of Islam* (Baltimore, Md.: Johns Hopkins University Press, 1955), 49–73.

14. Assad Nimer Busool, *Nisa Muslimaat Mujahimadaat* (Chicago: al-Huda, 1995), 35–37.

15. Quran 3:153. Verse 33:35 was revealed after she asked the Prophet about the rights

of women for performing duties of men, such as fighting in war. The verse, Surah Ahzab, is the first revelation that places men and women on equal footing in the eyes of God.

16. An Islamic Web page, www.nusaybah.com, is dedicated to Umm Umarah. She fought in numerous other battles and is remembered most for having defended the Prophet at a time when female fighters were rare. She also encouraged her four sons to die for Islam.

17. Ibid.

18. Busool, *Nisa Muslimaat Mujahimadaat*, 34.

19. Ibid., 39.

20. *Ibn Sa'd*, 8:430.

21. Jennifer Heath, *The Scimitar and the Veil* (Mahwah, N.J.: Hidden Spring, 2004), 199–200.

22. Ibid., 215.

23. Busool, *Nisa Muslimaat Mujahimadaat*, 34–35.

24. See David Cook, "Women Fighting in Jihad?" *Studies in Conflict and Terrorism* 28, no. 5 (2005): 375–84.

25. Saeed Ahmed Ansari, Abdussalam Nadvi, and Syed Suleman Nadvi, *Women Companions of the Holy Prophet and Their Sacred Lives* (Bombay: Bilal, 1997), 148.

26. Mail Khairabadi, "The Great Mothers," *Bhatkallys.com*, May 5, 2005, http://www .bhatkallys.com/article/article.asp?aid=1105 (accessed March 10, 2011); Ansari, Nadvi, and Nadvi, *Women Companions of the Holy Prophet*, 149.

27. Khairabadi, "The Great Mothers."

28. Jihad today is mistakenly seen as synonymous with "terrorism," "extremism," and "radicalism." No other term in the Muslim vocabulary has been flagrantly misunderstood in the West. It is a word that has been harmed by an unsound meaning of "holy war." Imam Muhammad Magid of ADAMS, a mosque and community center in Sterling, Virginia, says, "Nowhere in the Quran will you find holy war attributed to jihad." Correcting the misconceptions and the biases attached to the term requires a brief explanation of what it is, and what it is not.

29. Iraq has always been the center of conflict, or *fitna* (anarchy), in Islamic history, dating back to the caliphate of Uthman, Ali, and Yazid. Civil war erupted among the Muslims over the rightful leadership of the Muslim global community and reached a pivotal point in Iraq with the violent murder of Ali's son and Prophet Muhammad's grandson, Imam Hussein in Karbala.

30. http://www.islaam.net/main/display.php?id=1126&category=13 (accessed March 23, 2011).

31. Louay Fatoohi, *Jihad in the Qur'an: The Truth from the Source* (London: Luna Plena, 2009), 67.

32. Jalal Abualrub, *Holy Wars, Crusades, Jihad* (Orlando, Fla.: Madinah Publishers, 2002), 78–79. See also Rudolph Peters, *Jihad in Classical and Modern Islam: A Reader* (Princeton, N.J.: Markus Wiener, 1996).

33. Maher Hathout, senior advisor of the Muslim Public Affairs Council in Washington, D.C., says, "Historically, fighting back against aggressors [the pagan Quraysh tribe] was prohibited during the thirteen years of the Meccan period . . . [but] after the migration to Medina and the establishment of the Islamic state, Muslims were concerned with how to defend themselves against aggression from their enemies." After thirteen years of persecution and living in exile, the permission to fight enabled the early Muslims to protect themselves against the Quraysh and other enemies anxious to destroy the Islamic community. For background, see Abualrub, *Holy Wars, Crusades, Jihad*, and Peters, *Jihad in Classical and Modern Islam*.

34. Aslan, *No God But God*, 86.

35. Abdallah Azzam, *Defence of the Muslim Lands*, http://space.crono911.net/EBook/553_Religioscope_Azzam.pdf (accessed March 28, 2011). Azzam notes that bin Baz "declared in the mosque of Ibn Ladna in Jeddah and in the large mosque of Riyadh that jihad with your person today is *fard ayn*." The fatwa was also signed by other Saudi-based clerics, including Mohammed Bin Salah Bin Uthaimin.

36. Abdallah Azzam, "Join the Caravan," pt. 1, *al-Jihad*, December 1988, 23, http://www.religioscope.com/info/doc/jihad/azzam_caravan_3_part1.htm (accessed March 28, 2011).

37. Mohammed al-Shafey, "*Al-Sharq al-Awsat* Interviews Umm Mohammed: The Wife of Bin Laden's Spiritual Mentor," *al-Sharq al-Awsat*, April 30, 2006.

38. Abdallah Azzam, *al-Jihad*, November-December 1990.

39. "The Defense of Our Land," *al-Irshad*, April 1989. All magazines were acquired from a source in Peshawar, Pakistan, and translated by Afzaal Mahmood.

40. Azzam's sixth reason for waging jihad is to establish a solid foundation for Islam: "This homeland [Afghanistan] will not come about without an organized Islamic movement" ("Join the Caravan," 14). By stressing victory in Afghanistan, Azzam hoped to "change the tide of the battle, from an Islamic battle in one country, to an Islamic World Jihad movement" ("Martyrs: The Building Blocks of Nations," www.religioscope.com/info/doc/jihad/azzam_martyrs.htm [accessed March 10, 2011]). This would suggest that Azzam believed in spreading Islam, although his actions—and the bulk of his writing—indicated his focus was winning the battle in Afghanistan.

41. Abdallah Azzam, "Join the Caravan," pt. 2, *al-Jihad*, December 1988, 27, http://www.religioscope.com/info/doc/jihad/azzam_caravan_4_part2.htm (accessed March 28, 2011).

42. In contemporary Islamic reform movements, the founder of Wahhabism in present-day Saudi Arabia, Abdul al-Wahhab, first proclaimed the idea of jihad *kifayah*,

but he did not issue a blanket order to commit any and all violence. Al-Wahhab set limitations on violence as well as on killing and the destruction of property. For a complete biography, see Natana J. DeLong-Bas, *Wahhabi Islam* (New York: Oxford University Press, 2004). Contrary to accepted Western analysis, al-Wahhab never discusses martyrdom, paradise, or heavenly rewards in his writings on jihad; instead, he promulgates the sanctity of life, which is best reflected in his *Kitab al-Tawhid* (*Book of Monotheism*), colored with quranic verses and hadith.

43. Umayma al-Zawahiri, "Letter to My Muslim Sisters," February 26, 2001, http://www.jihadica.com/umayma-al-zawahiri-on-women%e2%80%99s-role-in-jihad (accessed March 10, 2011).

44. "MSM: An Interview with Defne Bayrak, CIA Agents Killer's Widow," January 8, 2010, *Tea and Politics*, http://teaandpolitics.wordpress.com/2010/01/08/msm-an-interview-with-defne-bayrak-cia-agents-killers-widow (accessed March 3, 2011).

45. Shama-il Tirmidhi chapter 011, hadith no. 006 (087).

46. Bruce Hoffman, *Inside Terrorism* (New York: Columbia University Press, 1998), 99. For a historical background on the Assassins, see M. J. Akbar, *The Shade of Swords: Jihad and the Conflict between Islam and Christianity* (New York: Routledge, 2002), 195.

47. Muhammad Asad, a Muslim scholar, translates the Arabic word as "one who is most pure" and "white" but refutes the idea that it has the denotation of "virgin."

48. Jihadist literature and terrorist organizations worldwide have emphasized the seventy-two virgins in heaven to provide the would-be martyr an additional incentive to sacrifice the pleasures of this life for the next. Most jihadists never question the authenticity of this hadith, partly because key figures like Azzam have accepted it and partly due to the lack of Islamic scholarship within the overall jihadi movement in the 1980s, which also holds true today.

49. For background on women's status in Islam, see Abdul Rahman al-Sheha, *Woman in the Shade of Islam* (Saudi Arabia: Islamic Educational Center, 2006); Asma Barlas, *Believing Women in Islam* (Austin: University of Texas Press, 2002); Fatima Mernissi, *The Veil and the Male Elite*, trans. Mary Jo Lakeland (Cambridge, U.K.: Perseus Books, 1987); Heath, *The Scimitar and the Veil*; Busool, *Nisa Muslimaat Mujahimadaat*.

50. *Sawt al-Jihad*, January 23, 2004. In this edition of the online magazine produced by al-Qaeda in Saudi Arabia, there is a new section dedicated to women and includes the glorification of Um Hamza, a woman who is a role model for other women wishing to join terrorist organizations.

51. See Paul Cruickshank, "Suicide Bomber's Widow Soldiers On," CNN, August 24, 2006, http://edition.cnn.com/2006/WORLD/asiapcf/08/15/elaroud/index.html (accessed March 10, 2011).

52. Judith Miller, "The Bomb under the Abaya: Women Who Become Suicide Bombers," *Policy Review* 143 (June 2007): 52.

53. Anat Berko, *The Path to Paradise: The Inner World of Suicide Bombers and Their Dispatchers* (New York: Praeger Security International, 2007).

54. Miller, "The Bomb under the Abaya."

55. Qtd. in "The Palestinian and Israeli Media on Female Suicide Terrorists," in *Female Suicide Bombers: Dying for Equality*, ed. Yoram Schweitzer (Tel Aviv: Jaffee Center for Strategic Studies, 2006), 47.

56. See Peter Bergen and Paul Cruickshank, "Lady Killer: Terrorism Is No Longer a Male-Only Preserve," *Center on Law and Security*, September 11, 2006, http://www.lawandsecurity.org/get_article/?id=54 (accessed March 10, 2011).

57. Farhana Ali, "Rocking the Cradle to Rocking the World," 26.

58. Miller, "The Bomb under the Abaya."

59. Al-Zahra is a Shia female unit that is now being trained in Iraq to conduct attacks against Sunni men and women; see Abdul Hameed Bakier, "Female Shiite Assassination Groups Dispatched to Baghdad," *Jamestown Foundation Terrorism Focus* 3, no. 45 (2006), http://www.jamestown.org/single/?no_cache=1&tx_ttnews%5Btt_news%5D=975 (accessed March 10, 2011).

60. See Chris Shumway, "Rise of Extremism, Islamic Law Threaten Iraqi Women," *New Standard*, April 27, 2007, http://newstandardnews.net/content/?items=1600 (accessed March 10, 2011).

61. Ibid.

62. Interview conducted in June 2007.

63. Eileen MacDonald, *Shoot the Women First* (New York: Random House, 1992), 74.

64. Ibid., 75.

65. "Ask the Scholar," *IslamOnline.net*, May 21, 2003.

66. "Salafi Jihadi Trend Theorist Turns against al-Qaeda and Issues a Religious Opinion of the Impermissibility of Suicidal Operations," *al-Sharq al-Awsat*, September 2, 2005.

67. Abualrub, *Holy Wars, Crusades, Jihad*, 209–11; Quran 32.

68. www.resalah.net (accessed August 2004).

69. www.islamweb.net (accessed June 13, 2006).

70. Fatwa Bank, *IslamOnline.net*.

71. Fatwa Bank, *IslamOnline.net*.

72. "Ask the Scholar," *IslamOnline.net*, March 22, 2004.

73. Abu Toameh Khaled, "Women May Be Terror Suicide Bombers, Muslim Scholar Rules," *Jerusalem Post*, May 25, 2003.

74. "Lebanese Muslim Cleric Ok's Female Suicide Bombers," *(Karachi) Business Recorder*, April 2, 2002.

75. "The Union of Good."

76. "Paper Cites al-Zawahiri's *al-Majallah* Interview, 'Sensational Revelations,'" *al-Arab al-Alamiyah*, December 17, 2001.

77. Qtd. in Bergen and Cruickshank, "Lady Killer."

78. The full text of bin Laden's fatwa can be found at www.pbs.org/newshour/terrorism/international/fatwa_1996.html.

79. Qtd. in introduction, in *Female Suicide Bombers: Dying for Equality?*, 11.

80. See "An Interview with the Mother of a Suicide Bomber," *MEMRI Jihad and Terrorism* special dispatch no. 391, June 19, 2002, http://memri.org/bin/articles.cgi?Page=archives&Area=sd&ID=SP39102 (accessed March 10, 2011).

81. Bloom, *Dying to Kill*, 62.

In almost every culture and every period of history, a she-devil
emerges as an example of all that is rotten in the female sex.
This Medusa draws together the many forms of female
perversion: a woman whose sexuality is debauched and foul,
pornographic and bisexual; a woman who knows none of the
fine and noble instincts when it comes to men and children;
a woman who lies and deceives, manipulates and corrupts.
A woman who is clever and powerful. This is a woman who
is far deadlier than the male, in fact not a woman at all.

— HELENA KENNEDY, *Eve Was Framed*

The Gendering of Women's Terrorism

Caron E. Gentry and Laura Sjoberg

There are as many myths and sensationalized stories about women insur-
gents and terrorists in history as there are women terrorists and insurgents.
One such myth grows out of the image of Leila Khaled with her machine
gun — she is the "sexy" poster girl for terrorism, like Farrah Fawcett for
Charlie's Angels. Helena Kennedy says that Bernardine Dohrn and Kathy
Boudin of the Weather Underground and Ulrike Meinhof and Gudrun
Ensslin of the Baader-Meinhof gang "have all provoked more interest and
speculation than their male comrades." Unfortunately, such attention has little
if anything to do with their politics and everything to do with "their sexual

liberation," which sparks the interest of "their male voyeur."[1] Another myth centers on the cold heartlessness of Marion Coyle, an Irish Republican Army member who, along with Eddie Gallagher, held Tiede Herrerma, a Dutch businessman, hostage. Unlike Gallagher, Coyle did not form a relationship with Herrerma. She shot at the police when they raided, while Gallagher cowered in a corner.[2] There is also Susanne Albrecht, of the Red Army Faction, who was involved in the murder of a family friend on his birthday. She is made out to be even more ruthless for knowing him, but what is often ignored is the fact that she was told he would not be harmed.[3] Many researchers—for example, H. H. A. Cooper, Luisella de Cataldo Neuburger and Tiziana Valentini, and Catherine Taylor—admit that contextualizing the female terrorist's violence is difficult. Thus, instead of trying to understand what can't be understood in relation to societal norms, researchers like Cooper, the anonymous author of "The Female Terrorist and Her Impact on Policing," and feminist Robin Morgan condemn and vilify the female terrorist more vehemently than they do male terrorists.

This chapter takes a broader look at women's violence and its reception, putting it in historical perspective and focusing in particular on the stylized narratives surrounding women's terrorism contemporary to it and the preservation of these gender-stereotypical accounts across time, space, and cultures. In reading women's terrorism historically, we seek to acknowledge the features of women's terrorism that have persisted across time as well as the recent evolutions in both women's relation to "terrorism" and in media, scholarly, and artistic responses to women, gender, and terrorism. This essay recounts a few stories of women terrorists in modern history and then turns to gendered stories about women terrorists in the literature on women terrorists. Two lessons emerge: 1) women were participants in terrorist activities long before it became popular to pay attention to them, and 2) gendered images of women in terrorism are as old and as timeless as women in terrorism.

After historically situating women's terrorism, this chapter provides a brief discussion of three twentieth-century cases of women's involvement in terrorism that counter the perception of women terrorists as Islamic self-martyrs. While it is fashionable now to think of women terrorists as right-wing (Islamic) religious extremists from outside the West, the women who figure in this chapter (who were members of the West German Baader-Meinhof gang, the U. S. Weather Underground, and the Peruvian Shining Path) come from countries that we do not usually think have women terrorists engaged in militancy on behalf of left-wing, political movements rather than religious ones. After discussing these women, we look at the early literature addressing these (and other) women terrorists and demonstrate that gendered expectations about and gendered interpretations of women terrorists do not just dominate research and public perceptions about Islamic terrorists but prevail in the thinking about women's participation in terrorism generally.

WOMEN AND TERRORISM IN HISTORICAL PERSPECTIVE

Women's terrorism is not a phenomenon exclusive to the twenty-first century. Nor is it in any way limited to Islamist terrorist groups. Women have been involved as terrorists in a large number of insurgencies and movements. It has been documented that women were affiliated with the Russian nihilist organization Narodnaya Vola in the late nineteenth century, as well as with the Socialist Revolutionary Party in the early twentieth century. Women have been involved in terrorist attacks carried out by Peru's Shining Path (Sendero luminoso), by republican and loyalist insurgent groups in Northern Ireland, by al-Qaeda, by the Liberation Tamil Tigers of Eelam (Sri Lanka), by the Kurdistan Worker's Party (Turkey), by HAMAS (Palestine), by the Zapatistas (Mexico), by Abu Sayyaf (Philippines), by the Symbionese Liberation Army (United States), by the Taliban (Afghanistan), by the Revolutionary Armed Forces of Colombia (FARC) (Colombia), and by a number of groups in the Iraqi insurgency. Women have had leadership roles in the Baader-Meinhof gang (Germany), the Red Brigades (Italy), Front Line (Prima linea) (Italy), the ETA (Basque separatist movement in Spain and France), the Japanese Red Army, the People's Liberation Front for Palestine, the Chechen resistance movement, and the Weather Underground (United States). A woman assassinated Czar Alexander II (Russia), and another blew up Indian Prime Minister Rajiv Gandhi. In addition to including women, the FARC, the Shining Path, and the Liberation Tamil Tigers of Eelam have expressed a commitment to gender equality as a part of their revolutionary goals. There is not space in this chapter (or in this book) to provide a detailed account of all known instances of women's terrorism in history, much less to take account of such instances that have fallen out of our history books and dominant accounts, but this chapter gives a brief overview of three cases.

The Baader-Meinhof Gang

The Baader-Meinhof gang lived a life of violence, rhetoric, fast cars, and stylish clothes. Their well-documented underground lives ended with arrest and prison, and their deaths were surrounded by a mystery that inspired conspiracy theories for years to come. The members of Baader-Meinhof constituted a revolutionary organization called the Red Army Faction (Rote Armee Fraktion [RAF]) that operated until 1992. The ideology of the Baader-Meinhof gang was based on Marxism-Leninism and, much as in many other Marxist-Leninist groups of the 1960s and 1970s, there was a high level of female involvement. In fact, two of the three people that made up Baader-Meinhof's triumvirate leadership were women—Ulrike Meinhof and Gudrun Ensslin.

Meinhof and Ensslin were both involved in the student movement before they formed the RAF, along with Baader, Horst Mahler, Astrid Proll, Irene Goergens, and Ingrid Schubert. Robin Morgan views Meinhof and Ensslin as "followers" who became revolutionaries merely for the sake of love—"a classic feminine behavior." The only reason Meinhof and Ensslin joined, according to Morgan, is so they could participate with their "men."[4] This view oversimplifies Meinhof's and Ensslin's roles in Baader-Meinhof. This section accounts for some of the complexities in Morgan's account.

After being trained in Jordan, the group returned to West Germany to begin their urban guerrilla struggle.[5] The next year and a half was spent robbing banks, stealing cars, searching for a support network, and losing members to arrest. They were essentially setting up operations. Over the course of time, the first generation would rob six banks, stealing DM 586,964.50. They broke into town halls to steal passports, identity cards, seals, and notepaper.[6] They lost a substantial portion of their membership to arrest, but their ideology was being galvanized. Meinhof was assigned the task of writing "The Urban Guerrilla Concept."[7] It was printed in April 1971. Meinhof spoke of the American "paper tiger," which she suggested could be defeated by pushing American military forces to overextend themselves. She defined the urban guerrilla as the "logical consequence of the negation of parliamentary democracy long since perpetrated by its very own representatives; the only and inevitable response to emergency laws and the rule of the hand grenade; the readiness to fight with those same means the system has chosen to use in trying to eliminate its opponents. The 'urban guerrilla' is based on a recognition of the facts instead of an apologia of the facts." The urban guerrilla would target "the state apparatus of control at certain points and put them out of action, to destroy the myth of the system's omnipresence and invulnerability." The RAF had wanted to combine grassroots mobilization along with guerrilla activity; however, "we have learned that individuals cannot combine legal and illegal activity."[8]

In December 1971, the police found a draft of a letter to the Labour Party of the People's Republic of Korea. Meinhof pleaded for funding, training, and weapons.[9] When Ensslin, Baader, Jan-Carl Raspe, and Gerhard Müller heard about the American Air Force's mining of North Vietnamese harbors, Ensslin suggested attacking the American military installations in West Germany. On May 11, 1972, three pipe bombs exploded in the officers' mess of the Fifth U.S. Army Corps in Frankfurt am Main. Thirteen people were injured; one was killed. May 12 saw two attacks. The first was on the Augsburg police headquarters; five were injured. Two hours later a car parked at the Munich federal criminal police office exploded. Sixty cars were demolished. On May 15, they targeted Judge Budenburg's car; instead of the judge, they severely wounded his wife. On May 19, the Springer Building was bombed; seventeen people were injured. After the Springer attack, the Second of June Commando (not to be confused with the Second of June movement) took responsibility. On June 24, two car bombs went off at the barracks block 28 at the European headquarters of the U.S. Army in Heidelberg. Three soldiers were killed: Clyde Bonner, Ronald Woodward, and Charles Peck; five were hurt. The letter claiming responsibility read:

> The people of the Federal Republic will not support the security forces in the hunt for the bombers, because they want nothing to do with the crimes of American imperialism and their condonation [sic] by the ruling class here; because they have not forgotten Auschwitz, Dresden and Hamburg; because they know that bomb attacks on the mass murderers of Vietnam are justified; because they have discovered that demonstrations and words are of no use against the imperialist criminals.[10]

By the end of June, the major players were arrested—Meinhof, Ensslin, Baader, Raspe, and Holger Meins.

The RAF members were able to stay in touch through their "info-system," whereby they passed notes and letters through their lawyers. It was developed by Ensslin in order to avoid a "balls-up," or leak. The info-system was used by the members of the gang as a way to engage in criticism and self-criticisms (a form of group brainwashing) and as a way to share ideological and technological information in the face of poor prison conditions and a hunger strike.

During her trial, Meinhof explained, "Terrorism operates amidst the fear of the masses. The city guerrilla movement, on the other hand, carries fear to the machinery of the state." The urban guerrillas would never direct their actions against the people. According to Meinhof, "They are always directed against the imperialist machine. The urban guerrilla fights the terrorism of the state." In mid-January 1976, the defendants admitted to belonging to an urban guerrilla group and took responsibility for the bombing attacks. They would not, however, take responsibility for the criminal aspect of their actions.[11] Bruce Hoffman writes that "violence is meant to be equally 'symbolic.'" The "purpose" of the terrorist "is not to destroy property or obliterate tangible assets, but . . . call attention to a political cause."[12]

For the leaders of Baader-Meinhof, the bombings were not criminal; they were political by-products of the legitimate war the RAF was waging against the West German state and the presence of the United States in West Germany. The RAF leaders tried "to put the trial on a political footing" by calling certain people—ex-president Nixon, former U.S. secretary of defense Melvin Laird, Willy Brandt, Helmut Schmidt, Ludwig Erhard, George Kiesinger, and Walter Scheel—to give evidence.[13] This happened on Meinhof's last day in court but only after she was allowed to leave after fighting with Ensslin. Meinhof was not in court to hear this call, and she was not there to hear Ensslin deny responsibility for the bombing of the Springer building. In refusing to assume responsibility, Ensslin was in effect rejecting Meinhof's leadership, since she was the one who had written the letter claiming responsibility. Gerhard Müller added insult to injury when he later testified that it was Meinhof who had planted the bombs. Meinhof committed suicide four days later.[14] On April 28, 1977, the three remaining defendants were found guilty of forming a criminal association and of committing three murders in conjunction with six attempted murders, one further murder in conjunction with one attempted murder, and twenty-seven other attempted murders in conjunction with bomb attacks. All were sentenced to life imprisonment.[15] On October 18, 1977, after a failed attempt by the RAF to have them released, Ensslin, Baader, and Raspe killed themselves. The extreme commitment of all of the leaders, men and women, cost them their lives.

The women's ideology truly shaped the group's ideology. Baader did not start to read and explore Marxist works until he was in prison for the first time.[16] Baader was a very strong leader, but his style was emotional, which left him dependent on Ensslin's people management skills and Meinhof's articulation of ideological strategizing. Together, the women, Meinhof and Ensslin, wrote the majority of the RAF's published ideological tracts after Horst Mahler was expelled from the group. Ensslin and Baader turned to Meinhof to write the history of the RAF, to ask the North Korean government for aid and weapons, and to justify their actions.

If the female revolutionary is simply a "mother" to the rest of the group, in accordance with Luisella de Cataldo Neuburger and Tiziana Valentini's maternal-sacrifice code, then we would see this in analyzing her group inter-actions.[17] If the female revolutionary is a "demon," whose anger and sexually unbalanced personality dominates others, not only would she be devoid of ideology but she would not be able to interact with other group members.[18] Instead, to a large extent, Meinhof and Ensslin were the true leaders of the RAF. They rallied the members, and they provided the ideology that went into shaping RAF tactics and strategies.

Weather Underground

The Weather Underground, another Marxist-Leninist group, had many female members. The students sought the overthrow of what they viewed as an out-dated government. They saw themselves as the vanguard Lenin wrote about; they would motivate the working class, the oppressed, to rise up and form a truly communist/utopian society or, at the very least, establish a free state for African Americans. The emphasis on racial and sexual equality played an important part in the group's thinking along with Marxist-Leninist ideology.

The Students for a Democratic Society (SDS) had begun as a peaceful movement committed to the ideals President John F. Kennedy set forth in his 1961 inaugural address, but by the mid-1960s this massive student organization was facing many challenges, particularly from more radicalized newer members. What would become the Weatherman faction (later the Weather Underground) began as the "revolutionary youth movement" that took control of the SDS in June 1969. The Weather Underground's early leadership laid out their ideology in their tract "You Don't Need a Weatherman to Know Which

Way the Wind Blows."[19] It took tactics and strategy to a new level of militancy.[20] It proved to be the wedge that split the SDS.

It was the Columbia University takeover that brought many of the future leaders, like Mark Rudd and ideologue John Jacobs (J. J.), of the Weatherman collective together. The police at the Columbia takeover arrested 712 students. The New York chapter of the National Lawyers Guild came to the defense of the students. Bernardine Dohrn, a recent graduate of the University of Chicago's law school, was among them. Susan Stern, product of a wealthy New Jersey childhood, became involved while she was doing her master's at the University of Washington in 1965. Kathy Boudin was the daughter of the well-known civil rights lawyer Leonard Boudin. The women moved into the organization the same way the men did. They were all involved in SDS activities. Yet in accounts of the group, the women are made out to be different—less committed to the group and more committed to their sexuality. This simply was not true. They not only embraced the basic ideology of the organization but wrote articles further articulating it and defending the Weathermen against their critics. Moreover, they were committed to discussing what was known as the "women's question"—where did women belong in the movement as a whole and how did they fit into the violent struggle against imperialism?

The Weathermen tract was thirty-thousand words typewritten by J. J. but edited and added onto by the rest of the authors: Bill Ayers, Jim Mellen, Dohrn, Rudd, Jeff Jones, Terry Robbins, Howie Machtinger, Gerry Long, Karin Ashley, and Steve Tapis.[21] It spoke of their advocacy of the National Liberation Front of Vietnam and their dislike of American imperialism. It barely addressed the women's question. The authors admitted as much, noting that the "SDS ha[d] not dealt in any adequate way with [it]" and acknowledging their "limited understanding of the tie-up between imperialism and [women]." The tract may not have given the "woman question" enough attention; however, several of their female supporters did. The "woman question" was thoroughly addressed in various articles before the Weather Underground officially addressed it in *Prairie Fire*.

For example, in the Weather Underground, the rejection of monogamy was seen as a way to empower and liberate women. The anonymous Weatherwoman who wrote the 1970 "Inside the Weather Machine" asserted that monogamous relationships were "built around weakness and dependency." She claimed that the women in them defined themselves "through their men" and saw such relationships as the only way to "feel secure and loved."[22] The tension that re-volved around sexuality is witnessed in the mechanisms of leadership. The men were known for sleeping with women in every city and site they visited as they traveled to raise support for their revolution. The women used sexuality as well. Dohrn is described as having dressed sexily, wearing miniskirts and high boots. Dohrn was not alone in this; Stern mentioned the kick she would get from acting sexy.[23]

Women's groups outside the Weathermen took a critical stance to the group's position on women. For example, the Bread and Roses collective is-sued a tract entitled "Weatherman Politics and the Women's Movement" that criticized the way women were treated in the organization.[24] Bread and Roses felt Weatherwomen were doubly oppressed: they were not only "told that their oppression . . . [was] less important . . . than the oppression of blacks or Vietnamese" but that they "must struggle in terms defined by men." A woman in Weatherman became a good revolutionary only when she was "a tougher, better fighter than the men."[25]

Other material suggests, however, that Dohrn was a national leader, if not *the* leader of the Weatherman collective. For example, Dohrn encouraged soli-darity with the black nationalist movement, a position she articulated in an article she wrote for *New Left Notes* in 1969.[26] She outlined the history and stance of the Black Panther Party and urged cooperation between the SDS and the Black Panthers. It would be "the best thing we [could be] doing for our-selves, as well as the struggle." The black liberation struggle was "instrumental" in bringing a "clearer understanding of imperialism, class oppression in the U.S. . . . [and] the need for armed struggle as the only road to revolution." Dohrn wrote that the repression of the Black Panther Party was aided "by the absence of substantial material support—power—by the white movement." She linked the two ideas—the revolutionary youth movement and black lib-eration—because to mobilize the working class was a way of providing the "necessary extension of the support" for the Black Panther Party. Weatherman leaders believed that the Revolutionary Youth Movement, a faction of the SDS had to fight racism not just because it continued to be an institutionalized practice in the South but also because African Americans were engaged in an anticolonial struggle within America.[27]

Toward the end of the summer of 1969, members of the Weather Bureau criss-crossed the country trying to drum up all the support they could for "the beginning of the end for the American state." It was Dohrn who rallied those who gathered. "A few buckshot wounds, a few pellets, means we're doing the right thing here," she stated. The fear the women felt then had "to be put up against the hunger, fear, death and suffering of black, brown and yellow people in this country and all over the world." Stern described watching Dohrn fight with the police: "I had seen her fighting with genuine rage. I had watched the women about her fighting just as hard. But she was still the high priestess." When Stern and Dohrn were in jail together, Dohrn held herself aloof, her face expressing her disdain for her surroundings, while she kept herself impeccably clothed in a "short black leather jacket, . . . purple blouse [and] boots—everything just so."[28]

Women played tactical and strategic roles as well in the Weatherman. During the Ave (the Haight-Ashbury of Seattle) riots of mid-August, the women emerged as the street-fighting force and destroyed the university's ROTC building.[29] Similarly, during the Pittsburgh "jailbreak" at South Hills High School in September 1969, women formed affinity groups—smaller, tactical groups that operated within the larger collective—each of which were led by a tactical leader.[30] Still, though women were highly visible in the Weatherman collective, writing ideological tracts and taking part in riots and bombings, it has to be acknowledged that the organization was indeed sexist. Stern, Morgan, and Dohrn all noted the sexist nature of the collective. Even Ayers conceded sexism was a problem and gave testimony on it.

The yearly December SDS national conference was renamed the War Council and held December 26–31, 1969, in Flint, Michigan. It was the last public meeting of the Weathermen. On the second day, the Weather Bureau announced their decision to take the organization underground. During 1970, there were approximately five thousand bombings across the United States. The Weather Underground claimed responsibility for several major ones. The first was the bombing of the New York City police headquarters on June 9, 1970 (which was carried out after the organization had sent out a "Declaration of a State of War" on May 21, 1970). The next day the Associated Press received a handwritten note signed by the group taking responsibility. There were several bombings in honor of Castro's seventeen years of revolutionary activity on July 26 and July 27. The Presidio army base in San Francisco was bombed the first day and the Bank of America on Wall Street in New York City was bombed on the second. On September 12, the organization helped Timothy Leary, LSD guru, escape from San Luis Obispo and smuggled him out of the country. The Weathermen began its fall offensive on October 8, by blowing up the police statue in Haymarket Square in Chicago to celebrate the one-year anniversary of the Days of Rage. It was coordinated with bomb attacks at the criminal courthouse in Long Island City in New York and the Hall of Justice in Marin County, California.[31] The Women's Brigade of Weather bombed the Center for International Affairs at Harvard on October 14 in a gesture of solidarity for Angela Davis, who had been arrested that day on charges of interstate flight and conspiracy to commit murder.[32] The communiqué was signed with the gender-neutral Weather Underground.[33]

The Weather Underground carried out its most destructive bomb attacks in the spring of 1971. In reaction to the U.S. invasion of Laos, Dohrn and Kathy Boudin planted a bomb in the women's bathroom at the U.S. Capitol on March 1. There was another bomb placed in the women's bathroom of the Pentagon on May 19 (Ho Chi Minh's birthday) to protest the mining of Haiphong Harbor. It destroyed the plumbing; the first floor flooded causing a computer that was a part of a global military communications network to shut down. It also ruined a computer tape archive storing highly classified information.[34] In late August the Weather Underground bombed California prison offices in San Francisco, which was followed by the September bombing of the New York Commissioner of Corrections Offices in Albany and the bombing of Vietnam War architect McGeorge Bundy's MIT offices in October. In January 1975, government offices in Washington, D.C., and Oakland, California, were bombed along with offices of the Agency for International Development in Washington. In June, the Banco de Ponce in New York was bombed. Weather Underground also hit Kennecott Corporation headquarters in Salt Lake City in October.

Dohrn and Ayers, who had been together as a couple since the early 1970s, surfaced in New York in 1980, where she was a waitress and Ayers was working in a preschool. They had two sons and were living as Lou Douglas and Anthony Lee. When they surfaced, they refused to apologize for their past. Dohrn stated she still believed "in the necessity of underground work."[35] Dohrn flew to Chicago to face her remaining charges (the ones against Ayers had already been dropped).[36] She received three years' probation and a $1,500 fine. During her sentencing, the judge scolded Dohrn, pointing out that "We have a system for change that does not involve violence." She retorted that they "had differing views on America." In 1981, Dohrn and Ayers were married. Dohrn is now a law professor and director of the Children and Family Justice Center at Northwestern University's School of Law. Ayers is a retired professor of education at the University of Illinois in Chicago.

The women who joined the Weatherman collective did not do so owing to some underlying problem with their fathers or to a nervous condition or simply because they were following their men. They did not join to impress someone and make this someone "want" them. The Weatherwomen were, or perceived themselves to be, equal partners with the men in their revolution, no matter how unsuccessful it was. The problem the Weatherwomen faced is the desire, implicit or explicit, on the part of those who have studied them to decontextualize their involvement. It's not just that the women were sexualized by their peers; their sexualization is also emphasized and/or remembered in historical accounts.

As more women began to take charge within the Weather Underground and as the organization came under more criticism, the group tried to establish policies and requirements that would liberate the women. The Pittsburgh "jail-break," the collective believed, had truly challenged the chauvinism of both men *and* women. A separatist women's struggle that refused to work with the other half of the human race could not gain any ground. Within the larger Weather Underground there was an acknowledgment that women were exploited, and the leadership urged them to take initiative and become full members.

In reading the material about these different women, from the interview with Boudin to Stern's autobiography, it cannot be inferred that these women became involved in the revolution by following their men. They make no mention of feeling neglected by their fathers or by society at large. They do not even mention being driven by erotic intentions. They do mention being persuaded by the ideological views of the organization. Dohrn and Boudin continue to be advocates for changing the American system. Dohrn is a child and family legal advocate. Boudin, from her prison cell, is leading a penal reform movement to improve the conditions for imprisoned mothers and to educate the prisoners about AIDS. If they had gotten involved in the collective for superficial reasons, these women would not still be fighting today but would have given up the New Left struggle long ago.

The Shining Path

In 1968, General Juan Velasco Alvardo came to power in Peru, leading the Revolutionary Government of the Armed Forces. It was reformist but top-down organization, and its changes were incomplete. His successor, Morales Bermúdez, continued the reform but with a significant right-wing bent. Several leftist groups legally protested the government, but others, particularly the Shining Path, became outlaw groups. The Shining Path, grounded in Maoist and Marxist-Leninist ideology, was led by Abimael Guzmán. Right before the 1980 elections for a civilian president, the Shining Path burned ballot boxes to signify the start of a revolutionary movement. A war between the Shining Path and the Peruvian state during the 1980s and 1990s ensued, during which about seventy thousand people died. For a short time, the Shining Path controlled substantial territory in the center and south of Peru.

In 1992, Maritza Garrido Lecca, formerly a prima ballerina, was arrested with Guzmán and videotaped with "raised fist and a fierce, hardened stare, shouting, 'Communism will take over the world!'"[37] Lecca, however, was not the only woman in the Shining Path. Nor was she even the only female Shining Path leader arrested that night. Nathaniel Nash reports that three other members of the Shining Path central committee were also arrested that night, as they were in the midst of "planning what was to be the most violent wave of killings yet in Lima," and they were all women.[38] Nash estimates that, at the time, at least eight of the nineteen members of the central committee were women. The Shining Path has claimed that at least 40 percent of its members are women. Women certainly made up a significant percentage of the Shining Path's membership in the 1980s, and their visibility was one of the most striking features of the movement.[39]

The 1992 arrests were not the first time women of the Shining Path had been in the news. In 1982, Edith Lagos, a member of the Shining Path, was killed by a police officer. She was mourned by tens of thousands of people, and her martyrdom served as an inspiration to Shining Path members.[40]

Still, gender dynamics in the Shining Path have been the subject of critique. Matilde Ureta de Caplansky has argued that women in the group "become almost like robots. . . . [T]hey give back to you ideas they are programmed with."[41] People who have visited the prisons where Shining Path women are incarcerated note that "despite the ferocity of women leaders, there is a strange stress on feminine qualities, such that they can be quite coquettish at times."[42] Nash reports that "those who have studied the role of women in the Shining Path" claim that statistics showing high numbers of woman in leadership positions in the group "do not necessarily mean they are treated better than women in the rest of Peruvian society, or that Latin machismo has been superseded by a sexless Shining Path communist society. But they add that there are strong reasons why Peruvian women, especially the dark-skinned women of the Andes, have sought a new identity in the ranks of the guerilla movement."[43] Still, some suggest that the Shining Path brought Peruvian women into the public sphere by giving them leadership roles within the revolutionary movement. Guzmán was known to refer to Mao's statement that women are half the world and that class struggle rather than struggle between the sexes would solve the problem of women's inequality. Guzmán established the Popular Women's Movement in 1965, which later became a part of the Shining Path and established a theoretical context for women's participation in Shining Path militancy.

Women have played a number of roles in the Shining Path, including as teachers who disseminate Shining Path philosophies and as fighters. Women are often leaders of armed guerilla groups. Nash describes one of many attacks perpetrated by women, explaining that, in a 1992 "attack outside of Ayacucho, 11 civilians riding in a bus and a car were killed. Lieutenant Colonel Carlos Romero Barestagui, operations commander at the army base there, said witnesses reported that a man had been shot in the arm and was crying. A Shining Path woman grabbed him by the hair, pulled back his head and cut his throat with a knife, Colonel Romero said."[44] Nash attributes "women's ruthlessness to group dynamics, where violence is considered an attribute. And in an effort to be accepted, women seek to show more ruthlessness, often trying to be 'more macho than macho.'"[45]

The Peruvian Truth and Reconciliation Commission found the Shining Path to be guilty of committing violence, though it also highlighted the deplorability of the government's and military's use of sexual violence toward women revolutionaries. Since the 1992 arrest of its leadership, the Shining Path has surfaced only rarely and in a limited capacity. Most of the women who were identified as in the Shining Path remain imprisoned for their insurgent actions.

GENDERED ANALYSES OF WOMEN TERRORISTS

Much of this book critiques and reconstructs the literature around women terrorists in the twenty-first century, but those gendered ideas, expectations, and stereotypes did not come from nowhere. They are entrenched in the early literature about how and why women participated in terrorism. In fact, the "deviant" woman terrorist is clearly vilified in one of the first articles written on female terrorists. "The Female Terrorist and Her Impact on Policing" published in 1976, is cited in many works on female terrorists, from those immediately following the publication of the article to a chapter in an edited volume published in 2000.[46] The author offers "erotomania" as the "primary cause of female terrorism," which arises, according to the author, because young women, or "girls," have been neglected by society in general "and the father in particular."[47] This links female "deviancy" with sexual misconduct. The author specifically blames the rise in female involvement on "pressure from disgruntled females who probably form a large majority of the women's liberation movement."[48] The author sums up the female terrorist in the following terms: "When [one] is dealing with a female terrorist one is usually dealing not with rational, but with emotional motivation. . . . Thus her violence will in all probability stem not from dedication to the particular cause which she appears to espouse, but from blind obedience to another more personal cause."[49]

The women in these groups are likened to women suffering from anorexia, because like anorexia, what causes a woman to join an underground organization is in effect a nervous condition. Thus, security forces should try to "cure" a woman of her involvement in an underground organization just as a medical doctor would "cure" a woman of anorexia. The author of this article never deviates from the belief that "girls," who are "less suited to the stresses and strains of an independent life," join subversive groups because "pop culture" has got its claws in them and that the absentee father of today's society has let them go the way of violence.[50] The article ends with this thought:

It must never be forgotten that the female terrorist is but one symptom of a massive syndrome of female unrest and discontent with the male, whose vitality and confidence this minority movement is sapping.

One awaits the outcome of this struggle for freedom from (largely mythical) male domination—a struggle which the majority of women probably do not wish to win.[51]

In his "Woman as Terrorist," H. H. A. Cooper admits up front that attitudes toward female terrorists may well be sexist. He acknowledges that "we are handicapped" because so few women are violent or involved in terrorism. "Terrorism is the ugly side of man and woman alike"; unfortunately, according to him, men are "conditioned" to look for physical or spiritual beauty in women, and so female terrorists offend this delicate sensibility.[52] Cooper claims that the horrified reactions to female terrorists is the product of classical patriarchal thought—"terrorism is simply not women's work."[53] Cooper states that "the female terrorist has not been content to just praise the Lord and pass the ammunition." Female terrorists "have consistently proved themselves more ferocious and more intractable in these acts than their male counterparts. There is a cold rage about some of them that even the most alienated of men seem quite incapable of emulating."[54]

Since such a woman is not content with hypothetical women's work, Cooper vilifies the female terrorist. Referring to Marion Coyle's "single-minded, fanatically inhuman behavior" toward Herrerma, which is seen as standing in contrast to Gallagher's humanity, Cooper describes it as "typical of the pitiless attitude many women terrorists are capable of assuming." Their attitude is one "that men find curiously hard to match."[55] This same sexism was also apparent during the 1986 IRA Brighton bombing court case. Martina Anderson and Ella O'Dwyer were singled out by the judge from their equally responsible male codefendants and chastised for their heartlessness.[56] The message is women are meant to care, men are not. Gallagher was an acceptable anomaly in his fraternal behavior. Female terrorists are characterized as the ultimate traitors for being less than compassionate and nurturing.

Cooper suggests that since the female terrorist has challenged "preconceptions . . . and patterns for response" through her "heinous activities," she should be "dealt with after the fashion of the Gorgon."[57] A female terrorist is no longer human: she is subhuman in her personality defects and superhuman in her strength. Women are "eager" to develop "skills and techniques of the violent terrorist." They "delight in aping" soldiers and in their "childish" motivation are "all too [ready to] surpass their masters in both violence and rhetoric."[58]

Women do not, according to Cooper, engage in terrorism for the same reasons as men. They become involved for personal reasons that have "obsessive [and] pathological" qualities. Therefore, "It is *useless* to inquire why women become terrorists."[59] Female terrorists, it seems, are not worthy of research, as their reasoning is completely unfathomable and therefore "useless" to the understanding of terrorism. This is reflected in Cooper's acceptance of "erotomania" the "primary cause of female terrorism." It is sexual relationships that lead women into terrorism. He cites Jane Alpert and Sam Melville, Gudrun Ensslin and Andreas Baader, and Carlos the Jackel and his host of women. Cooper ignores the fact that Gudrun Ensslin was the brains in that couple and that the women Carlos was involved with were not terrorists.

Yet this sexual relationship theory is something the feminist Robin Morgan espouses. Her book is based on Jungian psychology's hero journey—"the terrorist . . . [,] the ultimate sexual ideal of a male-centered tradition[,] . . . is the logical extension of the patriarchal hero."[60] Morgan dismisses the experts in the field, like Richard Clutterbuck, Anthony Burton, and Paul Wilkinson. Morgan writes from a feminist perspective and defines a terrorist as "the logical incarnation of patriarchal politics in a technological world."[61] Only she leaves the women out. If "sons" have learned violence from living in a violent society, so have the "daughters." Yet Morgan surprisingly refers to women as "token terrorists" and as participating in the harem of the demon lover, the male terrorist. Morgan finds "biological determinism" to be a "failure of intellectual nerve," and she does not mean to create a "mirror-image feminist version" by suggesting that "women are *inherently* more peaceable, nurturant, or altruistic than men."[62] Nonetheless, Morgan claims that "it is undeniable that history is a record of most women *acting peaceably*, and of most men *acting belligerently*—to a point where the capacity for belligerence is regarded as an essential ingredient of manhood and the proclivity for conciliation is thought largely a quality of women."[63]

She defines women as subsisting "outside the body politic, except as victims or tokens."[64] She denies that women are capable of making decisions for themselves. The "token terrorist" "is no more a true representative of women than the airbrushed Playboy centerfold."[65] A "'revolutionary' woman" buys into the "male 'radical' line" and "diassociate[s] herself from her womanhood[,] . . . her reality." The token terrorist defends her loyalty and her commitment while in denial to her true self.[66] Thus women who participate in armed struggles have made the wrong choice, forsaking the more humane path of feminism for male-dominated political violence. Morgan's thesis simply perpetuates the victimization of women by denying women any cause but feminism. Morgan diminishes the role of female terrorists by noting that the women in left-wing couples, such as Mara Cagol and Renato Curcio, who both started the Italian Red Brigades, only act as they do to secure "male approval and love."[67] Gudrun Ensslin and Ulrike Meinhof's roles in Baader-Meinhof are likewise distorted by Morgan, as we have already suggested. To reduce women such as Mara Cagol, Gudrun Ensslin, and Ulrike Meinhof to simply members of the "harem" of a male terrorist has the effect of suggesting that women, even terrorists, do not possess the ability to act on their own volition.

The anonymous author of "The Female Terrorist and Her Impact on Policing" and Cooper portray female terrorists as devoid of any emotion other than anger, vengeance, and bloodlust, while Morgan simply portrays them as empty-headed women gone wrong. This type of research has turned female terrorists into monsters, much more so than the males. The title of Eileen MacDonald's book *Shoot the Women First* comes from the West German GSG 9's command, which grew out of the idea that women are supposed to be that much more ruthless and aggressive than men. MacDonald, however, admits that the female terrorists she interviewed were "disturbingly normal" and after the first round of interviews she "stopped looking for their horns."[68]

Alison Jamieson's *The Heart Attacked*, which focuses on the Italian Red Brigade's kidnapping of Aldo Moro, tries to dismiss the myths surrounding female terrorists. "The driving force" behind female participation seemed "to conform largely to that of the male," according to Jamieson. In the Red Brigades, the sexes were united in their sense of injustice, hatred of an unequal society, and their embrace of violent revolution. The female terrorist's idealism, however, "stripped of the elements of fantasy, heroism and the bella morte . . . may be rawer, more acute and more passionately felt." Jamieson concludes that the "mythical female terrorist" is "more of a creation of the media" than of reality, even though she herself is a journalist.[69] One Milanese public prosecutor she interviewed felt that much of what is said about female terrorists is exaggerated and rejected the idea that "characteristics and motivations differ significantly between the sexes."[70]

Neuburger and Valentini's work also focuses on the Italian Red Brigade.

Their work highlights the high level of commitment on the part of the women members. Over time, the Red Brigade had twelve men and seven women in leadership positions. Sixteen percent of the men became penitents, while none of the women did.[71] They attribute the refusal of the women to recant to a heavier ideological investment in the organization.

Neuburger and Valentini refer to the "feminine 'way'" of living, the definition of which is that "women tend to develop their experience in accordance with an affective model based on sacrifice, on caring for others, on responding to others' needs and on protection."[72] This is what they call the "maternal-sacrifice code," and they use it to suggest that a woman's involvement in terrorist organizations derives from her desire to belong to something. In the interview they conducted with Mara Aldrovandi, she talked about the "collective aspect" and the wish not to be alone. Aldrovandi was satisfied with being "needed . . . and [she] let [her]self be used." In Aldrovandi's eyes, the women diverted conflict and brought the two sexes together.[73] However, her desire to belong corresponds to the experiences of other members in clandestine groups. Women may be more nurturing, but it is important to understand that they can join terror groups for the same reasons as a man: because of their strong belief in a cause and a particular organization. Neuburger and Valentini overlook a woman's desire to get involved in the terrorist organization based on her ideological beliefs. Bonnie Cordes, a researcher for RAND, concluded that both men and women join terrorist organizations to unite with like-minded individuals and for the community a group creates.[74] This echoes Donatella della Porta's contention that friendship and familial ties lead both sexes to join revolutionary groups.[75]

Leonard Weinburg and William Eubank theorize that Italian women did not seek out participation in terrorist groups but instead followed their husbands or brothers into the movement. They indicate "romantic or affectional ties" as a source of motivation. Yet one of the founders of the Italian Red Brigades was a woman, and female participation in said organization was close to 20 percent. In spite of this, Weinburg and Eubank conceptualize the role of women in terrorist groups as "housekeepers," which mirrors the "traditional female role in society" of providing support to men.[76]

Catherine Taylor is caught between the two sides. She tries to fight the stereotypical images of the female terrorist as either cold and deviant or supplicant and nurturing. Yet the overall tone of her piece puts her in Neuburger and

Valentini's camp. She sees a female terrorist as "a living contradiction — she has chosen to take life, not to give it."[77] These activities set her apart from society and her gender. Taylor also combats the reference to female terrorists as "girls." In her mind it serves two purposes: it denies the women political maturity and it "desexualises them," which has the effect of drawing less attention to the contradiction between their actions and their gender.[78] She sets the female terrorist apart by appealing to the stereotype that combines sex and violence in a titillatingly erotic mix.

Ulrike Meinhof served as the ideological leader of Baader-Meinhof without using her sex as a weapon. Nor did many of the other women who were members of Baader-Meinhof and the Red Army Faction.[79] The women in the Italian Red Brigades did not appear to do this at all. In the Palestinian groups, it is dangerous for a woman to be sexy, and she would be totally stripped of her power as a member of the organization for dressing or acting provocatively. Taylor does not back up her hypothesis with sufficient examples. She discusses the depiction of Maureen O'Hara, an IRA terrorist, who used her beauty "to lure British soldiers" to their death, but does not show a general trend.

The terrorist woman is, as Ann Lloyd titled her book, "doubly deviant"— both for breaking the law and the "unwritten code for proper female behaviour"— and "doubly damned."[80] The female revolutionary acts contrary to the norms that society has established for women and thus she is labeled a slut, a demon, a vulgar slap-in-the-face to all that femininity is supposed to be.

CONCLUSION

Putting women and terrorism in global politics in historical perspective shows that women's involvement in terrorism falls not only outside of gender stereotypes and expectations about women's ideal-typical behavior but also outside of stereotypes and expectations of what we typify as terrorist behaviors. The women in this chapter, and in this book, lead complex lives, both full of agency and fraught with constraints on that agency. This brief look into the history of women's terrorism demonstrates both that women were participants in terrorist activities long before it became popular to pay attention to them and that gendered images of women in terrorism are as old and as timeless as women in terrorism, facts that give us the background necessary to understanding women's participation in terrorism in the twenty-first century.

NOTES

1. Kennedy, *Eve Was Framed: Women and British Justice* (London: Vintage, 1992), 261–62.

2. Alison Jamieson, *The Heart Attacked: Terrorism and Conflict in the Italian State* (London: Marion Boyers, 1989), 65. See also H. H. A. Cooper, "Woman as Terrorist," in *The Criminology of Deviant Women*, ed. Freda Adler and Rita James Simon (Boston: Houghton Mifflin, 1979), 152.

3. Jillian Becker, *Hitler's Children* (London: Michael Joseph, 1977), 36.

4. Robin Morgan, *The Demon Lover: The Roots of Terrorism* (New York: Washington Square Press, 1989), 204–5, 208.

5. Stefan Aust, *The Baader-Meinhof Group: The Inside Story of a Phenomenon* (London: Bodley Head, 1985), 89–91. The first Baader-Meinhof communiqué chastised government officials: "Did they really believe that we would talk about the development of class struggle and reorganization of the proletariat without arming ourselves at the same time?" Those who did not join the struggle would be "buried alive in prisons, in reform schools, in the slums of worker districts, in the stone coffins of the new housing developments, in the crowded kindergartens and schools, in brand new kitchens and bedrooms filled with fancy furniture bought on credit" (Tom Vague, *Televisionaries: The Red Army Faction Story, 1963–1993* [Edinburgh: AK Press, 1998], 21).

6. Vague, *Televisionaries*, 25–31.

7. Aust, *The Baader-Meinhof Group*, 142–43.

8. Vague, *Televisionaries*, 26–30.

9. Aust, *The Baader-Meinhof Group*, 184.

10. Aust, *The Baader-Meinhof Group*, 210–13; Becker, *Hitler's Children*, 278–82.

11. Aust, *The Baader-Meinhof Group*, 337–38.

12. Bruce Hoffman, *Inside Terrorism* (New York: Columbia University Press, 1998), 159.

13. Aust, *The Baader-Meinhof Group*, 343.

14. Ibid., 344–45.

15. Ibid., 402.

16. When Baader was in prison for the first time, he finally began to read influential left-wing literature (Becker, *Hitler's Children*, 109).

17. According to Neuburger and Valentini, "Women tend to develop their experience in accordance with an affective model based on sacrifice, on caring for others, on responding to others' needs and on protection" (*Women and Terrorism* [London: Palgrave Macmillan, 2006], 81).

18. H. H. A. Cooper believes female terrorists are "more ferocious and more intractable" than their male peers ("Woman as Terrorist," 151).

19. A line from Bob Dylan's song "Subterranean Homesick Blues." The Weathermen paper was printed in the June 18, 1969, issue of *New Left Notes*.

20. Because of the proposed violent tactics of the Weathermen, Mike Klonsky prepared another paper, "RYM II," along with other national members. Thus, Weatherman was really the Radical Youth Movement renamed and the others became Radical Youth Movement 2. In order to defeat Progressive Labor, the Radical Youth Movement and the Radical Youth Movement 2 joined forces. When this common enemy was defeated, they split (G. Louis Heath, *Vandals in the Bomb Factory: The History and Literature of the Students for a Democratic Society* [Metuchen, N.J.: Scarecrow, 1978], 170).

21. By the end of the year, Ashley and Tapis were no longer associated with Weatherman.

22. "Inside the Weather Machine," *Weathermen*, ed. Harold Jacobs (New York: Rampart Press, 1970), 321–26.

23. Caron E. Gentry, "The Relationship between New Social Movement Theory and Terrorism Studies: The Role of Leadership, Membership, Ideology and Gender," *Terrorism and Political Violence* 16, no. 2 (2004): 274–93.

24. Bread and Roses, "Weathermen Politics and the Women's Movement," in *Weathermen*, 327–36.

25. Bread and Roses, "Weathermen Politics and the Women's Movement," 327.

26. Bernardine Dohrn, "White Mother Country Radicals," *New Left Notes*, July 29, 1968, 1, 5.

27. Heath, *Vandals in the Bomb Factory*, 126–27.

28. Susan Stern, *With the Weathermen: The Personal Journey of a Revolutionary Woman* (Rutgers, N.J.: Rutgers University Press, 2007), 143–44; Peter Collier and David Horowitz, *Second Thoughts: Former Radicals Look Back at the Sixties* (Lanham, Md.: Madison, 1989), 88–89.

29. Ibid., 79–80.

30. "Women's Militia," in *Weathermen*, 163–65.

31. Heath, *Vandals in the Bomb Factory*, 194–95.

32. For her attempt to free the Soledad brothers from jail in Marin County, California.

33. Jacobs, *Weathermen*, 123–24.

34. Collier and Horowitz, *Second Thoughts*, 103–6; Jacobs, *Weathermen*, 142.

35. "Dohrn Again," *New Republic*, October 14, 1985, 4–5.

36. A Justice Department investigation into Weatherman activities resulted in the indictment on July 23, 1970, of thirteen members — Rudd, Ayers, Dohrn, Boudin, Evans, Wilkerson, Dianne Donghi, Russell Neufield, Jane Spielman, Ronald Fliegalman, Larry Grathwohl (a police informant), Naomi Jaffe, and Robert Burlingham — on charges of conspiracy to bomb and kill. Several years later, these indictments were dropped because

of illegal FBI and police procedures. The first five in the list were also indicted by a federal grand jury in Chicago on April 2, 1970, along with Jones, Judy Clark, Robbins, J. J., Machtinger, Michael Speigal, and Lawrence Weiss on charges of conspiring to cross state lines to incite a riot, stemming from the Days of Rage (Heath, *Vandals in the Bomb Factory*; Committee of the Judiciary, U.S. Senate, 94th Congress, first session, January 1975, in *Weatherman*, 131).

37. Nathaniel C. Nash, "Shining Path Women: So Many and So Ferocious," *New York Times*, September 22, 1992, http://www.nytimes.com/1992/09/22/world/lima -journal-shining-path-women-so-many-and-so-ferocious.html (accessed March 11, 2011).

38. Ibid.

39. Feather Crawford Freed, "More than Half the Sky: The Power of Women in Peru," http://hiddentranscripts.wordpress.com/2008/08/15/women-and-the -shining-path (accessed March 11, 2011).

40. Robin Kirk, *The Monkey's Paw: New Chronicles from Peru* (Amherst: University of Massachusetts Press, 1997), 21.

41. Nash, "Shining Path Women."

42. Gustavo Gorriti, qtd. in Nash, "Shining Path Women"; Carol Andreas, "Women at War," *NACLA Report on the Americas* 24, no. 4 (1990–91): 21–25.

43. Nash, "Shining Path Women."

44. Ibid.

45. Ibid.

46. "The Female Terrorist and Her Impact on Policing," *Top Security* 2, no. 4 (1976): 242–45; Cooper, "Woman as Terrorist"; Catherine Taylor, "'And Don't Forget to Clean the Fridge': Women in the Secret Sphere of Terrorism," in *A Soldier and a Woman: Sexual Integration in the Military*, ed. Gerald DeGroot and Corinna Peniston-Bird (New York, Longman, 2000), 294–304.

47. "The Female Terrorist and Her Impact on Policing," 245.

48. Ibid.

49. Ibid.

50. Ibid., 244.

51. Ibid., 245.

52. Cooper, "Woman as Terrorist," 151.

53. Ibid., 151.

54. Ibid., 151.

55. Ibid., 152.

56. Kennedy, *Eve was Framed*, 262.

57. Cooper, "Woman as Terrorist," 152.

58. Ibid., 153.

59. Ibid., 154, emphasis added.

60. Morgan, *The Demon Lover*, xvi.

61. Ibid., 33.

62. Ibid., 27.

63. Ibid.

64. Ibid., 27–28.

65. Ibid., 59–60.

66. Ibid., 196–98.

67. Ibid., 204–5.

68. Eileen MacDonald, *Shoot the Women First* (London: Arrow, 1988), 11.

69. Jamieson, *The Heart Attacked*, 67–68.

70. Ibid., 67.

71. Neuburger and Valentini, *Women and Terrorism*, 3, 7–8.

72. Ibid., 81.

73. Ibid., 17.

74. Bonnie Cordes, *When Terrorists Do the Talking: Reflections on Terrorist Literature* (Santa Monica, Calif.: RAND, 1987), 8.

75. Donatella della Porta, introduction, in *Social Movements and Violence: Participation in Underground Organizations*, ed. Donatella della Porta (London: JAI, 1992), 7.

76. Leonard Weinberg and William Eubank, "Italian Women Terrorists," *Terrorism: An International Journal* 9, no. 3 (1985): 241–62.

77. Taylor, "'And Don't Forget to Clean the Fridge,'" 295.

78. Ibid., 296.

79. See Becker, *Hitler's Children*; and Aust, *The Baader-Meinhof Group*.

80. Ann Lloyd, *Doubly Deviant, Doubly Damned: Society's Treatment of Violent Women* (New York: Penguin, 1995), 19.

Women, Terrorism, and Contemporary Conflicts

Zombies versus Black Widows

WOMEN AS PROPAGANDA IN

THE CHECHEN CONFLICT

Alisa Stack

Terrorism has been called "propaganda of the deed."[1] Yet when women do the deed, the resulting propaganda often has more to do with the women than with their actions. The case of Chechen women involved in the conflict with Russia may be one of the most colorful examples of this dynamic. Until the Dubrovka Theater hostage taking in October 2002, Chechen women were primarily seen as victims of the Russian-Chechen conflict. In the Russian and Western press, Chechen women involved in the theater seizure emerged as vicious, sympathetic, strong, fanatical, foolish, and weak—sometimes all in the same portrayal. Two media depictions of the female Chechen terrorists are particularly compelling. One is the somewhat sympathetic "black widow," a woman suicide bomber who is forced into terrorism as a result of the deaths of the men in her life. The other is the "zombie," a woman drugged, raped, or tricked into terrorism by Chechen men. Chechen groups and the Russian government could use these images to promote their respective positions. However, neither has consistently harnessed the power of women as propaganda.

This chapter focuses on the unique propaganda value of acts of terrorism committed by women in the Russian-Chechen conflict. It is unclear to what extent Chechen terrorist leaders understand or control the propaganda that women's attacks generate. In certain instances, like the Dubrovka and Beslan hostage takings, they appear highly attuned to the use of women as both weapons and messages. In other instances, such as individual suicide bombings, they appear to let Russia and others tell the story. Rarely do the women speak for themselves. Even the stories of captured female terrorists are filtered through predominately male security services, which illustrates that the truth about women's motives, involvement, and roles in terrorist activities can be less important than the stories created about how they are understood in the public sphere.

THE RUSSIAN-CHECHEN CONFLICT

On November 2, 1991, Jokhar Dudayev, president of the Chechen-Ingush Autonomous Republic, declared Chechnya independent from the Soviet Union and the Russian Federation. In response, on November 9, President Yeltsin declared a state of emergency in the Chechen-Ingush Soviet Socialist Republic.[2] War came in November 1994, when Russian soldiers were captured with anti-Dudayev Chechen forces in an armored assault on Gronzy. When the soldiers were not released, the Russians launched extensive air strikes, which were followed by the invasion of Russian ground forces on December 11, 1994. The fighting continued until 1996, when both sides agreed to a ceasefire. The conflict resumed in 1999 after a series of bombings in apartment buildings throughout Russia.

Chechen field commanders, such as Shamil Basayev and Movzar Barayev, employed a number of tactics against Russian military and civilian targets; they took hostages, bombed infrastructures, and assassinated Russian targets using suicide bombers. Consequently, the U.S. Department of State listed three Chechen groups as foreign terrorist organizations: the Islamic International Peacekeeping Brigade (established by Basayev in 1998), the Riyadus-Salikhin Reconnaissance and Sabotage Battalion of Chechen Martyrs (also led by

Basayev), and the Special Purpose Islamic Regiment (led by Barayev until his death in 2002).[3] Of the field commanders, Shamil Basayev was the most prominent. He frequently solicited support from Muslim extremist groups and has been associated with foreign fighters, particularly the man known as Khattab, an Arab mercenary with possible ties to al-Qaeda.[4]

Rumors of female snipers and suicide bombers began appearing in the Russian press in 1994.[5] For example, the Russian television station NTV reported that a women's battalion was being established to prepare to fight Russian soldiers.[6] Such reports were given credibility by the occasional arrest of Chechen women and their visible involvement in some attacks. Despite the rumors and arrests, Russian security services paid greater attention to Chechen men than women, but the mythology of the wily female suicide bomber began to take shape early in the conflict.

In fact, a woman executed the first Chechen suicide bombing. In June 2000, Khava Barayeva and a companion drove a truck loaded with explosives into a Russian military base in Alkhan-Yurt.[7] Although there was relatively little reporting on Barayeva, the fact that she was the cousin of Arbi Barayev, a Chechen warlord known for his kidnapping skills, attracted some attention. The relationship of female Chechen suicide bombers to male Chechens is important in the black widow and zombie stories; the women are depicted as motivated either by the loss of men in their lives or hopelessness induced by being victimized and forced into terrorism by Chechen men. Aside from illustrating the propaganda value of Barayeva's family connection to Arbi Barayev, it also elucidates a common path by which women enter terrorist, criminal, and guerrilla groups.[8]

The attempted November 29, 2001, assassination of General Gaidar Gadzhiyev by a female suicide bomber in Urus-Martan received relatively little notice in the Western press. The bomber, Luiza Gazuyeva, whose husband had already been killed in the conflict with Russia, died in the attack, along with one of Gadzhiyev's guards. This incident may have been the first "black widow" attack, as it is the first time journalists reported that a Chechen woman had used suicide bombing against a Russian target in revenge for the death of a man in her life.[9]

While Chechen attacks on Russian targets continued throughout 2001 and 2002, the next attack in which women were visible did not take place until October 2002, when terrorists seized the Dubrovka Theater in Moscow. On

October 23, 2002, Movzar Barayev led forty-one people, including nineteen women, in taking about eight hundred theatergoers hostage for three days until Russian forces, aided by gas that killed both hostages and terrorists, took control of the building.[10] The Dubrovka Theater incident marks the point at which the "black widow" and "zombie" depictions took center stage in the international media and Chechen women gained global attention. The female terrorists at Dubrovka were filmed with bombs strapped to their bodies and interviewed by the press, one of the few times they had spoken for themselves.

After the Dubrovka attacks, women accounted for the majority of suicide attacks in Russia.[11] In May 2003, a woman took part in a suicide attack at a Chechen government building in Znamenskoye.[12] In the same month, two female suicide bombers attempted to kill Akhmad Kadyrov, the then leader of Chechnya, in a suicide bombing at a religious festival in Chechnya. Kadyrov survived the attack but died in a bombing in 2004. In June 2003, a woman suicide bomber threw herself at a bus headed to the Russian Prokhladny Air Force base. In July 2003, two women used suicide bombs at a concert at Tushino airfield near Moscow in attacks that injured at least fifty-one people and killed fourteen; nevertheless, the concert went on, with most of the forty-thousand-strong audience unaware of the violence.[13] In December 2003, a female suicide bomber detonated near Red Square.[14] In February 2004, two women assisted a suicide bomber attack on a Moscow metro.[15] Two women are blamed for suicide bombings that brought down two Russian passenger aircraft in August 2004. At least two women were involved in the Beslan hostage taking in September 2004. With each attack, the mythology of the black widows and zombies grew, and continuing attacks today only build on the lore. The airline bombings and siege at Beslan raised questions about what kind of a woman would do such a thing and what kind of group would allow it. These questions are central to the propaganda value of women in terrorism.

ZOMBIES VERSUS BLACK WIDOWS

The nineteen women at Dubrovka were responsible for both taking care of the hostages and threatening their lives. There are mixed reports from the hostages about the women:

> The *shakhid* woman sitting next to me said her brother was killed last year and she lost her husband six months ago. She said: "I have nothing to lose, I have

nobody left. So I'll go all the way with this, even though I don't think it's the right thing to do."[16]

They didn't talk politics. They said things which anyone could understand. They would say, "My whole family was killed. I have buried all my children. I live in the forest. I have nowhere to go and nothing to live for."[17]

Men and war is one thing. But if there are women . . . I realized that we might not get out alive. Most of the women were wearing black chador headscarves so I realized they must be extremists and it would be impossible to reason with them. . . . The women don't want to be involved in these attacks. They are drugged, raped, forced to do it. I understand they are not to blame.[18]

The women were more severe with us than the men. It was possible to speak with the men, but with the women I had no desire to speak. The women had read only the Koran.[19]

The first two statements speak to how the black widow is forced into terrorism by Russian violence. The last two statements reflect perceptions about the zombies, forced into terrorism by Chechen men and weak intellect.

Although the Chechen terrorist groups did not coin the terms "black widow" and "zombie" to describe their female members, Chechen terrorist leaders, such as Basayev, occasionally play up the black widow image, emphasizing the victimization of women. This has been effective both inside and outside of Russia.[20] Women's status as victims humanizes the conflict for a wide variety of audiences. If women are involved, there is an unspoken message that the conflict must be serious and the cause may be just.

Along these lines, even those they attacked generally forgave their female assailants. In a July 2003 survey, the Public Opinion Foundation of the All-Russia Center for the Study of Public Opinion found that 84 percent of Russians surveyed believed female suicide bombers were controlled by someone else (zombies); only 3 percent believe the women acted independently.[21] This belief exculpates the female terrorists. Women are seen as being acted on by Russian or Chechen men rather than as rational beings who choose terrorism as a tactic of national liberation.

By focusing on individual female motives and backgrounds, a terrorist group can highlight the political and social conditions they seek to change and attempt to gain sympathy and support. This tactic is also used with children but rarely, if ever, with individual male terrorists, who are instead depicted as heroic and virile. Women terrorists serve a uniquely feminine role in groups' communications by playing victims even when they are perpetrators. In the case of the black widow, however, the Chechen terrorist leaders have not capitalized on the sympathy the image can garner for their cause and groups, though perhaps they do not have to, as journalists have been doing it in their stead in the ways they portray political violence committed by women.

The Russian government, on the other hand, has relied on the zombie image to discredit Chechen men and the Chechen cause.[22] One of the best examples of a "zombie" is Zarema Muzhikhoeva, one of the few captured female suicide bombers. On July 9, 2003, Muzhikhoeva failed to set off her bomb at a café in Moscow. She was arrested and has been in Russian custody ever since. The Russian Federal Security Service released its interviews with her and allowed her to appear on Russian television.[23] Some of Muzhikhoeva's statements contradict; however, her basic narrative stays fairly consistent. She stated that she was married in her teens and had a child. Her husband died fighting the Russians, and in accordance with Chechen tradition, she and her child became the responsibility of her husband's family. Either desperate to escape servitude to her in-laws or marriage to her brother-in-law, Muzhikhoeva ran away, leaving her child behind. When she could not find work, she borrowed money. When she could not repay her debt, she became a suicide bomber to be absolved of the debt.

According to her account, she went to a terrorist camp in the mountains of Chechnya in March 2003 where Arabs taught Chechens Islam and insurgent tactics. She reported having sex with the camp leader and being beaten for dressing inappropriately. She also reported that other women in the camp were raped, beaten, and drugged. After a month of training, she was sent to Moscow to conduct an attack. In Moscow, she was confined to an apartment where two men told Muzhikhoeva how and when to conduct her attack.

Muzhikhoeva's story reflects the idea that women are physically and mentally weak that is important to the zombie mythology and common across cultures and time as explanations of women's violence. In an *Izvestiya* report on female suicide bombers, an interviewee notes that terrorist groups "bring into play God-fearing, weak-willed, sad little girls who are not very bright, sometimes virtually retarded. . . . It is easy for these recruiters in Chechnya; there is a lot of material to work with. . . . And there are plenty of dull young girls." In the same report, the deputy director of the Center of Social and Forensic Psychiatry stated that "the female *shakhids* [martyrs] are usually young, and that is no accident. In youth the instinct for self-preservation is lowered. . . . They are women, therefore creatures who are emotional from the beginning."[24]

The zombie story presents the Russian public with additional victims of Chechen and Arab terrorism rather than terrorists. It blames Chechen men and customs and foreign extremism for women's behavior. The zombie story ignores the possibility that Chechen women are freely volunteering for terrorist operations. In both the black widow and zombie mythologies, stereotypes about women and their behavior are instrumental to delegitimizing the enemy. Muzhikhoeva was a terrorist tool as a suicide bomber. Her story became a counterterrorism tool for Russia. In both cases, her femininity is central to her usefulness.

Recruitment is another area in which femininity is discursively deployed. There is some evidence that Chechen groups view the use of women in attacks as something of a failure and rely on it to attract men to the fight through shame. According to a 2003 story in *Pravda*, the loss of foreign fighters in combination with Russian victories in Chechnya forced Chechen groups to admit women to combat roles. Citing an extremist document for female terrorists, *Pravda* reported, "Women's courage is a disgrace to a lot of modern 'men.'"[25] Abu al-Walid, a commander of Arab fighters in Chechnya, strikes a similar note in attempting to recruit male fighters: "These women, particularly the wives of the Muhahideen who were martyred, are being threatened in their homes, their honor and everything are being threatened. They do not accept being humiliated and living under occupation. They say that they want to serve the cause of Almighty God and avenge the death of their husbands and persecuted people."[26]

Chechen women's involvement in terrorism is thus invoked to persuade men that they cannot abdicate their duty to protect their honor and their women. Chechen militant leaders, such as Basayev, rarely mention women. When they do, women are referred to as victims of Russian aggression who need men (and an Islamic state) to protect them. They spend a good amount of time trying to attract male fighters to the cause by highlighting women's sacrifices and the need for Muslim men worldwide to protect Muslim women in Chechnya.

While Chechen terrorist groups do not appear to be making an all-out effort to recruit women, the Russian media devotes a lot of ink to the idea that women are indeed being actively recruited for terrorism and particularly dwell on the idea that Chechen groups are seeking "Black Fatimas," the zombie makers. Muzhikhoeva's story conjures a somewhat familiar archetype of female violence—the poor, stupid girl who is taken advantage of by male terrorists. In contrast, Black Fatima, rather than being taken advantage of by men, preys on other women. She is the ugly, conniving female foil to Muzhikhoeva's stupid, pretty woman. In terrorist incidents such as the bombing at the National Hotel in December 2003, she is reported to be a middle-aged woman in a fur coat and hat with a hooked nose and matted, dark hair, who is "lurking on the edges."[27] This image plays on the stereotype of physically unattractive or older women as not quite female, perhaps even evil (like witches). It is another way to demonize Chechen society while absolving female terrorists of responsibility.[28]

Russia has taken steps that specifically address female terrorists. Notably, it expanded its cleansing operations to include women. Potential black widows—those women who have lost a male relative in the war—are targets.[29] According to one estimate, about one hundred Chechen women have disappeared in Chechnya since the Dubrovka hostage taking in 2002.[30] In 2003, the Ministry of Internal Affairs issued a directive to security forces to search women in headscarves or other traditional "Muslim" clothing.[31]

Moscow, however, has not been insensitive to the possibility that targeting women may produce more terrorists of both genders, and its response has taken into account the unique propaganda value of women. In statements explaining why women are targeted, Russian officials emphasize that Chechen groups prey on women in mourning to make them "zombies."[32] In this view, Russian detentions are meant to protect both Chechen women from becoming zombies and Russian society from the zombies. The Russian government, through its influence over the media, has been able to take advantage of the unique propaganda tools that women and perceptions of women offer in its counterterrorism strategy.

Just as terrorists can benefit from the sympathy women garner in the media, governments can use groups' ambivalence about female members and women's concern about their reputations to their advantage. Russia uses the stories of socially marginal women being exploited by Islamic extremist men to discredit terrorist groups and explain away women's violence. The stories excuse women from responsibility by depicting them as victims, reassuring society that their actions are aberrations while disgracing the men. These stories could be further exploited to delegitimize and fracture terrorist groups. Publicity about women's personal lives may discredit the use of women in terrorists' eyes, as this propaganda plays up women's unreliability and weakness. It may also deter women from seeking to join terrorist groups by making the women who do appear stupid, unfeminine, or promiscuous.

THE PROPAGANDA OF THE DEED?

Curiosity about female terrorists leads to one of their most important and perhaps unplanned roles—as propaganda machines. Women have served in a number of capacities in Chechen terrorism, but their most prominent and powerful roles have been as black widows and zombies. The pity the public feels for Chechen women can be used to discredit Russian operations in Chechnya. The black widows undermine public faith in the Russian government, because women's violence is seen as a symptom of a war gone out of control and a weak Russian government. Conversely, the zombies and Black Fatima discredit Chechen leaders. The belief that women are not making or capable of making a rational choice to engage in terrorism is also evident in other nationalist movements that use violence. In political violence, women are assumed to be pawns for male terrorist leaders, and the public looks for personal reasons to explain women's violence. Focusing on the women rather than the cause can be a benefit to the terrorist group because it can bring it sympathetic attention. It can also be a drawback for a terrorist group in that attention to the women can overshadow the cause. Leaders, when they recognize the dynamic, must balance the competing propaganda effects of women's violence.

In the Chechen case, assumptions about women's motivations are central to the effectiveness of the propaganda, but they do not necessarily reflect true group or individual motives. If the black widow story were true and the only motive for women's terrorism was revenge for the loss of male relatives, then one could expect to see far more female suicide bombers. Surely there are more hopeless women who have lost loved ones in the conflict with Russia than the less than approximately thirty-nine women who have taken part in suicide attacks to date. The existence of brutality on both sides of the conflict is not sufficient to explain why women become terrorists or why terrorists groups would want them.

Likewise, if the zombie story were true and Chechen men manipulate women into terrorism, one could also expect more female terrorists, as they would serve as wonderful disposable terrorists. If women were as malleable and available as the zombie story would have one believe, they would seem to be the perfect weapon, and male terrorists would no longer be needed.

The salience of the black widow and zombie narratives, however, derives from gendered assumptions about women's intents, capacities, and essential characteristics. That women are neither that simple nor that similar rarely comes into play. The facts are irrelevant to the effectiveness of a good story.

NOTES

1. See, for example, Walter Laqueur, *The New Terrorism* (New York: Oxford University Press, 1999), 43, and J. B. S. Hardman, "Terrorism: A Summing Up in the 1930s," in *The Terrorism Reader*, ed. Walter Laqueur and Yonah Alexander (New York: Penguin, 1987), 227.

2. Christopher Panico, *Conflicts in the Caucasus: Russia's War in Chechnya* (London: Research Institute for the Study of Conflict and Terrorism, 1995), 7.

3. U.S. Department of State, *Patterns of Global Terrorism 2003*, April 2004, http://www.state.gov/documents/organization/31912.pdf (accessed March 10, 2011).

4. For information on Khattab, see Reuven Paz, "Al-Khattab: From Afghanistan to Dagestan," International Policy Institute for Counter-Terrorism, September 20, 1999, http://212.150.54.123/articles/articledet.cfm?articleid=94 (accessed March 29, 2011); Marie Colvin, "Deadly Eye of the Believer," *(London) Times*, September 30, 2001; "History of Arab Mercenaries in Chechnya Conflict Viewed," *Kommersant-Dengi*, July 14, 2003.

5. Lawrence Sheets, "Defiant Chechens Prepare for War," *(Glasgow) Herald*, December 8, 1994. 4.

6. Ibid.

7. Accounts differ as to whether Barayeva's companion was female or male. Her attack and gender attracted relatively little media attention. Since then, however, one song has been written about her in Chechnya.

8. Entry into politics through male relatives is also common in legitimate movements and governments; for example, there is the phenomenon of widows being elected

to the U.S. Congress to replace their deceased husbands and the ascent of women to prime minister in Pakistan, Sri Lanka, and India.

9. Gazuyeva's husband was killed in "an operation" in Dagestan ("Female Suicide Bomber Identity Known," *RIA Novosti*, November 30, 2001).

10. Steven Lee Myers, "From Dismal Chechnya, Women Turn to Bombs," *New York Times*, September 10, 2004, www.nytimes.com/2004/09/10/international /europe/10chechnya.html?ex=1252555200&en=aa6112cc84d7ffe7&ei=5090&partner =rssuserland (accessed March 10, 2011). Again, family ties were important; Movsar Barayev is a nephew of Arbi Barayev and a relative of Khava Barayeva. Movsar's aunt, Arbi's widow, was one of the hostage takers.

11. Genevieve Sheehan ("Rebel Republic Russia's Chechen Conundrum," *Harvard International Review* 25, no. 3 [2003], http://hir.harvard.edu/leadership/rebel-republic [accessed March 29, 2011]) states that women committed six of the seven suicide bombings by Chechens in 2003. In 2004, the *Observer* reported that "almost all the more than 12 attacks on Russia in the past year have involved women" ("The Beslan Atrocity: The Black Widows: Women at Heart of the Terror Cells: Moscow Theatre Siege Survivors Say Female Terrorists out for Revenge Were Most Chilling of Their Captors," *Observer*, September 5, 2004, 4). I found evidence of seven attacks involving women in 2003 and four in 2004. Women appear to account for the majority of Chechen suicide bombers. There is insufficient data available to show the extent of their involvement in other bombings, sabotage, kidnappings, and anonymous attacks in 2003 and 2004.

12. Fred Weir, "Chechen Women Join Terror's Ranks," *Christian Science Monitor*, June 12, 2003, 1.

13. David Holley, "Suicide Bombers Kill 14 at Moscow Concert," *Los Angeles Times*, July 6, 2003, a5.

14. Kim Murphy, "Bomber Strikes at Heart of Moscow," *Los Angeles Times*, December 10, 2003, a3.

15. Mark Franchetti, "Russia Blames Saudi for Blast that Killed 39: Terrorist Linked to Chechen Rebels, also Believed to Have Masterminded Moscow Theatre Siege," *Ottawa Citizen*, February 8, 2004, a1.

16. Weir, "Chechen Women Join Terror's Ranks," 1.

17. "The Beslan Atrocity," 4.

18. Ibid.

19. Anne Speckhard, Nadejda Tarabrina, Valery Krasnov, and Khapta Akhmedova, "Research Note: Observations of Suicidal Terrorists in Action," *Terrorism and Political Violence* 16, no. 2 (2004): 319.

20. Russian opinion surveys indicate positive attitudes toward Chechens (see Public Opinion Foundation Database, http://bd.english.fom.ru/report/cat/societas/Chechnya

/chechenian/edo30429 [accessed March 11, 2011]). However, they also show that the majority of Russians think Chechnya should be part of Russia (see http://bd.english.fom .ru/report/cat/societas/Chechnya/stat_chechnya/eofo44806[accessed March 11, 2011]).

21. T. Yakusheva, "The Terrorist Attack in Tushino—'They Want to Face Us Down,'" Public Opinion Foundation Database, July 15, 2003, http://bd.english.fom.ru/report /map/edo32826 (accessed March 11, 2011).

22. Speckhard et al. offer an alternate explanation for witnesses' observations of the Chechen women's zombielike behavior: the Sufi practices of Chechen Islam aim at creating a trance state. The training to become a suicide bomber may make use of these techniques in order to assist the bomber in overcoming her fear. Going into the trance could be interpreted by the hostages as zombification. Additionally, the training required to become a suicide bomber involves giving up the self and identifying solely with the group. This training and going into a trancelike state may have also contributed to the women's failure to act independently at Beslan and Dubrovka ("Research Note," 321–22).

23. "Russian TV Interview with Jailed Would-Be Suicide Bomber," *RenTV*, June 24, 2004. Unlike other stories of Chechen female suicide bombers, this story emphasized financial benefit as a reason women might become bombers. The RenTV interview reported that Muzhikhoeva's family was to receive $1,000. The report also includes an interview with the sister of several of the women involved in the theater hostage taking. Russian authorities allege that her brother sold her other sisters to Basayev for several thousand dollars.

24. "Psychology of Chechen Woman Suicide Bombers Pondered," *Izvestiya*, August 5, 2003.

25. "Shamil Basayev Trains Female Suicide Bombers," *Pravda*, May 15, 2003, http:// english.pravda.ru/hotspots/conflicts/15-05-2003/2810-suicide-0/# (accessed March 11, 2011).

26. "Abu-al-Walid Says Chechnya War to Spread to Rest of Russia," *BBC Monitoring*, November 19, 2003.

27. "Andrew Meier Discusses Chechen Women Who Become Terrorists," *National Public Radio*, September 7, 2004.

28. Black Fatima has some symbolic ties to the "white stockings," another feminine vehicle for discrediting the Chechens. In the first Chechen war, there were reports of non-Chechen (often Ukrainian or Baltic) women fighting for the Chechen forces. These non-Chechen female fighters are occasionally referred to as "white stockings" and, like Black Fatima, are portrayed as cold and ruthless. Unlike Black Fatima, they are young and sexually alluring. Russian police arrested a female Ukrainian mercenary in January 2000 and heralded her as one of the white stockings. According to Russian reporting,

she reported joining Basayev's group in 1995 to earn money for her wedding. The white stockings recall Stalin's claim that the Chechens collaborated with the Nazis in World War II. See, for example, "Chechen Leader Basayev Profiled," *Rostov Voyennyy Yuga Rossii*, August 30, 1999; "7 Female Wahhabite Snipers Arrested in Dagestan," *Moscow Komsomolskaya Pravda*, October 2, 1999; "Russia: 18 Terrorists Arrested in Dagestan to Be Tried in March," *Russian Public Television ORT*, February 17, 2002; "Russians Pin Down Myth of Woman Sniper," *(London) Times*, January 14, 2000.

29. Kim Murphy, "Chechen Women Being Seized to Preempt Bombings, Rights Groups Say; Female Kin of Suspected Rebels are Reportedly Taken Away by Security Forces to Unclear Fates," *Los Angeles Times*, May 26, 2004, a3; Svetlana Alikina, "Russia: Chechen Interior Ministry Hunting Potential Women Suicide Bombers," *ITAR-TASS*, February 2, 2004.

30. Mark Franchetti, "Russians Hunt Down Potential 'Black Widows,'" *Australian*, September 27, 2004, 14.

31. "Russia: MVD Confirms Nationwide Operation to Check Muslim Women," *Moscow Gazeta*, July 23, 2003. As one of the Muslim leaders I cite in this chapter points out, searching women in traditional "Muslim" attire seems an unlikely way to prevent female terrorism, given that except for the Dubrovka suicide bombers, female Chechen suicide bombers have dressed like other Russians to escape notice.

32. "'Secret' Russian Unit Targets Chechen Terrorists, Potential Suicide Bombers," *Utro.ru*, February 11, 2004; Svetlana Alikina, "Russia: Chechen Interior Ministry Hunting Potential Women Suicide Bombers."

Aatish-e-Chinar

IN KASHMIR, WHERE WOMEN
KEEP RESISTANCE ALIVE

Swati Parashar

THE SUMMER OF DISCONTENT

A crescendo of agitation resulted in a bloody summer in Indian Kashmir in 2010. More than one hundred people died in clashes with the security forces, mostly young men between the ages of fifteen and twenty-five.[1] Protests and "stone rage" began on June 11, 2010, when a teenager was killed in police firing. Subsequently, ordinary Kashmiris took to the streets of the Kashmir Valley, shouting anti-India slogans and pelting security forces with stones. This popular agitation has been referred to as Kashmir's intifada, with all citizens—men, women, and children—dictating the agenda of the separatist politicians. Curfews and *hartals* (strikes) disrupted the semblance of "normal" life; schools were shut down and businesses were affected.[2] The popular character of the insurgency and agitation was further established by large-scale participation of women, a few of whom were killed in the crossfire or in their clashes with the security forces.[3] Large numbers of women were at the forefront of the protests, shouting slogans such as "Jeeway jeeway Pakistan" ("Long live Pakistan"); "Lashkar ayee Lashkar ayee, India teri mout ayee" ("The Lashkar is here, India your death is here"); and "Hum kya chahte, Azaadi" ("What do we want? Independence").[4] The female protesters included burqa-clad women wearing green bandanas, their eyes barely visible—women clearly comfortable in their Islamic religious identity—as well as women wearing traditional South Asian garb as colorful *salwar kameezes* (pantsuits) draped in *dupatta* (scarfs).[5] All were united in their common endeavor of securing Kashmiri independence (*azaadi*) (some even were advocating for its accession to Pakistan).

Via the protests of summer 2010, Kashmir's women once again brought their "private" into the "public" and demonstrated their political awareness, commitment, and responsibility to the nationalist cause. "We want freedom" and "Blood for blood" were heard in the women's protests, as they hurled stones and even utensils at the security forces. Other women participated indirectly by "carry[ing] drinking water to the protestors and also direct[ing] youth down escape routes as they fle[d] from baton charges, teargas, and gun fire."[6] Analysts claim that this is the new face of Kashmiri women and that Indian security forces are now faced with a new challenge in having to deal with women protestors. Even Manmohan Singh, the Indian prime minister, expressed shock and distress that women and children were at the forefront of these violent protests.[7]

However, close observers of the Kashmiri resistance would agree that women's presence in large numbers in popular protests was not a new phenomenon. Women were visible in large numbers in the 1989 popular insurgency and throughout the 1990s. As recently as July 2008 large numbers of Kashmiri Muslim women agitated in response to the governor of Kashmir's decision to hand over nearly a hundred acres of forest land to the Sri Amarnath Shrine Board to construct temporary shelters for the Hindu pilgrims (on their way to Lord Shiva's temple in Amarnath in the Kashmir Valley). Perceiving this as a deliberate attempt by the Indian state to change the demography of Kashmir by settling the Hindus in the valley, Kashmiri Muslim men and women took to the streets in protest. The protest was highly communalized, and Islamic symbols and slogans dominated. Women were seen at the forefront and made further news as mothers of "martyrs" who died during the protests. These mothers were publicly recognized and honored, as their dead sons received the Shaheed Maqbool Butt award for their "sacrifice."[8] This was an attempt to evoke "normative femininity" in the political movement and recognize women's gendered roles as wives, daughters, and mothers.[9]

WOMEN AND THE 1989 POPULAR INSURGENCY IN KASHMIR

In 1989, after a rigged election by India in 1987 and the emergence on the scene of the mujahideen fighters from the Afghan jihad against the Soviets, large-scale popular discontent in Kashmir was channelled into an armed insurgency and protest with considerable help from the mercenary muja-hideen and from the neighbouring state of Pakistan.[10] Early on, women were at the forefront—shielding militants, providing logistics, acting as couri-ers of messages and arms, and taking to the streets with slogans such as "Ay mard-e-mujahid jaag zara, ab waqt e shahadat aaya hai" ("O brave warrior, wake up, the time for martyrdom has come"), "Hum kya chahte? Azaadi!" ("What do we want? Freedom!"), "Yahan kya chalega? Nizam-e-Mustafa" ("What will work here? The rule of the Prophet"); and "Azaadi ka matlab kya, la ilaha illallah" ("What is the meaning of freedom, there is no God but Allah").[11]

Before we look closer at the role of women in the Kashmiri insurgency, it will be worthwhile to reflect on the nature of the movement and its particular objectives. There are multiple views on what the movement seeks to achieve, ranging from a territorial separation from both India and Pakistan and cre-ation of an independent Kashmir to a merger of Kashmir with Pakistan on account of their common religious identity and affinity; a complete merger with India as per the instrument of accession signed by the maharaja in 1947; a preservation of the status quo that recognizes the line of control as the in-ternational border, which would give more autonomy to Indian Kashmir, the withdrawal of the Armed Forces Special Powers Act, and more accountability on issues of human rights.[12] There is no consensus on the political objectives or the territorial aspirations of the Kashmiri movement, which remains one of its biggest weaknesses. There is a great deal of anger against India and over the continuous human rights violations by the Indian security forces. It is also important to note that *Kashmiriyat* (the syncretic and Sufi-inspired liberal, tolerant culture of Kashmir) has gradually been replaced by a firm adherence to a conservative and radical Islamist ideology that defines social, cultural, and political mores in purely religious terms.

Women have been at the forefront of resistance in Indian Kashmir and in many cases have accepted their roles as a natural extension of their domestic responsibilities. As Manisha Sobhrajani points out,

> Women repeatedly raised their voices against human rights violations in Kashmir. In the case of mujahids being killed or in anti-India rallies, women participated in a significant manner. According to a senior police officer, women often registered FIRS (First Information Reports) in Police Stations stating that a person had gone missing, when actually the person was operating as a militant. Women also pursued the cases of the release of their sons and/or husbands. This "activism" ran parallel to the Kashmiri "struggle for freedom."[13]

These activities did not require large-scale destabilization of conventional gendered norms and roles. The insurgency that began in 1989 was perhaps the most spontaneous phase of the resistance, and as Rita Manchanda, Manisha Sobhrajani, and, more recently, Seema Kazi have all mentioned, it saw large numbers of women participating in public protests.[14] Manchanda notes the congregations of women that gathered in the evenings in local mosques and sang the traditional *wanuwan* (Kashmiri songs) in praise of the mujahids. Kazi suggests that women's participation upheld a normative femininity of "sacrificing mothers" even though not all the women who came out on the streets had kin affiliated to militant groups. "Women's support derived from their political solidarity for the movement of azaadi. . . . It was an opportunity for political self-expression and an experience that was liberating."[15] During my interviews most women mentioned their *jazba*, or emotional commitment, to the movement, which was demonstrated in their spontaneous outpouring on the streets of Kashmir. It is still visible in the recent and ongoing protests in Kashmir during which women have come out in large numbers throwing objects at the Indian security forces and shouting slogans. But have women been part of the armed militancy, held guns, and handled grenades and bombs?

WOMEN IN THE ARMED MILITANCY

Though public demonstrations, stone pelting, sporadic attacks on police stations and security forces, the provision of safe escape routes to militants, and the shouting of communal/anti-India slogans remain the popular form of violent protest in Kashmir, armed militancy has a two-decade-long history there. Both the popular agitation and covert, as well as overt, militant attacks and bomb blasts continue to dominate the violent landscape of Kashmir. Armed militancy began in 1989, and extensive, long-term help from neighboring Pakistan and several militant organizations based in Pakistan have been instrumental in helping Kashmiris carry out attacks in Kashmir and in other parts of India.[16] Seema Kazi distinguishes between two phases of the armed militancy. The first, a more secular phase from 1989 to the mid-1990s, was dominated by groups such as the Jammu Kashmir Liberation Front that was anti-India in its rhetoric and focused on the independence of Kashmir. Dynamics changed in the second phase, when groups such as Hizbul Mujahideen and other more fundamentalist Islamist-jihadi groups like the Jaish-e-Mohammed and Lashkar-e-Toiba entered the Kashmir war theater. Among other factors that contributed to their redefinition of the Kashmiri liberation project in Islamic terms were the wide-scale support of Pakistan, the links of these jihadi groups with the Jamat-e-Islami, and the rise of Hindutva cultural nationalism in India.[17] Along with the Indian state, "un-Islamic practices/influences" were targeted, and Kashmir was to be purged of its Sufi influence. Recruitment from strictly within the indigenous population of Indian Kashmir to the armed militancy has gradually died out. As one former militant explained to me, Kashmiri men are not fighters by instinct but by training. Unlike the Afghan mujahideen, they are not capable of withstanding the harsh conditions that come with fighting a protracted guerrilla war.[18] And so cross-border infiltration by Pakistan-based Islamist militants has increased in the last decade. This has had a significant impact on the nature of women's mobilization and participation and in most cases has rendered them invisible and silent.

The more popular and perhaps more secular first phase of the insurgency saw women spontaneously helping with the logistics and embracing its militant ideology because "a euphoria and common ideology united men and women alike for a cause that seemed just and worth fighting for—the creation of an independent Kashmir. Women participated in large numbers leading public protests against the state and the army."[19] Militants were held in high esteem and were romanticized in popular discourse.[20]

The cross-border infiltration and the appearance of jihadist groups in the second phase had two major impacts. First, it ushered in "disillusionment especially among women who had suffered—and this was the time when women began to speak against the militancy and its damaging impact on their lives.

Women's ideological and logistical support to the militancy started to decline in the late 1990s, after the militants took to petty crimes in the Kashmir Valley and began to exploit the people for personal gain."[21] Second, it led to the emergence of conservative women's politics and women's groups such as the Dukhtaran-e-Millat (Daughters of Faith) advocating "freedom" strictly based on Islamic principles, enforcing the burqa, and pushing women into the private sphere.

In August 2001, a lesser-known Islamist group calling itself the Lashkar-e-Jabber threatened to punish women who did not wear the burqa in public places. Two young women were attacked with acid by members of this group, and a deadline of September 1, 2001, was set for adopting the burqa. While in 1992 similar efforts by militant groups were thwarted by mass protests, Lashkar-e-Jabber's call created panic and burqa sales in the valley went up. The Dukhtaran-e-Millat and its leader Asiya Andrabi backed this burqa-enforcement campaign, and it is believed in certain quarters that Dukhtaran-e-Millat created Lashkar-e-Jabber to revive its burqa campaign so that burqas could be used to hide weaponry with which to attack security forces.[22] While militant groups such as the Hizbul Mujahideen and the Lashkar-e-Toiba were critical of the burqa campaign in the beginning, and the burqa campaign was resisted by most people, it did succeed in promoting a kind of religio-politics that overshadowed the demands for *azaadi* as a purely political/territorial project. Jihad now had a dual nature: 1) to free Kashmir from Indian occupation; and 2) to purge the society of corrupt, un-Islamic influences and to work toward the creation of the Muslim *ummah*. This jihadist trend received a further boost after the 9/11 attacks, which were perceived by radical groups in Kashmir as a victory for Islam. Women like Asiya Andrabi and her Dukhtaran-e-Millat followers have contributed to this new religio-political militancy, ironically targeted at women.

Over the years, armed struggle has been legitimized in popular culture, in the memory of resistance, and in the nationalist narrative that celebrates the mujahideen.[23] Several former militants are now active separatist politicians who claim a legitimate political presence in any negotiations seeking to resolve the conflict.[24] What has, however, been wiped out of public memory or silenced by the dominant patriarchal religio-political discourse is the role played by women in supporting the militancy and keeping the armed struggle alive. As a "curious feminist" who has for years followed the developments in Kashmir, I am interested in the absence of women in narratives about the armed militancy and its possible consequences. While women's participation in the popular agitation is upheld as a clear indication of the mass base of the political movement, and very often women and children are encouraged to be prominent in the agitation, the women who have over the years contributed to the militancy are very rarely if ever acknowledged. The Islamization of the armed campaign in the last decade has further contributed to the public denial of women's involvement in the militancy.

WHAT THE WOMEN SAY

In my last two field trips to Jammu and Kashmir in 2007 and 2008, I interacted with several politically active women who pointed out that without women's support, armed resistance against India, which has one of the world's largest armies, would not have been possible. But they were unwilling to publicly acknowledge that they had held guns or assisted armed militants in one way or another. Asiya Andrabi's words reverberated through other conversations: "We have been victimized by India. . . . The women have the same role. We believe in the anti-India movement. We believe that Kashmir should gain independence from India."[25] It is these beliefs that led to the formation of the Muslim Khawateen Marqaz (Muslim Women's Center) during the early phase of the militancy. The group is still politically active and is a constituent member and the only representative of women in the All Parties Hurriyat Conference.[26] It is currently led by Yasmeen Raja, who is mostly seen with her group of burqa-clad women at protest demonstrations. It is common knowledge that the group was set up as the women's wing of the Jammu Kashmir Liberation Front to assist the militants when the armed insurgency began. Mohtarma Bhaktawar, the founder of the Muslim Khawateen Marqaz, mentioned to Manisha Sobhrajani in an interview that "they started as social workers in 1986. In 1990, after the Gaunkadal massacre, when security forces killed 60 people in a peaceful demonstration, they joined the *Azaadi* movement."[27] Bhaktawar explained that

Kashmir is occupied by both India and Pakistan. We are Kashmiri women. We have drunk the milk of Kashmir. We are committed to independent Kashmir. We respect all religions. We are not fundamentalists. People of all religions will

live side by side. Kashmiri Pandits should come back here, this is their mother-
land. We welcome them back and we will protect them if they join our struggle
for self-determination. The women of Khawateen Markaz believe in dressing
according to our conscience. They do not insist on burqa. They believe "jism pe
libaas is purdah," which means clothing which does not reveal the contours of
the body and a cloth which will cover hair.[28]

A former founding member of the group whom I interviewed and who does
not wish to be named argued that its members had been instrumental in providing medical aid and shelter to the militants, in carrying guns and messages
for them in the past, and in assisting militants in kidnappings and in other
covert activities. Anjum Zamrud Habib, another former member, garnered
immense mileage and became a household name after she saved the life of
Hamid Sheikh, chief of the Jammu Kashmir Liberation Front. She later served
a prison sentence after being charged with siphoning funds to militant groups.
However, she alleged that she had been implicated and sabotaged by members
of her own organization, who feared her powerful status and progressive politics.[29] She was subsequently released from prison and has been an important
political voice in the ongoing agitation for freedom. She calls her faction the
original Muslim Khawateen Marqaz. She is not, however, part of the conservative burqa politics. Even though she acknowledges the role of more conservative women, such as Asiya Andrabi, in the political movement, she disagrees
with their methods and objectives.

The other politically active organization in the Kashmir Valley is the
Dukhtaran-e-Millat headed by Asiya Andrabi, a radical Muslim woman whose
activism is deeply rooted in her conservative religious ideology and personal
convictions. A highly educated, upper-class woman, whose family has a liberal
background (most members of her family are highly educated, and some are
even settled abroad), Andrabi chose to don a burqa as a young woman. She
married a militant (a regional commander of the Jamait-ul Mujahideen) and
has been arrested under the Public Safety Act several times. She has remained
underground for much of her life while also raising her two sons. Andrabi is
not merely interested in the independence of Kashmir from "secular" India but
sees its accession to Pakistan as the first step toward creating a Muslim *ummah*.
Her group is made up exclusively of women and is referred to as a soft terror
outfit by some analysts.[30]

There are allegations that the burqa-clad members of Dukhtaran-e-Millat act as couriers of guns and messages for militant groups.[31] The group has been involved in vandalizing and moral policing in the name of upholding and promoting Islamic values. Andrabi has personally led her followers in the destruction of cinema halls and beauty parlors. She has also thrashed women in public places who are uncovered or in unknown male company. She denies charges that she has attacked women with acid but did admit to me that her group throws paint on women who do not wear the burqa.[32] She was also supportive of Lashkar-e-Jabber's burqa-enforcement campaign in 2001. Andrabi denied her son the opportunity to play cricket in India, which she describes as the "oppressor" and "enemy." Andrabi protested against schools remaining open in the valley during the ongoing agitation even though her own son has applied for an Indian passport to study abroad.[33] She contradicts herself in various ways, but for her, Kashmir is in a state of war in which men, women, and even children have a role.

Farida Dar is another publicly active woman, who heads the Jammu Kashmir Mass Movement, an organization of largely male members. She also wears a burqa and has served a jail sentence for her alleged role in the Lajpat Nagar blasts in Delhi in 1996 in which thirteen people were killed.[34] Dar's brother was a militant, and in her interview with me she stated she had been tortured because she was suspected of shielding her brother. She also described the problems her sons have faced because of the events in her life. She is widely respected as the mother figure in her organization and is referred to as *behenji* (respectful term for elder sister).[35]

Hameeda Nayeem, a professor of English at Kashmir University in Srinagar, is an important voice in the Kashmir movement and is married to separatist leader Nayeem Khan. She described to me the trauma that women in Kashmir have suffered. She said that women as wives and mothers had made tremendous sacrifices during the armed struggle and militancy. Women had even celebrated the martyrdom of their sons at the same time that they mourned for them. She, added, however, that women's issues, if prioritized, would distract the movement, and so it would be better if they were addressed and resolved once freedom had been secured. She does not agree with Asiya Andrabi's religious views and mentioned to me that Andrabi had even sent her threatening messages for not wearing the burqa. But, like Andrabi, she is in favor of Kashmir's merger with Pakistan.[36]

THE CONTESTED ROLE OF WOMEN

There is no doubt that women have served as ideological and logistical support systems in the Kashmiri militant uprising, and many women I met during my fieldwork corroborated this. Some even admitted that shielding militants, carrying guns and messages, and nursing the wounded was vital to the uprising.[37] Many see armed militancy as simply a necessity. A resilient Kashmiri society, otherwise known for its Sufi traditions and passivity, adopted armed resistance and adapted to it, perceiving it to be in their community and "national" interest to do so. As Asiya Andrabi reminded me, "The fact that our issue is being recognized is because of militancy and jihad. Otherwise no one was listening to us. From 1947 to 1988 we were talking slowly at the political level but no one was listening. It is because of the military might shown by our mujahids that the world has recognized our problem and began to think that there is something wrong."[38]

However, there remains some ambiguity with regard to women's more direct roles in handling weapons and bombs. Asiya Andrabi argues that jihad, is primarily a man's job alone. Women have a role in it and that role is to take care of the families and the destitute.

> In 1988 anti-India movement started here. Our contribution in '88–89 was that I, through the newspapers, told the women that they should not participate in the militancy. If you participate our social set up will get destabilized. If men want to participate let them go ahead. You should not take part as far as militancy is concerned. Allah has given the responsibility of jihad on men. I don't think it is [women's participation] needed right now. By Allah's grace I feel that it would be better if this should be left to men. This will create more issues for us. See, I am telling you, if I was in jihad, what would have happened to my children? At least my children are studying. . . . At least if the father is not there the mother is there to look after them. That's why this field is not for women. Leave it to men . . . but men must keep getting moral support from women so that they can continue.[39]

Andrabi's religious beliefs dictate that women's participation in jihad should be limited to support roles. She reminded me that during the Prophet's time, his favorite daughter, Hazrat Fatima (whose husband Hazrat Ali was the Prophet's most prominent mujahid and commander), would accept responsibility of the entire house during jihad. Fatima herself used to spin yarn on the wheel; she used to make the dough and prepare bread for the children, Andrabi said.[40] When the militancy started, many women came to her to request permission to go to the other side (Pakistan) for gun training. Andrabi dissuaded them because, in her view, jihad demanded that they stay back and take care of the families and preserve the society. She is convinced that there are enough muja-hideen (men) who can fight for Kashmir and that there is no need for women to actually take up arms, but she did say that if the situation changed, women would not be reluctant to wield arms.[41]

Periodically, there have been reports of women being condoned members of militant *tanzeems* (groups) based in Pakistan, some of whom have also claimed to have active women's wing. The Lashka-e-Toiba's women's wing has often made news for organizing gatherings of women in Azaad Kashmir, where mothers of martyrs enthral female audiences with stories of their son's mar-tyrdom.[42] For instance, "the Lashkar chief, Hafiz Saed, has often been heard in conventions and rallies appealing to the sacrifices of the mothers in Islam in the cause of jihad. Motherhood provides greater justification for jihad, as appeals are made to the 'mothers of Islam' to sacrifice their sons—who are, in turn, supposed to protect them."[43] Periodically, the Indian media reports on intelligence inputs that suggest women may be involved in militant operations in Kashmir. In May 2008, the Indian forces claimed to have killed an "active" woman militant of the Lashkar-e-Toiba. Her husband, deputy divisional com-mander of the outfit, was also killed during the encounter. The slain woman, Samreena Bano, had apparently joined the Lashkar only a few months prior to the encounter. Before that, she had worked as an over-ground operative for militants and had confessed her involvement in militancy-related activities in a police enquiry. Later, she secured bail and formally joined Lashkar-e-Toiba.[44] In April 2009, General Deepak Kapoor, Indian army chief, stated that he believed there would be large-scale infiltration by women *mujahidaat*. Just a few days after he made this statement, Zahida Bano, a member of Lashkar-e-Toiba, was killed along with her lover in an encounter between Indian security forces and militants in Pulwama district of Kashmir.[45]

Women operatives attract less attention as they commit the act and they bring publicity when they succeed. A senior army officer was cited in the same report as that of Indian army chief as having said that "women arouse less sus-picion. Searching and questioning them are also quite complex. So far, women have served as informers for terrorists or provided shelter in India." The officer added that attacks by women brought publicity.[46] Indian army intelligence reports from September 2010, when the protests in the Kashmir Valley were ongoing, reveal that the militant outfit Lashkar-e-Toiba was planning to trigger blasts using trained women "terrorists" who would intermingle with protestors. According to the inputs that were received, Lashkar-e-Toiba operatives had "sought permission from their handlers across the border to lob grenades or explode IEDs during demonstrations to trigger large scale casualties and incite protesters to resort to violence."[47] No such blasts have occurred so far. But Lashkar-e-Toiba is known to be a group that constantly improvises and the idea that women were being recruited for such operations cannot be completely rejected.[48]

THE "BODY" AND THE BOMB

Security analyst Sudha Ramachandran pointed out in 2002 that "the profile of a suicide bomber in Kashmir is male (so far, no women have participated in a suicide attack) between fifteen and twenty-five years of age, and from a deeply religious background. Interestingly, less than 2 percent of the suicide bombers are local Kashmiris. Most of them are said to be Pakistanis and Afghans, and they are not necessarily from the lower socio-economic strata."[49] Suicide bombing is not seen as a legitimate Islamist resistance strategy in Kashmir and does not have the approval of most people, a conclusion I have drawn from my fieldwork. It has become a common mode of attack in Pakistan, but Kashmir has still not witnessed suicide bombings and the use of human bombers on a large scale. At a meeting in Lahore, Pakistan, in 2005, fifty-eight clerics belonging to different schools of thought issued a unanimous fatwa (decree) according to which considering suicide attacks a kind of jihad was *haram* (forbidden) in Islam.[50] Ramachandran did not speak to anyone in Srinagar who wanted their children to join the suicide squads. These included people who are deeply religious and believe in jihad: "Some praised the sacrifice made by those who participated in suicide missions, but the idea of a loved one blowing himself up, whatever the cause and the rewards, was repugnant to all."[51]

In order to ensure religious legitimacy, militant Islamist groups, such as the Jaish-e-Mohammed and the Lashkar-e-Toiba operating from Pakistan, refuse to designate their suicide operations as such. "The Lashkar-e-Toiba refers to them as *fidayeen* (or those who make the supreme sacrifice) and the Jaish calls them *khudkush shaheed dusta* (or voluntary martyrs' squad)."[52] The *fidayeen* have been projected as jihadis whose death is inevitable in the mission they undertake. Unlike suicide bombers from the Liberation Tigers of Tamil Eelam who assassinate, Kashmiri suicide bombers act "to gain entry or to blast their way into high-security government installations," as when a Jaish-e-Mohammed suicide bomber rammed an explosives-filled vehicle into the gate of the Jammu and Kashmir state assembly building in October 2001.[53] However, suicide bombings are certainly not popular modus operandi of militant groups in Kashmir.

Given these perceptions, the reactions of locals to the news that a young Kashmiri woman who had explosives strapped to her body had blown herself up was predictable. In October 2005, it was reported that Yasmeena Akhter, a twenty-two-year-old Kashmiri woman who allegedly belonged to Banaat-e-Ayesha (Daughters of Ayesha, named after the Prophet's wife), the women's wing of Jaish-e-Mohammed, blew herself up on the highway near an army camp in Avantipora.[54] A Jaish-e-Mohammed spokesperson called up the local BBC office in Srinagar and claimed responsibility for the attack carried out by their first female suicide bomber. The lack of any documented "history" of women combatants in the armed militancy in Kashmir meant that there was a scramble to "explain" her actions. During my own fieldwork I received several explanations from locals, all of whom denied that her intention was to blow up. Most concluded that she had been probably coerced into acting as a courier and that the explosions were entirely accidental. This incident is still referred to as a mysterious one, with no conclusive evidence.

In a detailed study of Akhter's case, noted Kashmiri journalist Basharat Peer suggested that she had secretly romanced a Pakistani militant and married him. She subsequently left home to join the militants. Peer's investigation also suggested that there were nasty rumors about her "affair" with a militant. Interestingly, Peer's study reveals that there are social taboos against girls willingly marrying Pakistani militants, and if they do, they are no longer acceptable to the conservative and patriarchal Kashmiri society. A psychiatrist Peers consulted during his research argued that Akhter was suffering from adjustment problems. She was denied paternal love (her father was arrested and imprisoned when she was young) and shared a close bond with her militant husband. Upon his arrest, she was bound to be suicidal in the absence of any emotional support or security. Peer's conclusion is that even if Akhter had preferred to go back to her family and lead a normal life it would not have been easy due to social pressures. Akhter's grieving mother told Peer, "I will tell you why she died like that. A martyr's death was the only honourable option for my daughter. Thousands came here to congratulate me on her martyrdom."[55] Peer's conclusion is firm: Akhter's tragic family history and her reckless heart had pushed her into dangerous militant terrain. He does not take up the act itself and whether it could be considered a suicide bombing. He reminds us that an act like hers is unusual, and he constructs his evidence in such a way as to project the "victimhood" of a woman whose own story we might never know. Peer refers to another woman's actions in drawing his conclusions. Firdausa, a Kashmiri woman from Shopian who married a Pakistani militant, was arrested and later returned to her parents. Peer suggests that her actions created a great deal of discomfort for those around her, who thought of her as a wayward woman, a prostitute whom no one would marry.

There have been no other women who have blown themselves up in Kashmir, but the debate around Akhter's life continues to highlight the multiplicity of views on the armed militancy in Kashmir. The ultraconservative Asiya Andrabi of the Dukhtaran-e-Millat was severely critical of Jaish-e-Mohammed for claiming Akhter as their suicide bomber. She maintained that "it is against the dignity of a Muslim woman that the parts of her body be strewn in a public place. If a combatant or suicide bomber is a woman, her dead body is bound to fall or be scattered in a place full of men."[56] Andrabi also expressed her shock at this incident and suggested like others that she had perhaps been serving as a courier and her bombs went off accidentally. Glorifying her death and claiming her as a suicide bomber is unacceptable to Andrabi, even though she has had no issues with male *fidayeen*. She believes that female modesty must be preserved even in death.[57] In 2007, I had a conversation on suicide bombings with Andrabi when I interviewed her in Srinagar. Even though she is against women's direct participation in the militancy, in this interview she did not reject suicide bombings by women (or men) as such but rather just rejected it as a strategy for Kashmir. She told me of her meeting in 1997 with the imam of Baitul Maqdis, who at the time was also a prominent leader of HAMAS.[58] She apparently asked him about Kashmiri women's roles in the "Hindustani mukhalif mujahati tehreek" ("anti-India movement") and reported that he had told me that if you want to go for arms training you can go. Islam has permitted you in these circumstances that you are facing. I had a threadbare discussion with him and I told him that the circumstances are like this. If we also go out for armed struggle what do you think will happen? Will our jihad move forward or will it face a setback? Then I explained to him that our family set-up system stays protected because of this. The imam agreed that I was right and that the matter of Palestine is different. They don't have homes and they are living in camps. They have a different system so they could be permitted. They are going. You call it suicide bombing? We call it self-sacrifice![59]

When I asked her if suicide bombings could be a legitimate form of resistance given that suicide itself is considered un-Islamic, she argued that the Quran permits it.

Allah says in Quran that those people are the best who leave their homes. There is the conception of *hijrat*, that you leave your home and go to some other place. Those who leave their homes for the religion of Allah are the best people among you. They die themselves and also kill the enemy. The self-sacrifice movement that is going on in the world today, what we call suicide bomber, that person is martyred but also causes huge damage to the enemy. He is not committing suicide for himself but for some issue or problem that bothers him. He has gone out to kill the enemy. This is allowed in the Shariah. Therefore, when in Palestine, even some women went for suicide attacks and we allowed that. But it depends upon the circumstances and the situation. God forbidding if those circumstances come in here [in Kashmir], we would also have to think if we need to get directly involved. But right now, I do not think that this is needed.[60]

Normative femininity has to be maintained even in times of armed resistance. Women, thus, can contribute to the resistance and jihad but should not be allowed to transgress the boundaries of expected gendered roles, except perhaps in emergency situations. Basharat Peer's account of Yasmeena Akhter's life reveals women's direct participation in the militancy tends to be mediated through men, and even then, a woman opting for a life in the armed struggle or choosing her own partner is frowned upon, unless balanced by the woman's unwavering commitment to conservative religious values. The choices for women like Asiya Andrabi, Yasmeen Raja, Anjum Zamrud, Farida Dar, and Hameeda Nayeem have been arduous. They speak with different voices and their politics and aspirations diverge, even though they are all women from the same conflict milieu. However, what they do share is an acceptance of traditional feminine norms and gender roles (as mothers, sisters, and wives), norms and roles that they applaud, endorse, and personally uphold even while recognizing that without women's participation and support, the militancy in Kashmir would have never been successful. For women like Akhter and Firdousa, especially because they transgressed the gender norms and fell in love with a "militant," there is no mercy, no acceptance even if they did serve the cause in their own way.

WOMEN IN THE HINDUTVA MILITANCY

Kashmiri Muslim women's militancy and violent protests cannot be analyzed in isolation. It is the Hindutva women who have been the harbingers of militant resistance in India.[61] The protests by Muslims in the Kashmir Valley over the land transfer to the Amarnath Shrine Board in July 2008, ignited protests by Hindus in Jammu. They were angry at the state's constant "appeasement" of Kashmiri Muslims and at the marginalization of the Hindus (especially the Kashmiri Pandits who had been driven out of the valley by the Islamist militancy) in Jammu. Interestingly, Hindu women in Jammu, who had remained very passive until then, came out in large numbers to participate in the violent protests. The women "[beat] their chests, display[ed] swords and trishuls (tridents), and [took] the pledge that they would keep the struggle going till the land was restored back to the Amarnath Shrine Board."[62] The protests on both sides gradually subsided after the government revoked the land transfer order.

In October 2008, more information came to light about Hindu women's participation in "terrorist" activities. A young Sadhvi, Pragya Singh Thakur, was arrested for her role in the September 2006 bomb blasts in Malegaon in Maharashtra's Nashik district in which thirty-seven people were killed on the eve of the Muslim festival of Eid.[63] Even before this arrest, it was common knowledge that women's roles in Hindutva vigilante groups had been pronounced, and women had also participated in sporadic political violence such as the communal riots in Gujarat in 2002. The arrest of Sadhvi Thakur and also of Maya Kodnani (the government minister in Gujarat who supported the anti-Muslim riots of 2002) demonstrates that women are not merely spectators and silent supporters of religio-political violence in the Indian subcontinent but are real actors and perpetrators who act in accordance with their religious and political views.

This shift in Hindutva politics that has allowed women to be more directly involved suggests that religio-political and cultural nationalisms are perhaps paving the way for women to embrace a more radical politics. Any comparison of Hindutva politics with the Kashmiri movement is beyond the scope of this chapter, but the overlaps, especially of women's roles (as mothers, wives, and sisters) and "sacrifices," reveal aspects of the nature and character of women's militant activities within the framework of religious ideologies. It is also important to note that the rise of Hindutva cultural nationalism and militancy in India has contributed immensely to the radicalization and Islamization of the armed resistance in Kashmir and to the increasing Islamist attacks against prominent Indian targets.[64] Both of these religio-political movements are communal in nature, derive legitimacy from religious identity, and construct the "self" in opposition to the "other." The "enemy-other" is often (re)presented as a ruthless occupying force, whose aim is not just territorial control but moral, psychological, sexual, and religious subjugation of the community. Not surprising, then, is the claim by both sides that the "enemy" aims in particular to corrupt women and to rob them of their honor and modesty. This highly gendered discourse around the "enemy-other" that ultimately plays out on the bodies of women also impacts women's participation in these religio-political projects.[65]

SUBVERSION OR CONFORMITY?

Popular protests and demonstrations are the most effective ways that women participate in the Kashmiri political struggle. However, the faith in the military campaign of the mujahideen is still intact among the women in Kashmir. Asiya Andrabi sums up the mood of a certain section of Kashmiri women, who continue to believe in the legitimacy and effectiveness of the armed campaign as the savior of Islamic societies:

> By Allah's grace we feel that if militarily we are very sound we can teach the
> West a lesson. We need to be militarily strong and we should have the conviction.... Some years back it used to sound like dream of the madmen. Now I feel
> that there is some weight in what we are saying. People have started thinking and
> there is no place in the world where work is not being done for this (Islamist)

ideology. Somewhere in the name of jihad or in the name of *dawat* . . . some people are working in the name of jihad and some for education. Muslims should have military might. We feel that since the time Muslims gave up the sword, the West started its campaign against us. The ideology of jihad is emerging in the world today.[66]

As we have seen, though, despite this unwavering belief in the legitimacy of the armed militancy, Kashmiri women have not been openly and fully accepted as combatants. Women have mostly been engaged in support roles and have provided much needed social and political legitimacy as well as a mass base to the Kashmiri movement. Although they are part of the larger project of subversion, they have had to conform to the rigid demands of a patriarchal society and polity, which are gradually adopting conservative religious values. As this study shows, women like Asiya Andrabi (and her group) have even willingly upheld the "silencing" of other women and have colluded with patriarchal strictures to push women out of public spaces.

Women's involvement in the Kashmiri militancy has thus not seriously undermined patriarchal norms, which in reality deter women from talking about their involvement in the armed resistance, restrict their agency, and prevent them from having strong and meaningful voices in the peace processes. Participating in the armed militancy validates the masculinity, courage, and "self-sacrifice" of men. But Kashmiri women's participation has been sporadic, equivocal, and limited by the norms of femininity that consigns them to their traditional roles as wives, mothers, and sisters. Moreover, narratives about women's participation have been suppressed in a strictly patriarchal society where deviant roles (as a militant, for example) have to be legitimized by way of reference to established cultural and social norms. Women's "sacrifices" have been recognized through the discourse of "victimhood" (which validates the immense suffering of women in the culture of violence and militarization) but not through their "agency" in the armed militancy.

My attempt in this ongoing research has been to "locate" women's multiple voices and bring to light the narratives of their participation in the Kashmiri resistance, given that they continue to be marginalized in mainstream political processes. As Seema Kazi aptly suggests, "The contradiction between women's involvement in *azaadi* on the one hand, and their political marginalization on the other, is a painful one."[67] For women to have a voice in peace, they need to be first heard and made visible in war stories. As a feminist, I consider this an important political project. My attempt is not to speak on behalf of these women (for they also speak in different voices and tell different stories) but to merely (re)present their stories, which have been unheard for too long, stories that highlight the complexities of a society and polity continuously and ruthlessly engaged in conflict between the "self" and "other" as well as among the different "selves."

NOTES

I am very grateful to the Jebsen Center for Counter-Terrorism Studies at the Fletcher School for its initial support of and interest in this research. It provided a generous grant that allowed me to undertake a field trip to Indian Kashmir in March 2007. I am grateful to the women and men in Kashmir who have opened their hearts to me and extended enormous warmth and hospitality despite their anger at my country. Special thanks to Christine Sylvester, who has been a remarkable source of strength and intellectual companionship ever since our first conversation at Lancaster University in September 2006.

Aatish-e-Chinaar, the phrase used as the title for this chapter, means the fire or even the spark of the *chinaar* (a tree with a spreading crown that adds beauty and character to Kashmir). *Aatish-e-Chinaar* is also the title of the autobiography of Kashmiri leader Sheikh Abdullah, whose grandson, Omar Abdullah is now the chief minister of the Indian state of Jammu and Kashmir. I use this phrase here to refer to the women of Kashmir as the spark or fire of *chinaar* who have kept alive the political resistance in Kashmir, through their participation in every activity including militancy. Yet they remain silenced in all dominant discourses or are represented as mourners and victims. It is assumed that like the *chinaar* they have no voice.

1. For the death toll in the 2010 violence in Kashmir see "100+ Days, 100+ Deaths: Summer Uprising 2010," *Daily Rising Kashmir*, September 10, 2010, http://www.risingkashmir.com/news/100-days-100-deaths-1539.aspx (accessed October 6, 2010).

2. See Danish Nabi, "104 Days of Shutdown, over 104 Killings; Current Shutdown Longest in Kashmir's History," *World Kashmir Awareness*, September 23, 2010, http://www.kashmirawareness.org/Item.aspx?id=3838 (accessed December 24, 2010); "Kashmir's New Revolt," CNN, August 7, 2010, http://www.youtube.com/watch?v=oKvJmPV96rw& feature=related (accessed October 6, 2010).

3. The exact number of women casualties is not known. See Soutik Biswas, "The Angry Housewives Setting Kashmir Ablaze," BBC, August 15, 2010, http://www.bbc .co.uk/news/world-south-asia-10961577 (accessed September 21, 2010). A list of injured can be found in Javid Iqbal, "Women in Conflict," *Rising Kashmir*, September 23, 2010, http://www.risingkashmir.com/news/women-in-conflict-1690.aspx (accessed December 24, 2010).

4. See "Freedom Slogans in Kashmir: 'Jeeway jeeway Pakistan,' 'Lashkar ayee Lashkar ayee, India teri mout ayee,'" CNN IBN, November 20, 2009, http://www.youtube.com /watch?v=rzPL6_idjlQ (accessed September 22, 2010).

5. *Salwar* is a loose pant; *kameez* is the loose and long top worn over the *salwar*. The *dupatta* is a scarf worn around the neck and shoulders; it usually covers the breasts and is often referred to as a garment of modesty.

6. See "The New Face of Kashmiri Women," *Kashmir Global*, August 12, 2010, http:// kashmirglobal.com/content/new-face-kashmiri-women (accessed October 4, 2010).

7. See "Manmohan Singh 'Shocked' by Kashmir Protests, Urges Dialogue," *Dawn. com*, September 15, 2010, http://www.dawn.com/wps/wcm/connect/dawn-content -library/dawn/news/world/04-apc-india-on-kashmir-qs-05 (accessed October 9, 2010).

8. I was doing my fieldwork in Kashmir and witnessed protests in both Jammu and Srinagar in which women participated in large numbers. Kashmir expert and well-known journalist Praveen Swami told me in an interview in July 2008 that mothers of the youths who died in the protests were given the Shaheed Maqbool Butt award and recognized in a public ceremony. The awards are named after Maqbool Butt, a Kashmiri militant and founder of the Jammu Kashmir Liberation Front who was hanged in February 1984. Swami suggested that this was an interesting development aimed at publicly recognizing women as participants in the freedom struggle, if only as mothers and daughters.

9. For more on normative femininity and religio-political movements in South Asia, see Swati Parashar, "The Sacred and the Sacrilegious: Exploring Women's 'Politics' and 'Agency' in Radical Religious Movements in South Asia," *Politics, Religion and Ideology* 11, no. 3 (2010): 435–55.

10. For more on the causes/nature of the Kashmiri conflict, see Swati Parashar, "Gender, Jihad, and Jingoism: Women as Perpetrators, Planners, and Patrons of Militancy in Kashmir," *Studies in Conflict and Terrorism* 34, no. 4 (2011): 295–317.

11. Ibid.

12. The line of control is the military control line between India and Pakistan in the province of Kashmir. Originally known as the "ceasefire line," it was redesignated the "line of control" after the Simla agreement, formalized in December 1971. Indians refer to their portion of the territory as Jammu and Kashmir, while Pakistanis refer to their portion of the captured territory as Azad (free) Kashmir.

The Armed Forces Special Powers Act was extended to Kashmir in 1990 when the armed insurgency broke out. It conferred special powers upon the armed forces in Kashmir that in turn became part of the "disturbed areas" along with the northeastern states of India. Security personnel enjoy unlimited powers under this act, which enables them to use force as per their discretion and to detain and arrest people with impunity. Kashmiris have opposed this act over the years, but the government of India has called it a security necessity to deal with armed militancy, especially given cross-border infiltration from Pakistan. This act has been abused by police, army, and paramilitary stationed in Kashmir, who have consistently violated the human rights of ordinary Kashmiris.

13. Manisha Sobhrajani, "Jammu and Kashmir: Women's Role in the Post-1989 Insurgency," *Faultlines* 19 (2008), http://www.satp.org/satporgtp/publication/faultlines/volume19/Article3.html (accessed February 20, 2009).

14. See Rita Manchanda, "Guns and Burqa: Women in the Kashmir Conflict," in *Women, War and Peace in South Asia: Beyond Victimhood to Agency*, ed. Rita Manchanda (New Delhi: Sage, 2001), 42–101; Sobhrajani, "Jammu and Kashmir"; Seema Kazi, *Between Democracy and Nation* (New Delhi: Women Unlimited, 2009).

15. Kazi, *Between Democracy and Nation*, 140.

16. In a recent revelation, former Pakistan president Pervez Musharraf has admitted that Pakistan played a key role in supporting the Kashmiri mujahideen groups since 1989. These groups continue to enjoy great support in Pakistan. See "Kashmiri Militancy Fathered in Pakistan: Musharraf," *Rediff News*, February 26, 2010, http://news.rediff.com/report/2010/feb/26/kashmiri-militancy-fathered-in-pakistan-musharraf.htm (accessed October 7, 2010). On militant groups in Kashmir and jihadi ideology, see Amir Mir, *The True Face of Jihadis: Inside Pakistan's Network of Terror* (New Delhi: Roli, 2006); Pravin Swami, *India, Pakistan, and the Secret Jihad* (New York: Routledge, 2007); Navnita Chadha Behera, *Demystifying Kashmir* (Washington, D.C.: Brookings Institute Press, 2006); Wilson John, *Coming Blowback: How Pakistan is Endangering the World* (New Delhi: Rupa, 2009).

17. Kazi, *Between Democracy and Nation*, 140.

18. Interview with a former militant, Srinagar, July 2008.

19. For more on the different phases of the militancy and women's involvement see Parashar, "Gender, Jihad, and Jingoism."

20. In some of my interviews in Kashmir, women mentioned the romantic images of militants during the early phase of the militancy. Young women and teenage girls kept photos of militants and perhaps even dreamt of marrying them. They sang songs of their bravery and sacrifice. Being a militant was not an awful thing. On the contrary, it was a noble sacrifice held in high esteem.

21. See Parashar, "Gender, Jihad, and Jingoism."

22. See A. M. Sofi, "Militant's Threats Force Kashmiri Women Take to Burqa," *Economic Times*, August 27, 2001, http://www.hvk.org/articles/0801/8.html (accessed September 30, 2010). See also the profile of Lashkar-e-Jabber at the South Asia Terrorism Portal, http://www.satp.org/satporgtp/countries/india/states/jandk/terrorist_outfits/lashkar-e-jabbar.htm (accessed October 3, 2010).

23. See, for example, "20 Years into Gun Life, Salahuddin Still Popular in Kashmir," *Kashmir Watch*, January 4, 2008, http://www.jammu-kashmir.com/archives/archives2008/kashmir20080104d.html (accessed September 20, 2010).

24. Notable militants turned politicians are Hashim Qureshi, Zafar Bhat, and Yasin Malik. They are all part of the Hurriyat Conference, which is a lose conglomeration of separatist parties.

25. Interview with Asiya Andrabi, Srinagar, March 28, 2007.

26. The All Parties Hurriyat Conference, created in 1993, is a political front of all separatist groups in Indian Kashmir united for self-determination. However, the Hurriyat's political activism has been undermined due to the internal factionalism and differences among the groups and their leadership.

27. See Sobhrajani, "Jammu and Kashmir."

28. Ibid.

29. Interview with Zamrud Habib, Srinagar, July 2008.

30. See for example, Sudha Ramachandran "Women Lift the Veil on Kashmir Struggle," *Asia Times Online*, March 7, 2002, at www.atimes.com/ind-pak/DC07Df01.html (accessed October 1, 2010).

31. Ibid.

32. Interview with Asiya Andrabi, Srinagar, March 28, 2007.

33. See Maroosha Muzaffar, "The Rebel Son, Both Fan and Prisoner of His Mother's Politics," *Indian Express*, August 24, 2010, http://www.indianexpress.com/news/the-rebel-son-both-fan-and-prisoner-of-his-mothers-politics/664127/0 (accessed October 4, 2010).

34. See "Delhis Lajpat Nagar Blast Three Get Death Sentence," *Times of India*, April 22, 2010, http://timesofindia.indiatimes.com/city/delhi/Delhis-Lajpat-Nagar-blast-Three-get-death-sentence/articleshow/5843924.cms (accessed September 29, 2010).

35. Interview with Farida Dar, Srinagar, July 2008.

36. Interview with Hameeda Nayeem, Kashmir University, Srinagar, July 2008.

37. Field notes, Srinagar, July 2008.

38. Interview with Asiya Andrabi, Srinagar, March 28, 2007.

39. Ibid.

40. Ibid.

41. Ibid.

42. See Farhat Haq, "Militarism and Motherhood: Women of the Lashkar-e-Tayyaba," *Signs: Journal of Women in Culture and Society* 32, no. 4 (2007): 1023–46; C. M. Naim, "The Mothers of the Lashkar," *Outlook India*, December 2008, http://www.outlookindia.com/fullprint.asp?choice=1&fodname=20081215&fname=naim&sid=1 (accessed February 8, 2009).

43. See Parashar, "Gender, Jihad, and Jingoism."

44. See Arun Sharma, "First J-K Woman Militant Killed in Encounter: Cops," *Indian Express*, May 29, 2008, http://www.indianexpress.com/news/first-jk-woman-militant-killed-in-encounter-cops/315858/1 (accessed October 8, 2010).

45. See Rahul Singh, "Women Terrorists Looking to Infiltrate India: Army," *Hindustan Times*, April 15, 2009, http://www.hindustantimes.com/Women-terrorists-looking-to-infiltrate-India-Army/Article1-400479.aspx (accessed October 5, 2010).

46. Ibid.

47. See "LeT's Femme Fatale in Kashmir," *MSN News*, September 24, 2010, http://news.in.msn.com/national/article.aspx?cp-documentid=4421765 (accessed October 9, 2010).

48. We saw Lashkar-e-Toiba's innovative capabilities in the planned operation in Mumbai in November 2008 when multiple targets were attacked by the *fidayeen* squad.

49. See Sudha Ramachandran, "Suicide, Just Another Way to Fight in Kashmir," *Asia Times*, July 24, 2002, http://www.atimes.com/atimes/South_Asia/DG24Df02.html (accessed October 7, 2010).

50. See "Suicide Attacks Are Haram, Clerics Decree," *Daily Times*, May 18, 2005, http://www.dailytimes.com.pk/default.asp?page=story_18-5-2005_pg1_4 (accessed October 8, 2010).

51. See Ramachandran, "Suicide."

52. Ibid.

53. Ibid.

54. Most Kashmiris as well as strategic analysts believe it was not a suicide bomb attack but a case of bombs on her body blowing up accidently. She was probably serving as a courier of those bombs. Neither the claims of the Jaish-e-Mohammed nor the suggestion that she was a bomb courier have yet been conclusively verified.

55. See Basharat Peer, "The Bride with a Bomb," *Guardian*, August 5, 2006, http://www.guardian.co.uk/world/2006/aug/05/pakistan.weekend7/print (accessed October 7, 2010).

56. Ibid.

57. Ibid.

58. Baitul Maqdis (al-Aqsa) is the third largest Mosque in the Islamic world and is located in Jerusalem. It is from here, Muslims believe, that their Prophet ascended to Heaven. The imam's name that Asiya mentions who came to India and who is a supporter of Hezbollah is not clearly audible. It could be Sheikh Akrama Sabri who visited India some years ago and who has often given theological insights on suicide bombings.

59. Interview with Asiya Andrabi, Srinagar, March 28, 2007

60. Interview with Asiya Andrabi, Srinagar, March 28, 2007. *Hijrat* refers to emigration; Muslims believe that when they are not allowed to worship Allah according to their faith in their native place, when they are subjected to restrictions and prohibition, and a when ban is imposed on proclamation and preaching of Islam, they should emigrate from such a place to such areas where they can worship Allah and propagate their religion freely. "Self-sacrifice movement" here refers to suicide bombings.

61. *Hindutva* is the ideology of the Hindu radical groups and political parties affiliated with the Sangh Parivar, which rejects Indian secularism and wish to establish a Hindu state where Hindu way of life and religion would be privileged. *Hindutva* is the true essence of Indianness, they claim, and they treat Christianity and Islam as foreign religions that are not/cannot ever be part of Indian culture.

62. Mohita Bhatia, "Women's Mobilization in the Jammu Agitation: Religion, Caste, Community and Gender," *Economic and Political Weekly*, June 27, 2009, 448.

63. Sadhvi is a female Hindu ascetic who has renounced worldly pleasures in pursuit of higher spiritual goals.

64. These attacks by Islamist militants include the attack on the Red Fort (a cultural and political symbol from where the Indian prime minister addresses the nation on Independence and Republic Days) in Delhi in December 2001, the attack on the Indian Parliament (political symbol) in December 2001, the attacks in the city of Varanasi in 2006) and on the Akshardham temple in Gandhinagar, Gujarat, in 2002. In the most recent such attacks in November 2008, Islamist militants from Pakistan, carried out a warlike siege in November 2008. The Mumbai attackers, who been trained in the militant camps in Pakistan, engaged in random firing at unarmed civilians in restaurants and at the railway station and also held people hostage at the Taj Palace hotel and in the Nariman house, a Jewish place of congregation. One militant who gained access to the media in the Mumbai siege said that the attacks were in response to the treatment of Kashmiri Muslims under Indian "occupation."

65. For more on "self" and "other" in religio-political movements in South Asia, see Parashar, "The Sacred and the Sacrilegious."

66. Interview with Asiya Andrabi, Srinagar, March 28, 2007

67. Kazi, *Between Democracy and Nation*, 147.

The Committed
Revolutionary

REFLECTIONS ON A CONVERSATION
WITH LEILA KHALED

Caron E. Gentry

In March 2002, I had an opportunity to interview Leila Khaled. A Palestinian born in 1944, Khaled vividly remembers the shelling of Haifa by the Israeli Defense Forces and her family's subsequent flight from Palestine.[1] Raised in a politically active family, Khaled has been a member of the Popular Front for the Liberation of Palestine (PFLP) since 1967. After joining the PFLP she carried out two hijackings for them, in August 1969 and September 1970.[2] She now lives in Amman, Jordan, with her husband and two sons. At the time of the interview, she was still only a member of the PFLP's Central Committee, as her fame does not allow her to move higher up into the organization.[3] My intention in this chapter is to first place Leila Khaled's own justifications for her choices in the context of what is written about her, material that often denies Khaled political motivation and culpability, and then allow her own words to speak for themselves.

My interest in Khaled is twofold. Not only is she an internationally recognized female voice for Palestinian resistance, often identified as a female
terrorist because of the two hijackings, but much is made of her femininity
and attractiveness. In fact, so much is made of her womanhood that it often
detracts from her ability to participate in the PFLP, dismissing as it does her
personal and political reasons for committing acts of violence and her commitment to the Palestinian cause. For example, an article at Wikipedia, the
controversial yet finger-on-the-pulse-of-pop-culture informational website,
asserts that the character of "Leela the Savage Warrior" in the 1970s British
television show *Dr. Who* is based on Leila Khaled.[4] Leela was a scantily clad
"alien" skilled in the art of killing and unable to communicate (because she
was a "savage") with the rest of the crew. Another more credible source draws
a comparison between Khaled and a celebrity figure: "The iconic photograph
of Leila Khaled, the picture which made her the symbol of Palestinian resistance and female power, is extraordinary in many ways: the gun held in fragile hands, the shiny hair wrapped in a keffiah, the delicate Audrey Hepburn
face refusing to meet your eye."[5] According to this source, Khaled's image
is powerful and enduring because she encapsulates "beauty mixed with violence."[6] The references to her beauty, her Middle Eastern Palestinian identity, and her participation in political violence serve to construct a Leila
Khaled who is an "uncivilized," titillating, non-Westerner. Needless to say, this
is problematic.

But this style of analysis is not confined to mass-media or journalistic
accounts. Robin Morgan, for example, a well-respected researcher, studied
Khaled and concluded she was a "token terrorist." Morgan labels Khaled as
such because she has "never spoke[n] about women" and she "has not survived
being female," because Khaled once said, "When I speak at an international
conference . . . I represent Palestinians, not women."[7] Furthermore, Morgan
declares that women become terrorists in order to join a male terrorist's harem. Women become terrorists for "love's sake" and "for male approval and
love."[8] When I presented Khaled with this idea, she could scarcely believe it,
especially as it came from a feminist. Khaled, a Palestinian woman, who has
struggled for almost forty years on behalf of her people, was, to say the least,
offended by the suggestion that not only was she a sex symbol but that she also
had not "survived being female."

IN HER OWN WORDS: LEILA KHALED'S COMMITMENT
TO THE PALESTINIAN CAUSE

Before I met Khaled in Amman, I had emailed her questions covering different topics such as background, group involvement, observed and felt gender issues within the group, group and personal ideology, justifications for armed struggle, and group dynamics. Therefore, this account of my interview with Khaled concentrates on her own motivations, her belief in the Palestinian cause and how that led to political violence, and her own approaches to womanhood. We began with her background and why she became and remains politically active.

Khaled addressed her belief in the Palestinian cause first: "Armed struggle is not an individual choice. It's a people's choice for the cause that they are struggling for. . . . [A]nd in our case, our land is occupied. . . . Armed struggle is the means to achieve the goals of the people. That's why for the man and the woman [it] is the same. [Our] country is occupied, for us, part of our people are under occupation, part are refugees."

Khaled joined the Arab National League (ANL) at the age of fifteen in 1959. She stayed in the ANL until the PFLP was formed in 1967. She mainly attributes her early involvement to her family. She was the sixth child of twelve and her older brothers and sisters were all involved in Palestinian causes.

She explains, "So I was involved too. . . . Our goals were to go back to Palestine. . . . [W]hen the war broke out in 1967, in August, this was all occupied, . . . [and] this meant we had to go further not only by political means. . . . Armed struggle was declared at that time [and] so I joined the armed struggle. And that was a dream for us because we learned . . . as . . . student[s] [that people] can't have their freedom or their land or have their sovereignty over their land unless they fight for it. . . . I was convinced . . . and that's why I left . . . Kuwait . . . and came here to Jordan to the training camps. I was trained to use arms." Khaled did face familial and social resistance to her participation. Her mother was very protective of Leila because of her young age and her gender. Her mother also was reluctant to allow Leila's older sisters to join, but because these sisters were closer in age to Khaled's eldest brother, he was able to act as guide and chaperone in a manner approved of by their mother. However, all had their father's support. Eventually, Khaled's mother accepted her participation but still was unhappy because "she [didn't] want the entire family to fight. . . . She [knew] that we may go to jail or . . . be killed. Even though at that time [it was] not a revolution." Khaled's mother knew the risks "because of her experience . . . in Palestine. . . . [B]ut, I think it was because, more or less, I was a woman." The ambiguity in her mother's attitude reflects both her belief that participation in the political struggle was important and a simultaneous desire to protect her youngest daughter.

Even though her mother wanted to protect Khaled, Khaled still described her as proud of Khaled and her siblings for defending the cause of Palestinian nationalism. "My mother . . . always spoke about Palestine—that we have to go back: there we can have a better life, a better situation. We can have everything there. . . . [S]he planted this in us." When they joined the struggle, her mother "couldn't contradict herself [even though] as a mother she was afraid. At the same time . . . she came to me and . . . said, 'Do not be afraid, we are all with you.' So she was supportive [the whole time]."

Leila says that although it was her family who mainly inspired her to become active in the Palestinian cause, the social influence of Nasserism was also important.[9] "Most people" around Leila "were involved in general activities. Teachers [in our schools] were mostly from the ANM [Arab National Movement], so they always supported and encouraged us to go [to] activities." This included distributing pamphlets, which risked arrest. "[I]t was a challenge for us as students. . . . But for a woman, it was a challenge for us as members to prove . . . that we can do the same thing. . . . But, in society [at large], women" were limited; only so many women could participate and their participation was circumscribed. It was acceptable for a woman to go to an "event, or to celebrate, or go [to] a demonstration [once] . . . but not every time." Thus, "it was . . . doubl[y] challeng[ing] for us to prove . . . that we can do the same thing."

When asked if this feeling of needing to prove oneself made a woman's action more intense than a man's, Khaled responded, "No, no. Because [in theory] in the party . . . women are equal [to] men with their duties and their rights." In reality, "to prove themselves as members of the organization, [women] have to work hard. Because if they retreat a little bit, they will be looked at as [lesser] members" and be treated as if "they don't deserve to be given other missions. That's why I think women have hard work to do. For two reasons, to prove to themselves and [to] prove to others." It is intensity in commitment, not action.

Khaled also spoke about her life in the PFLP, both as a woman and as a part of the community more generally: "PFLP women are members the same as men. They have the same rights and the same duties. But, in fact, they are not [the same]. There is still all this inheritance of old traditions and the culture of our society, affecting the people, even in our organizations. But when . . . the majority [of] men . . . see that some of the women are . . . determined and [the women] do their work . . . with the same efficiency as men [then the women] are looked upon as equal to men. If not . . . women always come second."

However, Khaled has always felt the support of her group: "In all of the stages that we have passed [through], my group and the organization [were supportive of me] all [of] the time." When Khaled was detained in London after her second hijacking failed, the PFLP had no other "means except to hijack a plane" in exchange for Khaled. This was a successful mission, and during her detention it also provided needed emotional support for her. And when the PFLP decided that hijacking was no longer an effective strategy, Khaled was a part of that decision.

In the PFLP, "all members should discuss the [politics], the strategies, the tactics of the group itself. That's why I don't feel [that] they tried to impose their ideas [on] me. Because I [always] had the opportunity . . . to discuss it and to have my [own] opinion." The group is democratic, and before becoming a member, "one should accept the program and the rules of the group itself. When you accept that then the minute you are a member you have the opportunity to discuss everything in the group." This gives a member "the opportunity to reveal his ideas." But once the discussions have taken place and a policy is decided on, Khaled said, "even though they are not my ideas . . . I have to defend the decisions that are [made]. . . . [T]his does not give me the opportunity to speak . . . to the public [about my own views]. . . . This teaches us . . . how to be faithful to the group . . . and to the goals of the organization, irrespective of your own ideas."

Khaled describes her experience in the PFLP as enriching. She is adamant in her belief that "this is a just cause. We can reach our goals. [Participation has] hardened my heart and my mind to this. But in my daily life, I feel more humane, more passionate. For example, last night I didn't sleep at all. . . . I was thinking [to] myself . . . of the mothers of the children who were killed. If I lost my child the same way that woman lost her child, the woman who lost her husband, or her brother—this makes me more passionate and sometimes I weep. I cry. To see these inhumane pictures on the TV and what's going on inside [the Palestinian Territories]. Although I don't know the people I feel as if they are my family."

While many secondhand accounts claim that Khaled and other women who have been involved in insurgent operations were manipulated or forced into participation, Khaled flatly denies that. Her participation is, she states, voluntary and it is the calculated manifestation of her political beliefs. Khaled has never regretted her participation: "I'm . . . an educated person who is totally committed to the cause."

Marxism is Khaled's guiding ideology. Marxism "strengthened the idea of armed struggle as the means to reach the goals of the people." Ideology "is the basis of the actions—not the actions the basis of ideology—of course, they interact. But at the same time, being involved [in] political violence . . . made my attitudes and beliefs [stronger]. . . . [I]t should be this way and not any other way." The commitment of the organization to Marxism has been a process: "But even after the foundation of the PFLP and adopting the ideology, it took us years to understand what Marxism-Leninism means."

The PFLP's goals include, according to Khaled:

- the return of the refugees to their homeland;
- self-determination; and
- the right to establish an independent state with Jerusalem as its capital.

Khaled defines the right of return "according to the UN resolution which calls upon Israel" to allow "the Palestinians to go back to their homeland and to be compensated for the sufferings that the Israelis have inflicted upon us." As the "conflict is about . . . existence itself," Khaled has never considered the right of return would be easily or quickly granted. "We never thought that it's going to be very near. . . . It's a historical conflict. . . . [The conflict] is going to be [passed] from one generation to another."

While some feminists have insisted that just resistance is necessarily non-violent, Khaled disagrees. Violence, Khaled says, "is always, always justified when there is injustice. . . . What an injustice that . . . we were uprooted from our homeland and we were driven out and then the other part of our people are under occupation all the time." According to Khaled, "killing, by itself, is something inhumane." But "it is justified that we defend ourselves, we can defend ourselves by declaring . . . that we are living under harsh circumstances. It's war—to be killed or to kill is justified. Because . . . our people are attacked by tanks, F-16s, Apaches, raids and so on. They have to defend themselves by using arms to kill the Israeli soldiers." As a Marxist group, the PFLP has resisted a a two-state solution that would split the contested territory between Israel and the Palestinians, instead insisting on the right to a violent struggle to create a single state with an Arab identity in which all people can live.

When asked if political violence is compatible with the role of women in society Khaled responded that "it depends upon the society women are living in. Now in Jordan, it's of no use to use political violence. With peaceful means, people—women—can struggle. But in other circumstances, the Palestinian situation, their role first is to defend themselves, to defend their people, their children, their houses, their families. And at the same time, they [demonstrate that] women can be recognized on an equal basis with men, when they come to achieve the goals of the society itself."

When asked about the complexity of being an armed woman in her society, Khaled says that "there's [not] a contradiction between being a female [and] hold[ing] arms. . . . I have the same authority as men; I [have] the same motives; we are living in the same situation." The only time she feels a contradiction is when others imply there's something wrong with a woman who holds arms. But she herself does not feel this contradiction because of the injustices she has witnessed.

I interviewed Khaled after two of the four female suicide bombings in 2002 (Wafa Idris on January 27 and Darin Abu Aysheh on February 27). I asked Khaled what this signified in Palestinian society. She attributes suicide bombing in general to a feeling of powerlessness and desperation, noting that "there are women now who have reached [the point where] the distance between life and death is minimized because of [the] powerlessness [of the] situation they are living in. . . . The first woman [Wafa Idris] . . . saw how she gathered the parts of the people who were killed—and [saw] many wounded and so on. She reached [the point where] it is no use just living, just collecting the parts of the people who were killed. So she was convinced she could go and do something to hurt the enemy and she did it. The second one [Darin Abu Aysheh], the same thing. She used her body as a weapon too. . . . In general our people look highly upon this. . . . At the same time, for women to reach that, and young women—not old women who have lived their lives. . . .[She was] a student in a university and she still ha[d] future in her life."

However, Khaled contrasts self-martyrdom with her own conscious decision to engage in activities that are risky but not necessarily a death sentence: "I may be killed while defending myself or [my children and family]. . . . I am ready for it. . . . I am ready always to die for my people." She makes a clear distinction between this readiness and suicide bombing: "But . . . death is [not] the final goal for me. No. Because it is very dangerous to reach [the point where] death is the goal. Then it means we are a desperate people. [It means we] are not reaching for [the] future and for peace and for our children. That's why I don't think . . . we should all go and die in this struggle. No, we are looking forward for the future, so we have to live. . . . And to prove myself as a woman, to [end] my life is easier than to struggle. . . . [Women] have to struggle to be a part of this."

Initially she thought that her hijackings would be the apex of her career within the PFLP, but they were "just the beginning." For Khaled, her highest point has been her "work in the woman's group. To give [women's issues] more attention and to have more time to give [to] the women's issues [was a big achievement]. At the beginning, I just didn't think of it [at] all. It was about the armed struggle." Yet, after she joined the General Union of Palestinian Women (GUPW) in 1974, the importance of women's issues grew. Therefore, she has worked very hard "to mobilize women, to work with women, [and] to discuss women's issues."

She maintains the GUPW platform, which some see as problematic, as the GUPW has placed national liberation above women's liberation. Khaled said, "[For] women in Palestinian society, the main issue . . . is . . . independence":

> So whatever we speak about women's issues, as long as we don't have a state to practice of our own, then it is nonsense to speak about women's role or women's issues *only*. Although we discuss women's issues . . . , what is the first priority for us? First . . . , to achieve the goals of the society itself, the people itself.

And through it, "women can achieve also." There is concern that women's issues will always remain secondary. Some find the Palestinian situation too close to the Algerian case for comfort. Women's issues were secondary in the

Algerian struggle; instead, equality was promised to women when the revolution was successful. Yet, in the end, nothing came of these promises. At the same time, Khaled objects to treating women's issues as more important than that of national independence, because, how can women in the West Bank and Gaza "speak about their issues when their houses are destroyed? [When] they are living [in] war conditions? They cannot speak about [women's issues] now; they speak about how to stop this aggression; and then, to think of the future of the second generation." To Khaled, this is feminism; that idea that to focus on national liberation is to put women's issues on a metaphoric "back-burner" does not have much sway in her mind. Women cannot be liberated until the entire nation is liberated.

When asked if she feels she has sacrificed a family to be a part of struggle, she answered: "Yeah, of course. First of all, I think I sacrificed . . . the old ideas that bound women to the family and to their role in the family only. Which I don't think is a big sacrifice." Instead it allowed female participants to break all the old bonds in society and in the family. She admits, "I was privileged that I could have a family, even though I was involved in armed struggle." She has been married twice. Her second husband is also a member of the PFLP. Together, they have had two sons who are now in their twenties.

In many ways Khaled sacrificed her personal life and anonymity: "From the beginning, I was very well known to the public. It made me . . . [responsible] in such a way that [the PFLP] was my first priority." Most of her friends were a part of the organization, and most of the time she was away from her family. Her work came first, and this was "thirty years ago, when women [were] not allowed to go out by themselves, and to live on their own." Yet Khaled "was given a special role and [is] very well known. . . . I was looked upon, always, as . . . one who is committed totally to her work and not to her social life."

It was only after she became a mother that she found "the balance between my work and being a mother. Before marriage, it was always whatever I have to do . . . according to my missions, and then . . . to my social relations." Khaled gave up the armed struggle in 1982 when she was in Syria and became a mother for the first time. Because of her celebrity-esque status, she no longer conducts missions, although for this very same reason she does participate in demonstrations and give speeches. She does not ever foresee giving up her membership in the PFLP.

Khaled elaborated on the balance she had to find in her life:

> It took me time to [find] the balance between my social life and work. Sometimes, it depends upon the situation and the circumstances. Sometimes I am totally away from the family and . . . then I remember . . . I'm not by myself. I have children to take care of, a husband and so on. In general, of course, [my participation] has affected my life in a way sometimes I feel I'm proud of. Sometimes it hinders me from doing things that any other human being can do. But I can't do it because I'm committed [to the cause]. But in general, it gave me the opportunity to be one who is, all the time, asked about the whole struggle and women in particular. I feel it is good for us, as women, to discuss our issue in the stream of the struggle. But it was difficult for me. Yeah, it was difficult. Sometimes, I can't go . . . places because . . . of the past. . . . But I don't have any regrets . . . never.

BEYOND THE INFAMY

Leila Khaled is perhaps one of the most mythologized proponents of political violence. While her politically violent actions are nowhere in league with Carlos the Jackal or Osama bin Laden, she joins their ranks because of her gender. But the myths surrounding her actions do not make her out to be a person willing to go to extremes for her cause; instead the myths depict her as a beauty queen or as a person who has betrayed her gender.[10]

In her own words, Khaled not only refutes Morgan's description of her but also inadvertently addresses her celebrity status. Khaled's involvement in the PFLP is far more intricate than the comparisons to Audrey Hepburn would suggest. She made a commitment to the Palestinian cause that has guided her actions throughout her life. By justifying political violence and by being able to defend her choices she portrays herself as an intelligent woman who made a choice forty years ago. This is not the countenance of a woman who fell into the armed struggle to be with a man, nor is this a woman who can be dismissed as a star. In Khaled's case, her experiences as a refugee and as a member of a politically active family awakened her sense of injustice and motivated her to join the armed struggle.

NOTES

1. Leila Khaled, *My People Shall Live: The Autobiography of a Revolutionary* (London: Hodder and Stoughton, 1973).

2. Philip Baum, "Leila Khaled: In Her Own Words," *Aviation Security International*, October 2000: 5–13; see also Khaled, *My People Shall Live*.

3. Personal interview with Khaled in 2002.

4. "Leela (Dr. Who)," *Wikipedia*, http://en.wikipedia.org/wiki/Leela_%28Doctor _Who%29 (accessed May 1, 2007).

5. Katharine Viner, "I Made the Ring from a Bullet and the Pin of a Hand Grenade," *Guardian*, January 26, 2001, sec. G2, 2.

6. Ibid., sec. G2, 2.

7. Robin Morgan, *The Demon Lover: The Roots of Terrorism* (New York: Washington Square Press, 1989), 210–11.

8. Ibid., 204–5, 208.

9. Nasserism is a form of pan-Arab and Arab nationalism as espoused by former Egyptian president Gamal Abdel Nasser. It was meant to unify all of the Arab world under a form of socialism and was popular during the late 1950s and 1960s.

10. Viner, "I Made a Ring," sec. G2, 2; Morgan, *The Demon Lover*, 210–11.

"In the war front we never think that we are women"

WOMEN, GENDER, AND THE
LIBERATION TAMIL TIGERS OF EELAM

Miranda Alison

Since Sri Lankan independence in 1948, conflict between the majority Sinhalese and the minority Tamil population has been largely continuous, leading to armed struggle from the 1970s on and civil war from 1983 on, with many Tamils desiring the establishment of an independent Tamil state or some form of federal or autonomous region political structure. While there are many distinct dimensions of this ethnic/nationalist conflict, this chapter focuses on the kinds of roles considered appropriate held by the major separatist group the Liberation Tigers of Tamil Eelam (LTTE) for women in nationalist struggles and in society more generally. The LTTE included women in their military and political struggles, a very unusual practice at the time that remains a

131

standout in nationalist struggles. Despite the 2009 defeat of the LTTE and the apparent end of the Sri Lankan civil war, LTTE ideas about women and gender have been influential in Sri Lankan Tamil society for decades and arguably remain so. This chapter, then, looks at women and gender in the LTTE militant movement.

The chapter starts with a brief section outlining the conflict the LTTE fought in and the goals and causes of the organization. The second section discusses the LTTE's policy of inclusion of women and the gender dynamics of the organization's recruitment of and use of women in its ranks. The chapter assumes that LTTE's willingness to include women is only part of the story, and so a third section uses personal interview data to look at why women joined the LTTE. A fourth section discusses gender dynamics among members of the LTTE, particularly how women were conceptualized, framed, and treated within the LTTE's military and political structures. A fifth section critically relates the gender dynamics in the LTTE to the LTTE's explicit commitment to feminism, looking at the concepts of feminism it deployed and the results of its commitment to feminism both within its ranks and in Tamil society more generally. A sixth section then explores the potential for the LTTE's ideas about gender (generally and in regard to LTTE women specifically) to continue to have impacts on Tamil (and Sri Lankan) society after the war. The chapter concludes with a discussion of the implications of women's militant action as members of the LTTE for analyzing women and gender in twenty-first-century militant and terrorist movements and global politics writ large.

THE CONFLICT IN SRI LANKA

Sri Lanka is a small island with an ethnically diverse population currently estimated to be slightly over twenty million.[1] According to the 1981 census, the population was 74 percent Sinhalese, 12.6 percent Sri Lankan Tamil, 5.6 percent Indian Tamil, and 7.5 percent Muslim.[2] Sri Lanka has an ancient and complicated history that is highly politicized and contested; competing myths of the past have become hugely significant in contemporary nationalisms. While a number of the national/ethnic groups in Sri Lanka make primordialist nationalist claims, it is clear that contemporary Sri Lankan nationalisms have a fairly recent history. Important to their development was the formation of racialist and racist ideas, attributable to the impact of developing European ideas of "race" that British rule brought. The British maintained (eventually) that the different groupings in Sri Lanka were different "races," taking various combinations of language, religion, custom, and clothing to be racial markers.

These categorizations of "race" and nationality were somewhat incoherent, inconsistent, and variable over time.[3] Only a few of these racial categories came to be politically significant. In the late nineteenth and early twentieth centuries, developing identities in Sri Lanka "were primarily directed against, and mediated by, the British," and it was only after independence that "the British were to be replaced by the Tamil as the 'dangerous other' [for Sinhalese]."[4] Contemporary Sinhala-Tamil conflict is, however, at least in part the result of processes begun by British colonialism: the unification of the country, the introduction of a unitary bureaucratic structure, and the import of Western ideas of "race" and its relation to "nation." The conflict also owes in part to the impact of mass media and state education, which were likewise developed under British colonial rule.

After independence in 1948 the construction and reaffirmation of a predominantly Sinhala-Buddhist national identity, and the concomitant process of the marginalization of Tamil and other minority identities, contributed to the mobilization of Tamil nationalism. The Tamil nationalist movement in turn threatened Sinhalese hegemony and stimulated a Sinhalese crisis of identity and security.[5] The Citizenship Act of 1948 and the Indian and Pakistani Residents (Citizenship) Act of 1949 disenfranchised Indian Tamils and made them aliens in their own country. Language and education policies have been extremely significant; in 1956 a "Sinhala only" policy made Sinhala the sole official language, and from 1970 on higher education policies were seen to disadvantage Tamil students.[6] Another important feature was the entrenchment of Buddhism within the state and Constitution. Employment and economic factors have also contributed significantly to ethnic tensions and the development of both Sinhala and Tamil nationalisms.[7]

The Tamil population first peacefully protested against these state policies and was met with varying degrees of state repression. As conflict intensified in the 1970s, "Tamil secessionism became an active phenomenon."[8] In response, the 1972 Sri Lankan Constitution entrenched the exclusivist policies of the state. Tamil political organizations subsequently proposed the establishment of a sovereign state of Tamil Eelam and declared Sri Lankan Tamils "a nation distinct and apart from the Sinhalese."[9] Tamil armed struggle, initially on a small scale, began in about 1972.[10] (The beginning of the civil war is generally taken as being 1983, when the violent riots that year "opened a floodgate" of young Tamils to militant groups.)[11] Of the five militant groups that initially fought against the Sri Lankan state, the LTTE was the only one that continued to fight for an independent Tamil Eelam until their brutal May 2009 defeat.[12]

THE LTTE'S INCLUSION OF WOMEN

Women have been active in all the Tamil nationalist groups, but research into their military participation has focused on the LTTE because they established their presence as combatants in substantial numbers in 1990s, by which point the LTTE had attained primacy among the groups. The LTTE "continued to aggressively recruit women into their fighting cadres."[13] Initially, these women disseminated propaganda, administered medical care, gathered information and intelligence, raised money, and recruited members, but they were soon given military training and began participating in combat. In interviews, female former LTTE combatants generally credited the LTTE's gender-liberal approach to women's participation jointly to the leader of the LTTE, Velupillai Prabhakaran, who was open to it, and women's active pursuit of an armed role in the Tamil nationalist struggle.

The LTTE policy seems to me to have been the result of (1) a strategic need for more fighters owing to an insufficient number of men; (2) the ideological need to demonstrate that the LTTE was an all-encompassing mass social movement; and (3) the pressure from young Tamil women themselves.[14] Despite its openness to women's participation, the LTTE is among those militant nationalist groups around the world that have not hesitated to draw on gendered cultural expectations of women's appearance (traditional saris or loose dresses) and behavior (nonviolent, nonthreatening) to gain access to targets for suicide bombers.[15] Still, though tactical reasons matter, incorporating women into nationalist military organizations is also a way of symbolically showing women's equal status in the collectivity and, therefore, showing that the movement is truly a mass social movement concerned with all members of society.[16] The LTTE presented itself as a revolutionary movement seeking not just independence from the Sri Lankan state but widespread change within Tamil society; its insistence on women's equality and the elimination of caste discrimination were an integral part of this program.

WOMEN'S CHOICES TO JOIN THE LTTE

The LTTE's decision to include women among its ranks does not in itself explain or account for women's participation. Women also chose to be involved. There are a range of different and often intersecting reasons why women chose to join militant groups; most of these are likely to be common to both female and male combatants, while others will be gender specific to women. There was rarely one single identifiable motivating factor in women's decisions to enlist in the LTTE; more usually, a number of interlocking factors that I have tried to identify and separate out here were responsible.

A significant reason for LTTE women enlisting was Tamil nationalism. Of the sixteen women I interviewed who said they had voluntarily joined the LTTE, nine referred explicitly to nationalist ideas of freedom for the Tamil nation, self-determination, land, and/or rights for Tamils (though this was not always expressed in terms of a desire for a fully independent state) as part of or as the main reason why they had enlisted. Two others explicitly articulated nationalist ideas they had come to view as important since joining the Tigers. For example, Thamilvily, who enlisted in the LTTE in 1995 at the age of seventeen, explained that

> we have witnessed the adverse effects of shelling and military action; we have seen people die and be injured. When we ask why, we see it is that we are not free and are at the mercy of the military. This is common to all Tamil people. So I joined the LTTE. . . . Everyone . . . in this country needs peace, especially the Tamil people need peace because since 1948, since independence, they have been discriminated against.

However, it seemed to me that nationalism or nationalist ideology was a meta-reason for enlistment, beneath which there were other factors, many of which intersected with or fed into nationalism.

Another motivation to enlist, intimately intertwined with nationalist ideology, was the experience and perception of Tamil suffering, oppression, and injustice. Sometimes this was related to personal or family experience; sometimes it had been received as a part of the Tamil narrative of oppression and suffering, borne out by the experience of one's friends and neighbors. My research suggests that a sense of communal Tamil suffering seemed to be an even more significant factor than direct personal or family loss in persuading some women to join the movement. Four women discussed the death of an immediate family member. Six women mentioned that their families had been displaced, and this was clearly a contributory factor for many in their decision to enlist. Ten cadres I interviewed spoke of their areas coming under attack by the military during the war, their anger over the suffering of people in their communities, and/or witnessing violence, and gave this as a partial or primary reason for enlisting. As Sudarvili told me, "Our people have been suffering. . . . The common places and the churches and the *kovils* [Hindu temples] was bombed by the government, without any reason. . . . [W]e don't have anybody to save us, and what we feel is if we have someone to safeguard us then there won't be any problem. Because of the occupation of the army we have been forced to take arms in our hands."

A third reason that women might have joined the LTTE was educational disruption and restrictions. Given that Sri Lankan policies of "standardization" had effectively discriminated against Tamils with respect to university entrance, I was expecting this to be given by some of the interviewees as a motivating factor for joining the LTTE. In a Panos oral testimony project, the standardization system is mentioned as one reason for young Tamils to take up arms.[17] However, my research revealed that the general disruption to all levels of education caused by the war, which was particularly linked to experiences of displacement, was perhaps more significant. Eight of the interviewees discussed disruption to education (either their own or more generally) as a result of displacement and war. Four of these women specifically mentioned educational disruption as part of the reason they joined.

Poverty is another factor that is often associated with people's decision to join insurgent groups, and the LTTE is no exception. Nevertheless, most of the people I interviewed were the rough equivalent of lower middle class. It seemed to me that the war-related disjunctures between past and present, between aspiration and reality, were at least as significant, or more so, as was outright poverty. Still, four of my interviewees spoke to the importance of economic motivations. For example, Thangachi explained that "I was a child. . . . I thought that if I join LTTE I would lead a better life. We were struggling even to get food. If I join the LTTE, at least these basic needs of mine would be taken care of . . . but, after joining LTTE, worries about my family started. I was getting good food. They took care of me very well. But worries about my family grew every day."

All of the reasons for enlisting in the LTTE that I have so far described are equally applicable to men and women. I also found, however, that there were some reasons for taking up arms that are gender-specific to women. One is sexual violence against Tamil women. Sexual violence against Tamil women by Sinhalese military members and police was a long-standing problem during the conflict, and many say it persists in the postconflict period.[18] Ten women discussed the fear and reality of rape as being a reason in general to join the LTTE and fear of or anger about this was part of their own reasoning for four of them. In the context of a question about whether she thought that being in the LTTE had been good for her, Barathy volunteered that "particularly in the Jaffna Peninsula, Tamil girls are raped by the Sri Lankan army" and declared that it was a part of her motivation for joining.

A number of researchers have suggested that women joined the LTTE for a variety of reasons related to women's emancipation and the desire to expand their life opportunities. A commitment to women's liberation is part all Tamil militant groups' commitment to national liberation. According to Sarita Subramaniam, the LTTE regarded "its female cadres" as "the ultimate symbol of women's liberation" and believed that women "achieve liberation from oppressive gender roles through active combat."[19] The majority of the women I interviewed said they had not been aware of issues relating to women's social conditions, women's rights, or equality before joining the movement. However, all of their awareness on this front had been raised since being with the movement and many of them expressed a clear commitment to wanting to improve life for Tamil women.

All of these matters, gender-specific or otherwise, pertain to voluntary enlistment. It is important, however, to note that the LTTE also forcibly recruited by conscription, and one of the women I interviewed had not enlisted voluntarily.[20] Noncombatant Tamils I spoke to were divided in opinion on conscription; some seemed to believe this was a lie made up to slander the image of the LTTE, while others (including some who supported the LTTE on the whole) asserted that it had certainly happened. Kavitha reported that she was forcibly conscripted by the LTTE from her Batticaloa boarding school in 1990, at the age of only fifteen, but was released after ten months and sent home. She was immediately arrested for having been in the LTTE and was then imprisoned for a year, during which time she was beaten and tortured with electrical currents.

Despite her conscription, she supports the LTTE's political agenda, though not their methods.

GENDER RELATIONS AND EXPERIENCES IN THE LTTE

In 1991, the Women's Front of the LTTE, which had been trying to publicize the unequal position of women in Tamil society, formulated the following ambitious aims: to secure the right to self-determination of the Tamil Eelam people and establish an independent democratic state of Tamil Eelam, to abolish oppressive caste discrimination and divisions and customs like dowry, to eliminate all discrimination against Tamil women and all other discrimination, to secure social, political, and economic equality, to ensure that Tamil women control their own lives, and to secure legal protection for women who are sexually harassed, raped, and subjected to domestic violence.[21]

Though the LTTE had a formal commitment to women's equality, separate organization of men and women fulfilled Tamil cultural expectations prohibiting fraternization between young men and women, reduced the perceived problem of sexual relations between cadres, and gave young women the opportunity to develop skills and grow in confidence in a supportive environment. Thamilvily explained that "men and women train and live separately because the movement is very conscious of discipline. Society is not quite happy to have women join the movement, so to have men and women train together would raise eyebrows. . . . Also because the LTTE is so strong on discipline, they want to avoid questionable behavior."

Through experience fighting alongside female cadres, the men, Adele Ann claims, came to accept and respect them, and "as mutual confidence and comradeship grew from the battle experience the gender distinctions in the allocations of responsibilities and military duties started to melt away."[22] Many of my interviewees, particularly those who joined the LTTE after 1990, said things like "we were treated as equals and we did not have any difference between us. We were like brothers and sisters" (Geetha enlisted in 1993).

Margaret Trawick argued in 1999, however, that "[s]ome of the men are conservative, and uncomfortable with the idea of sisters in trousers."[23] Thamilini maintained that "when we do something then men get to know about our capabilities, but our country's attitude towards women is different and men are always praised for doing harder and cleverer jobs, so on seeing women doing the work it will kindle the men's ego and ego tends to stop women's growth in this aspect, but on that situation we need to be courageous and patient." Six of the women I interviewed discussed specific social restrictions on women, and they were all happy that within the LTTE they had the opportunity to do things that they were raised to believe were inappropriate or dangerous for women. Geetha explained that the LTTE experience was "good for me" and credited the LTTE with giving women the ability to "seek livelihood for ourselves by working in other jobs." Furthermore, many non-LTTE women told me that the organization opposed domestic violence and punished offenders.

The war and recruitment of women into militant groups also produced changes in the lives of some nonmilitant Tamil women, who started behaving unconventionally.[24] There was some backlash against this, however, both within the LTTE and in society more generally. The concern over women's appropriate attire, the disparity between women within and without the LTTE, and the difficulties that come with attempting to balance significant social change against more traditional community attitudes and expectations in the context of nationalist mobilization all tie into the issue of the representation and rationalization of women cadres.

Early in the Tamil movement, the idealized Tamil woman was a mother who sent her son to fight in the war. Appeals to the importance of motherhood have also been used in militant Tamil depictions of state family planning as a genocidal plot. The change from "brave mother" to "woman warrior" in the construction of "woman" was a "categorical shift" although the significance of motherhood was not abandoned.[25] In fact, in the mid-1990s, Sitralega Maunaguru was arguing that a "mother-warrior" construction of Tamil womanhood had emerged, resulting in gun-and-baby representations.[26] The conjunction of motherhood and combat and the challenges and ambiguities this presents all seem to have made their way into popular representations of the Tigers as well.

The mother-warrior conjunctive image clearly stands in stark contrast to maternalist feminism, which argues for motherhood as a basis for peace and nonviolence. In the context of worsening state repression in the northeast in the 1980s, Tamil women organized themselves as mothers in groups such as the Mothers' Front. While groups like the Mothers' Front show how the "social mother" manifestation of maternalist feminism can be actualized, the mother-warrior (image and reality) illustrates that this is far from being an automatic link. Other scholars have identified a construction of LTTE women as "armed virgins" that works in conjunction with (yet also stands in contrast to) the Tamil mother-warrior construction that Maunaguru discusses.[27] Radhika Coomaraswamy and others view this construction extremely negatively, arguing that it denies women sensuality, sexuality, and love and enforces androgyny.[28] Peter Schalk, however, sees it as strategically brilliant. He explains that "the role of the fighting woman is thus implicitly rationalised with reference to an old classical societal value. This rationalisation creates a special type of woman, namely the armed virgin, a Tamil Saint Joan of Arc, who has no precedents in Tamil culture, but is a hybrid creation born of the conflict of introducing a new social role to an old culture."[29]

Some express concern that the acceptance of this "creation" may signal a Tamil nationalist "patriarchal bargain."[30] The reality of the "armed virgins," however, is a little more nuanced. Although marriage was originally forbidden for LTTE members of either sex, this policy changed at some point, and Trawick notes that "young people fall in love and get married, subject to the permission of their elders within the organization."[31]

I found that female cadres rejected the "armed virgin" representation of themselves as being a misguided interpretation by outsiders rather than an LTTE ideal. Certainly many of the women I interviewed were keen to refute this image of themselves and stressed that cadres could marry (with permission) after the appropriate age had been reached. Nonetheless, it is true that this in no way suggests that unmarried cadres would be likely to view premarital or extramarital or, probably, homosexual sexual relations as acceptable, nor would they likely be accepted by their leadership. The LTTE even sometimes arranged marriage for its members, and I was also told a number of times about LTTE child care centers in the Vanni, where children could be left when both parents were LTTE members. Arranged marriages both allowed the LTTE to follow local cultural practice and to circumvent the problem of LTTE women not being seen as suitable wives by many outside the movement. There is, however, a gender distinction in terms of marriage; some male cadres married women in the movement, but many married women who were not, whereas female cadres generally seem only to have married men in the movement. Once again, this reflects a divergence between LTTE women and "normal" Tamil women, as well as arguably a similar divergence between LTTE men and "normal" men.[32]

Finally, the female fighters in the LTTE earned a fearsome reputation and have often been represented in the media and discussed among ordinary people (Tamil and Sinhalese) as being more violent and more terrifying than male Tigers. Young men described themselves as "absolutely terrified of the women cadres of the LTTE. The physical maltreatment meted out by the male cadres was a pale shadow to what the female cadres did."[33] One "rather common" explanation of this is that "female cadres have to be more tough, ruthless and less-sympathetic—in a word, more macho—in order to compete for the status and recognition in a traditionally patriarchal context."[34] Whether the women really were more violent than the men is, of course, hugely debatable (and difficult to establish empirically), but the very fact that such claims are made is interesting, signaling as it does the operation of the "monster" narrative about politically violent women.[35]

Certainly the LTTE did expect its female cadres to act and present themselves as fierce and fearless warriors in the same way as was expected of male cadres; equality here is arguably about women emulating constructed/expected masculine qualities. For example, Kalaivily explained that "in our history, women are generally known for their soft nature. Women are full of mercy and kind hearted. . . . In our day-to-day normal life we are still treated like this. Also qualities such as love, affection, caring are all quite natural to us. But in the war front we never think that we are women and we are soft by nature. These disappear from our mind. In the war front we have only our aim in our mind, our aim to get an independent nation. We never think that we are killing someone. We think that we are doing our duty . . . to get an independent nation."

LTTE FEMINISMS (?)

If women in the LTTE considered themselves to have a similar mission to men on the battlefield, this is consonant with the LTTE's official position on women's equality and the training that the organization offered to women. Although, as I have noted, the vast majority of my interviewees said that they had not been aware of issues pertaining to women's social conditions, women's rights, or equality before they joined the movement, all of them came to think about these issues while within the movement. Most mentioned being taught about women's social oppression in LTTE political classes as well as through their individual experiences contributing to the change. Kalaivily spoke of the LTTE teaching the "common people" about women's liberation and empowerment. Eleven of the seventeen women appeared now to possess a genuine interest specifically in working toward improving the lives of Tamil women and in securing more opportunities for them. Unsurprisingly the intellectual conceptualization of and ability to articulate such issues varied from woman to woman, but the depth of their commitment to women in their communities was unquestionable, though arguably the nature of the commitment was such that it might also be autocratic in some contexts.

It seemed to me that the type of feminist ideas the women expressed were, while tied to their nationalism, largely of a liberal variant with some cultural specificities, in which women and men are conceived of as essentially having the same potential capacities and qualities. What was often stressed was the idea that people, regardless of their sex, vary in their abilities and talents and that all people should have the chance to develop their particular talents. A few (in higher LTTE positions) also demonstrated awareness that cultural variation between countries is significant and that the problems women face are different in different places. Thamilini asserted that "even in the developed world . . . women will be facing some problems, but the problems are different for different countries. This depends on the country, life, development, and the environment and culture; the problem varies." She also spoke of the high divorce rate in Western countries and argued that this had a negative impact on children and families. She did not want Tamils to emulate the Western pattern and was concerned about Tamil diaspora communities in other countries, whom she perceived as struggling and as neither integrated entirely into one culture or another.

Kalaivily also talked about gender rights in a culturally specific way. She spoke of how Tamil society raises girls to think that there are boundaries to the kind of jobs that they can do, that they are only fit for cooking and household work. She mentioned how women are expected to be home by 6 p.m. and are not allowed to look at men while walking in public, and so on. In her view, these things "suppress the natural qualities of women." However, she was keen to stress that there are cultural limits to change; "if there are changes to our basic culture such as the way women dress, it won't be acceptable." Her comments imply that the impetus for changes to the gendered order stems from the LTTE and that "ordinary people" resist some of them; there is no acknowledgment of the potential for Tamil society to set its own agenda for change independently of the LTTE.

Although LTTE feminism is certainly tied to Tamil nationalism and it is assumed that freedom for women will not/cannot/should not come *without* national freedom, at the same time not all the LTTE women seemed to fall into the classic trap of believing it would automatically come *with* national liberation either. Banuka said "even if we get the nation's freedom, unless there are equal rights for women in the fields of education and employment there won't be real freedom. So it is our responsibility to ensure women are getting their rights."

According to the late LTTE leader Prabhakaran, "The ideology of women liberation [*sic*] is a child born out of the womb of our liberation struggle."[36] The women's liberation movement, he said, is an integral part of the greater Tamil struggle.[37] Prabhakaran was careful to state, however, that "the struggle against male chauvinistic oppression is not a struggle against men. It is an ideological struggle against the ignorance of men."[38] He claimed that "our struggle shines as a superb paradigm of women's ability to accomplish anything."[39]

Many non-LTTE feminists and other commentators have questioned the ideology of women's liberation that was expounded by the LTTE. They are skeptical of Tamil nationalist ideology in relation to women and the idea that participation in militant groups can or has brought improvements for Tamil women as a whole. Vidyamali Samarasinghe argues that through women's participation in armed struggle in civil war they "become actors in the public arena."[40] The question (especially as the armed conflict appears to be over, at least for the present) is whether this public sphere activity was temporary and transitory, ending with the war, or "whether the gains they made in times of war" can be "consolidated in terms of gender equity in times of peace."[41] She reminds us that "women's participation in the public arena of the armed struggle is certainly no guarantee that women have finally penetrated into the public sphere of activities on the basis of gender equality."[42] I would not dispute this; nevertheless, the participation of women as soldiers and the expressed ideological commitment to women's equality in Tamil nationalism are significant sociopolitical changes.

Women's wings of militant Tamil organizations *and* autonomous women's groups tried to use the opportunities created by nationalist lip service to feminism to raise issues relating to the subordination of women and "extended the discourse beyond the boundaries of ethnic repression."[43] Still, in 1990, Rajan Hoole and his coauthors asserted that the women's wings of Tamil militant groups, or at least of the LTTE, had failed to address issues surrounding sexual violence, though this does not seem entirely fair.[44] For example, for the 1986 International Women's Day, a joint march by various women's groups used the slogan "Let us forget the Four Virtues [modesty, charm, coyness and fear]/ Let us own a fighting spirit."[45] One feminist gain from this, Maunaguru says, was a new understanding of and activism around the issue of sexual violence against women. While Tamil militant groups saw the rape and sexual harassment of Tamil women in Tamil-majority areas where there was a large military presence as a means of racially oppressing the Tamil community, the women's activist groups viewed rape as an issue linked to gender and power and stressed the relationship of sexual violence against Tamil women to a general violence against women. This represents one way that "Tamil women used the new context created by militant nationalism to articulate their interests as women."[46]

Evidence suggests that the LTTE commitment to women's liberation has done more than just raise awareness of sexual violence. Sumantra Bose asserts that "the liberating impact of Tiger struggles on the lives of young Tamil women thus should not be underestimated, especially if one remembers that this is a society where women have historically been totally excluded from the public arena. The confidence and poise of leading Tiger women is impressive indeed."[47] This was also something I noticed during my fieldwork. Tiger women have an air of quiet assurance and confidence that is not necessarily obvious in other women; even the way they walk and carry themselves is different. Still, it is important to look at feminism within the LTTE with caution. Bose reminds us that changes within Tamil social formation in regard to women and in other areas "may not necessarily have been consciously *intended* by the leaders of the LTTE, though they have definitely been the concrete *result* of specific strategies of mass mobilization pursued by these same leaders."[48] Conversations with LTTE activists left him feeling that they welcomed these social changes if only because they realized that they were necessary to achieving the unified national movement that would bring about Eelam. He believes that overall these changes to the preexisting Tamil social order were seen by the LTTE leadership as simply incidental to the ultimate goal of an independent state of Eelam.

Similarly, Samarasinghe argues that there are "several tensions present be-tween the articulated elements of women's emancipation and the reality of women's actual positioning within the revolutionary/militaristic praxis" of the LTTE, tensions that could prevent women's gains from extending to the post-conflict era.[49] First, because women's revolutionary role is commonly under-stood to have been subject to the direction or command of the male leader of the LTTE, she views this role as more "like a set of orders to be followed, rather than spontaneous activation by society in general."[50] Second, after the conflict, "the priorities of governance and statehood change, and with that the agenda for women may also change. Evidence from other liberation move-ments illustrates that often times women are politely told to go back into the reproductive sphere and to the kitchen."[51] LTTE women have not, she suggests, created a public space for women that can be sustained in peacetime. This is all the more problematic given that it appears that the LTTE has *lost* the war, which brings up a question of what (if any) influence their ideas about ap-propriate gender roles can have in a postconflict Sri Lanka. Finally, on the one hand, female soldiers were glorified by the LTTE and postrevolutionary gender equality it envisaged; on the other, leadership of the LTTE in Samarasinghe's view remained "almost exclusively Tamil male."[52]

Although Samarasinghe makes valid points, particularly in respect to the open question of whether women's expanded roles will be preserved in peace-time, there are some indicators that her assessment is too negative and that the LTTE built some potentially lasting structures for women's rights. Many LTTE women were very actively involved in a wide range of women's development and community development programs. During a 2002 interview, Thamilini (the most senior figure in the women's political wing) told me that there were (at the time) twelve members on the LTTE Central Committee, five of whom were women.[53] When I asked her about the allegation that there were more women who took part in military activities than in decision making, Thamilini claimed that this was largely false bad press from the Sri Lankan government but also implied that there was some truth to the claim, since she maintained that women were beginning to rise through the political ranks. It is likely that the main thrust of the LTTE project was defined by men, but it is worth reemphasizing that women have "nationalistic aspirations" as well and that women in the LTTE viewed these as being of primary importance. While some people see feminism as "true" only when it puts women's rights before nationalist goals or insists that they are separate from those goals, many women in nationalist struggles all over the world have shown that in their position, this strategy is not only questionable but undesirable. Commitment to what one sees as the needs or interests of one's perceived nation or ethnic group is viewed as being just as important, or more so, than one's needs or interests "as a woman." The debate over whether LTTE women are agents or victims, liberated or subjugated, emancipated or oppressed strikes me as an unnecessary and unsophisticated binary.

TAMIL WOMEN "AFTER" THE CONFLICT

The links between the LTTE's nationalism and feminism and the harnessing of women's hopes to Tamil Eelam's hopes look different now that it appears the LTTE has been militarily defeated and with it its hopes for an independent Tamil state. It is arguable that if women's rights were a flagship cause and symbol of the LTTE, the repression of Tamil women in Sri Lanka now is a potent symbol of the LTTE's defeat. There are accusations that war crimes, human rights abuses, and other violations of international law were committed by both the Sri Lankan security forces and the LTTE in the final months of the war, and the International Crisis Group, Amnesty International, and Human Rights Watch have jointly called for an independent international investigation into such matters.[54] The question of what happens to both the women of the LTTE and Tamil women generally in these uncertain times is an important one.

Reports of possible sexual violence against LTTE women by the security forces during the last stages of the war and of Tamil women in the internal displacement/internment camps and Tamil-majority areas since the end of the war suggest that the sex-specific consequences for Tamils of the civil war are no less severe "postwar" than they were during the war.[55] Although all Tamil women are at risk of being sexually abused by state forces, precedent suggests those most at risk are internally displaced women, women who are or were members or suspected members of the LTTE, and female relatives of male LTTE members or suspected members.[56] Food, water, shelter, sanitary and medical provisions have been wholly inadequate at the overcrowded and militarized so-called welfare centers or welfare villages, where over 280,000 Tamils were interned for months during the war and where around 73,000 remained a year after the war ended.[57] There have been reports of prostitution networks in the camps in which the collusion of Sri Lankan security forces has been impli-cated, and of destitute women trading sex for food, money, and supplies.[58]

Human rights organizations were also seriously concerned about extraju-dicial killings of Tamils suspected of having been LTTE members, subsequent arbitrary arrests of those still alive, and a lack of due process in the prosecution of LTTE suspects. There were, as of February 2010, around eleven thousand suspects (including over five hundred children) who were being held in gov-ernment "rehabilitation centers" after having been "screened" from the Tamil population in the government camps and at checkpoints.[59] It is unclear what proportion of these detained LTTE suspects are women or girls, though ap-parently male and female suspects were separated into different camps, and there have been allegations of sexual violence against the female suspects.[60] A recent media report states that the Sri Lankan military official in charge of "rehabilitating" former Tigers is planning a mass wedding for about twenty couples as a precursor to those couples being moved to another government-run center in Jaffna where ex-LTTE families are living.[61] Although it is claimed the mass wedding will be performed with the consent of all those involved, in the current circumstances it is hard to rule out coercion. Most LTTE members or suspected members are being held incommunicado in "irregular" (unofficial) detention centers run by Sri Lankan security forces and affiliated anti-LTTE Tamil paramilitary groups, increasing the risk of serious human rights viola-tions being committed against those being held.[62]

Still, there is also the suggestion that Tamil women and LTTE feminism remain influential. As Feizal Samath documents, the LTTE "helped women . . . take a closer look at themselves and take on roles and ways other than those dictated by society," which is still resulting in women "slowly being freed from the strict roles and ways imposed on them by tradition,"[63] Because of women's participation in the conflict and their taking up new roles that war thrust on them, "the rest of society began to give women more space."[64] In the April 2010 parliamentary elections, the people of the Jaffna peninsula elected a fe-male Sri Lankan Tamil MP, Vijayakala Maheswaran (from the United National Party).[65]

It is difficult to get a sense of to what extent the LTTE (and particularly the Tamil women's organizations within it) remains organized underground after its military defeat and the destruction of "virtually the entire political and mili-tary leadership," as well as the arrest in August 2009 of Prabhakaran's would-be successor.[66] There are suggestions that the Tamil resistance movement has not fought its last day, particularly outside the country, in Tamil Nadu and in Western diaspora communities, where a self-proclaimed Tamil Eelam transnational government was elected in May 2010. These developments may keep the issue of women's equality alive.[67] Still, a complicated set of variables means an uncertain future for Sri Lankan women generally and Tamil women specifically, as it remains a question whether LTTE feminism will continue to provide opportunities for Tamil women postwar and whether the Sri Lankan government's treatment of Tamils generally and Tamil women specifically will improve either in the wake of the military conflict or in the event of its renewal.

LEARNING OF AND FROM THE WOMEN OF THE LTTE

Arguments for a special connection between women and peace (and men and war) are empirically hard to sustain, as is illustrated by the many cases in this book. To be a feminist (or a woman) is not a necessary or sufficient condition for being a pacifist, just as being a pacifist is not a necessary or sufficient condition for being a feminist. Just as being a woman or a feminist is not a sufficient condition for being a pacifist, it is also not a sufficient condition for being antinationalist. Women are intimately involved in national projects and mobilizations not just as symbols of the nation or as passive recipients of nationalist ideology but as nationalist (and antinationalist) actors themselves. The specific relationship(s) between feminism(s) and nationalism(s) within the LTTE and anywhere is highly variable according to political, social, and cultural context(s) and historical period(s).

That women in the LTTE are nationalist actors does not mean, however, that they are completely free agents making totally independent choices about their lives. There is no such thing as "pure" or "complete" agency (for LTTE women or anyone else); we are all constrained and impacted by the structures and discourses of our societies and the events of our lives. In this "relational autonomy" choice exists but is dependent on context; we make choices but our choices "are not independent of the gendered social and political contexts of . . . local and global worlds."[68] Relational autonomy can be seen at work in the lives of the LTTE combatant and ex-combatant women in this chapter. Almost (though not quite) all of the women emphasized that they *chose* to become involved, that they *wanted* to be there; the desire to be seen as agents is clear and deserves attention. Nonetheless the contexts that shaped and constrained their decisions is also apparent and at least implicitly acknowledged by most. Relational autonomy, however, does not take away from the fact that LTTE women (and men) made choices and see themselves as political actors.

Possibly the theme that recurred the most in my interviews with LTTE women was that of respect and, tied to this, of women proving themselves (*to a masculine standard*) to earn respect. How many times in how many ways and in how many varied places, and at what cost do women have to keep proving themselves worthy of respect? The fact that women succeed in militaries in large part by taking on a masculine gender role and by denying or subsuming gender differences means that the movement's politics, no matter how liberatory it considers itself to be, will not *automatically* be genuinely or consistently interested in or effective at addressing systematic gender inequality in a wider society, *especially* given its apparent defeat. Addressing systematic gender inequality requires a direct challenge to existing gender ideologies and practices and a chipping away at the often narrow concerns of the Tamil nationalist movement. Although the very presence of women in nontraditional combat roles in the LTTE may have been the drip of water that opened up a crack in the rock, to split it wide open requires a constant feminist assault that is not characteristic even of this formally feminist nationalist movement.

NOTES

1. "Sri Lanka" is generally used to refer to the country, to save confusion, even when discussing the colonial period when it was called "Ceylon." It has been argued that the 1972 change of name from Ceylon to Sri Lanka was done without the consent of Tamils (Alfred J. Wilson, *The Breakup of Sri Lanka: the Sinhalese-Tamil Conflict* [London: Hurst, 1988], v). I use "Sri Lanka" because that is how most people outside the country know it.

2. Chris Smith has suggested that as a result of the war, Sri Lankan Tamils now make up only 8 percent of the population (*In the Shadow of a Cease-Fire: The Impacts of Small Arms Availability and Misuse in Sri Lanka*, Occasional Paper no. 11, [Geneva: Small Arms Survey, Graduate Institute of International Studies, 2003], 3). "Sri Lankan Tamils" are sometimes referred to as "Ceylon Tamils" while "Indian Tamils" are also known as "hill-country Tamils," "plantation Tamils," or "up-country Tamils"; they are

the descendants of south Indians brought over as indentured labor by the British to work the plantations in the central hills in the mid-nineteenth century. "Muslims" are considered a separate ethnic group, sometimes called "Moors." I use "Sri Lankan Tamils," "Indian Tamils," and "Muslims" here. This is not intended as a political judgment, and certainly the distinction between "Sri Lankan" and "Indian" Tamils does not imply that Indian Tamils have any less of a right than Sri Lankan Tamils to live in Sri Lanka.

There is an inconsistency in the literature about when it is best to use "Sinhalese" and when to use "Sinhala," and some use the terms interchangeably. In accordance with the pattern that seems the most logical and most consistent in the literature, I use "Sinhala" for the language and the variant of nationalism and "Sinhalese" for the people.

3. Darini Rajasingham-Senanayake, "Ambivalent Empowerment: The Tragedy of Tamil Women in Conflict," in *Women, War, and Peace in South Asia: Beyond Victimhood to Agency*, ed. Rita Manchanda (New Delhi: Sage, 2001), 14–20.

4. Elizabeth Nissan and R. L. Stirrat, in "The Generation of Communal Identities," *Sri Lanka: History and Roots of the Conflict*, ed. Jonathan Spencer (London: Routledge, 1990), 32.

5. Serena Tennekoon, "Newspaper Nationalism: Sinhala Identity as Historical Discourse," in *Sri Lanka*, 205.

6. Neil DeVotta, "Illiberalism and Ethnic Conflict in Sri Lanka," *Journal of Democracy* 13, no. 1 (2002): 86–89.

7. See Siri Gamage, "Post-Independent Political Conflicts in Sri Lanka: Elites, Ethnicity, and Class Contradictions," South Asia-Journal of South Asian Studies 20, no. 1 (1997): 359–95, and Deborah Winslow and Michael D. Woost, eds. *Economy, Culture and Civil War in Sri Lanka* (Bloomington: Indiana University Press, 2004).

8. Wilson, *The Breakup of Sri Lanka*, 86.

9. M. R. Narayan Swamy, *Tigers of Lanka, from Boys to Guerillas* (Delhi: Konark Publishers, 1994), 31–32. The term "Eelam" (or "Ilam") is an old name for Sri Lanka. In the 1920s and 1930s the term "Tamil Eelam," which referred the areas inhabited by the Tamils and considered to be traditional homelands, came into increasing usage. The term was widely used in the late 1930s and is currently used by Tamil nationalists to mean "belonging to the Tamils" (Dagmar Hellmann-Rajanayagam, "The Politics of the Tamil Past," in *Sri Lanka*, 114).

10. Purnaka L. de Silva, "The Growth of Tamil Paramilitary Nationalisms: Sinhala Chauvinism and Tamil Responses," in *Conflict and Community*, 97.

11. Narayan Swamy, *Tigers of Lanka*, 96.

12. The period from July 1983 until the 1987 Indo-Sri Lanka Peace Accord (or until

the collapse of this in 1990) is sometimes described as the first "Eelam war." The second "Eelam war" was fought between 1990 and 1995 with a brief ceasefire in 1995. The third "Eelam war" was fought from 1995 until the start of the ceasefire at the end of 2001. The fourth "Eelam war" began in 2008 and ended in May 2009.

13. Vidyamali Samarasinghe, "Soldiers, Housewives, and Peace Makers: Ethnic Conflict and Gender in Sri Lanka," *Ethnic Studies Report* 14, no.2 (1996): 213.

14. Miranda Alison, "Women as Agents of Political Violence: Gendering Security," *Security Dialogue* 35, no. 4 (2004): 447–63.

15. Ibid.

16. Nira Yuval-Davis, *Gender and Nation* (London: Sage, 1997), 98.

17. Olivia Bennett, Jo Bexley and Kitty Warnock, eds., *Arms to Fight, Arms to Protect: Women Speak Out about Conflict* (London: Panos, 1995).

18. Amnesty International, *Sri Lanka: Rape in Custody Must Be Stopped Immediately*, 2002, ASA 37/001/2002, http://www.amnesty.org/en/library/asset/ASA37/001/2002 /en/2c91e5d4-d8a7-11dd-ad8c-f3d4445c118e/asa370012002en.pdf (accessed May 20, 2010); Amnesty International, *Sri Lanka: Torture in Custody*, 1999, ASA 37/10/99, http://www .amnesty.org/en/library/asset/ASA37/010/1999/en/eaoed8ee-e1d8-11dd-a03a -6b5b1e49bce3/asa370101999en.pdf (accessed January 18, 2001).

19. Sarita Subramaniam, "Women Lead Rebel Attacks, but Tiger Leaders are Men," *Inter Press Service*, August 11, 1997, www.oneworld/org/ips2/aug/srilanka.html (accessed February 16, 2002); Margaret Trawick, "Reasons for Violence: A Preliminary Ethnographic Account of the LTTE," in *Conflict and Community*, 141.

20. Human Rights Watch, *Living in Fear: Child Soldiers and the Tamil Tigers in Sri Lanka*, HRW 16, no. 13 (2004), www.hrw.org/reports/2004/srilanka1104/srilanka1104.pdf (accessed April 16, 2007).

21. Peter Schlak, "Women Fighters of the Liberation Tigers in Tamil Ilam: The Martial Feminism of Atel Palacinkam," *South Asia Research* 14, no. 2 (1994): 169.

22. Adele Ann, *Women Fighters of the Liberation Tigers* (Jaffna: LTTE Publication Section, 1993), 100.

23. Trawick, "Reasons for Violence," 145.

24. Sitralega Maunaguru, "Gendering Tamil Nationalism: The Construction of 'Woman' in Projects of Protest and Control" in *Unmaking the Nation: The Politics of Identity and History in Modern Sri Lanka*, ed. Pradeep Jeganathan and Qadri Ismail (Columbo: Social Scientists' Association, 1995), 169.

25. Ibid., 163–64.

26. Ibid., 164.

27. Peter Schalk, "Birds of Independence: On the Participation of Tamil Women in Armed Struggle," *Lanka* 7 (1992): 44–142.

28. Radhika Coomaraswamy, "Tiger Women and the Question of Women's Emancipation," *Pravada* 4, no. 9 (1997): 8–10.

29. Schalk, "Women Fighters," 178.

30. See Deniz Kandiyoti, "Bargaining with Patriarchy," *Gender and Society* 2, no. 30 (1988): 274–90.

31. Trawick, "Reasons for Violence," 158.

32. See also Alisa Stack, "Lions, Tigers, and Freedom Birds: How and Why the Liberation Tigers of Tamil Eelam Employs Women," *Terrorism and Political Violence* 19, no. 1 (2007): 51–52.

33. Purnaka L. de Silva, "The Efficacy of 'Combat Mode': Organisation, Political Violence, Affect, and Cognition in the Case of the Liberation Tamil Tigers of Eelam," in *Unmaking the Nation*, 184.

34. Ibid.

35. See Laura Sjoberg and Caron Gentry. *Mothers, Monsters, Whores: Women's Violence in Global Politics* (London: Zed, 2007).

36. Velupillai Pirapaharan, "Tamil National Leader Hon V. Pirapaharan's Women's International Day Message," EelamWeb, March 8, 1993, www.elamweb.com/leader /messages/women/1993/ (accessed May 21, 2002).

37. Ibid.

38. Ibid.

39. Ibid.

40. Samarasinghe, "Soldiers, Housewives, and Peace Makers," 217.

41. Ibid.

42. Ibid., 213.

43. Maunaguru, "Gendering Tamil Nationalism," 164–65.

44. Rajan Hoole et al., *The Broken Palmyra: The Tamil Crisis in Sri Lanka, an Inside Account* (Claremont, Calif.: Harvey Mudd Press, 1990), 324.

45. Maunaguru, "Gendering Tamil Nationalism," 165–66.

46. Ibid., 167.

47. Sumantra Bose, *States, Nations, Sovereignty: Sri Lanka, India, and the Tamil Eelam Movement* (New Delhi: Sage India, 1994), 112.

48. Ibid., 115.

49. Samarasinghe, "Soldiers, Housewives, and Peace Makers," 218.

50. Ibid.

51. Ibid.

52. Ibid., 219.

53. It has been claimed that Thamilini was killed in combat in 2009 (Satheesan Kumaaran, "Demise of LTTE Commanders and Its Implications," *TamilCanadian*, May

21, 2010, http://www.tamilcanadian.com/page.php?cat=266&id=5905 [accessed May 22, 2010]).

54. International Crisis Group, *War Crimes in Sri Lanka*, ICG Asia Report no. 191, 2010, http://www.crisisgroup.org/~/media/Files/asia/south-asia/sri-lanka/191%20War%20Crimes%20in%20Sri%20Lanka.ashx (accessed May 19, 2010); Human Rights Watch, *War on the Displaced: Sri Lankan Army and LTTE Abuses against Civilians in the Vanni*, HRW 1-56432-443-5, 2009, http://www.hrw.org/en/reports/2009/02/19/war-displaced (accessed March 3, 2009); Human Rights Watch. "Sri Lanka: Repeated Shelling of Hospitals Evidence of War Crimes," *HRW News*, May 8, 2009, http://www.hrw.org/en/news/2009/05/08/sri-lanka-repeated-shelling-hospitals-evidence-war-crimes (accessed May 19, 2010).

55. Human Rights Watch, "Sri Lanka: New Evidence of Wartime Abuses," *HRW News*, May 20, 2010, http://www.hrw.org/en/news/2010/05/20/sri-lanka-new-evidence-wartime-abuses (accessed May 21, 2010); International Crisis Group, *Sri Lanka: A Bitter Peace*, ICG Asia Briefing no. 99, 2010, http://www.crisisgroup.org/~/media/Files/asia/south-asia/sri-lanka/b99%20sri%20lanka%20a%20bitter%20peace.ashx (accessed May 22, 2010); Amnesty International, *Stop the War on Civilians in Sri Lanka: A Briefing on the Humanitarian Crisis and Lack of Human Rights Protection*, 2009, ASA 37/004/2009, http://www.amnesty.org/en/library/asset/ASA37/004/2009/en/36e63f0d-f0be-4ccc-87c0-862f0c0f62a8/asa370042009en.pdf (accessed July 3, 2009), 9; "Regular Rapes, Killings, Degrading Interrogations in Internment Camps," *TamilNet*, April 18, 2010, http://www.tamilnet.com/art.html?catid=13&artid=29085 (accessed May 22, 2010); "Vanni in the Year after War: Tears of Despair and Fear," *Groundviews*, May 26, 2010, http://www.groundviews.org/2010/05/26/vanni-in-the-year-after-war-tears-of-despair-and-fear/ (accessed May 26, 2010); Gethin Chamberlain, "Sri Lankan Guards 'Sexually Abused Girls' in Tamil Refugee Camp," *Observer*, December 20, 2009, http://www.guardian.co.uk/world/2009/dec/20/tamil-tigers-sri-lanka-refugees (accessed May 22, 2010); "Credentials of IC Challenged While Widespread Rape by SLA Alleged in Vavuniyaa," *TamilNet*, November 24, 2009, http://www.tamilnet.com/art.html?catid=79&artid=30672 (accessed May 22, 2010).

56. Amnesty International, *Sri Lanka: Rape in Custody*, 3. See also Amnesty International, *Unlock the Camps in Sri Lanka: Safety and Dignity for the Displaced Now*, 2009, ASA 37/016/2009, http://www.amnesty.org/en/library/asset/ASA37/016/2009/en/c612ddea-1786-413b-97c6-6021ebfead8d/asa370162009eng.pdf (accessed May 19, 2010).

57. Amnesty International, *Unlock the Camps in Sri Lanka*; Internal Displacement Monitoring Centre, *Sri Lanka: Continuing Humanitarian Concerns and Obstacles to Durable Solutions for Recent and Longer-Term IDPs*, IDMC, November 10, 2009, http://www.internal-displacement.org/8025708F004BE3B1/(httpInfoFiles)/E52F8EDB6E

C95876C125766A0045F597/$file/SriLanka_Overview_Nov09.pdf (accessed May 20, 2010); Nita Bhalla, "One Year On, Conditions Worsen for War-Displaced Sri Lankans," *AlertNet*, May 19, 2010, http://www.alertnet.org/db/an_art/55867/2010/04/19-154627-1 .htm (accessed May 22, 2010); Integrated Regional Information Networks, "Sri Lanka: UN Calls for Faster Screening Process, Greater Access," IRIN, May 14, 2009, http:// www.irinnews.org/Report.aspx?ReportId=84377 (accessed May 25, 2010); Integrated Regional Information Networks, "Sri Lanka: One Year Later, 'Some Kind of Peace,'" IRIN, May 18, 2010, http://www.irinnews.org/Report.aspx?ReportId=89166 (accessed May 25, 2010).

58. International Crisis Group, *Sri Lanka: A Bitter Peace*, 5.

59. Human Rights Watch. *Legal Limbo: The Uncertain Fate of Detained LTTE Suspects in Sri Lanka*, HRW 10-56432-592-X (2010), http://www.hrw.org/en/reports/2010/02/02 /legal-limbo-0 (accessed May 12, 2010); Amnesty International, "Sri Lanka's Displaced Face Uncertain Future as Government Begins to Unlock the Camps," *AI News*, September 11, 2010, http://www.amnesty.org/en/news-and-updates/news/sri-lanka -displaced-uncertain-future-government-unlock-camps-20090911 (accessed May 12, 2010); Amnesty International, *Stop the War on Civilians in Sri Lanka*. The 566 alleged child soldiers have now been released (Charles Haviland, "Tamil Tiger Child Rebels Go Home," *BBC News*, Colombo, May 26, 2001, http://news.bbc.co.uk/1/hi/world /south_asia/10165563.stm [accessed May 26, 2010]).

60. International Crisis Group, *Sri Lanka: A Bitter Peace*, 5; "Grand Scale Murder, Rape of Screened Civilians Feared, TNA MP Alerts," *TamilNet*, February 14, 2009, http://www.tamilnet.com/art.html?catid=13&artid=28413 (accessed May 22, 2010).

61. Charles Haviland, "Sri Lanka Former Tamil Tiger 'Mass Wedding' Planned," *BBC News*, Colombo, May 19, 2010, http://news.bbc.co.uk/1/hi/world/south_asia/10125414 .stm (accessed May 20, 2010).

62. Amnesty International, "Sri Lankan Army Clashes with Detainees," *AI News*, September 24, 2009, http://www.amnesty.org/en/news-and-updates/news/sri -lankan-army-clashes-detainees-20090924 (accessed May 12, 2010).

63. Feizal Samath, "How the War Gave Tamil Women More Space," *Inter Press Service*, April 21, 2010, http://www.ipsnews.net/news.asp?idnews=51132 (accessed May 22, 2010).

64. Ibid.

65. Parliament of Sri Lanka, directory of members, http://www.parliament.lk /directory_of_members/ViewMember.do?memID=3185 (accessed May 27, 2010).

66. International Crisis Group, *Sri Lanka: A Bitter Peace*, 14.

67. "New Political Party in Tamil Nadu Vows to Fight for Tamil Eelam," *TamilNet*, May 19, 2010, http://www.tamilnet.com/search.html?string=New+political+party+in

+Tamil+Nadu+vows+to+fight+for+Tamil+Eelam (accessed May 20, 2010); "Government Blacklists Transnational Government of Tamil Eelam Representatives," Terrorism Update of the South Asia Terrorism Portal, May 10, 2010, http://www.satp.org /satporgtp/detailed_news3.asp?date3=2010%2F5%2F10&image2.x=0&image2.y=4#26 (accessed May 22, 2010); "LTTE Threat Shifted from Field of Battle to Field of Diplomacy, Says External Affairs Minister G. L. Peiris," Terrorism Update of the South Asia Terrorism Portal, May 7, 2010, http://www.satp.org/satporgtp/detailed_news3 .asp?date3=2010%2F5%2F7&image2.x=2&image2.y=11#20 (accessed May 22, 2010); "Tiger Foreign Network Intact," *Daily Mirror*, April 22, 2010, http://www.dailymirror .lk/index.php/news/3289-tiger-foreign-network-intact.html (accessed May 25, 2010); "S. Lanka Vows to Prevent Tiger Revival," *Bangkok Post*, May 20, 2010, http://www .bangkokpost.com/news/asia/178537/s-lanka-vows-to-prevent-tiger-revival (accessed May 25, 2010).

68. Sjoberg and Gentry, *Mothers, Monsters, Whores*, 17.

PART THREE

Women, Gender, and al-Qaeda

Al-Qaeda's Use of Female Suicide Bombers in Iraq

A CASE STUDY

Jennie Stone and Katherine Pattillo

Over the past decade, there has been a significant increase in the use of suicide bombing as a terrorist tactic and of women as perpetrators of these attacks. At least seventeen organizations have used women as suicide bombers, including the Liberation Tigers of Tamil Eelam, the Kurdistan Workers Party, Chechen rebels, the al-Aqsa Martyrs Brigade, the Palestinian Islamic Jihad, HAMAS, and al-Qaeda. These groups have claimed responsibility for female suicide bombings across the globe, in places such as Lebanon, Sri Lanka, Chechnya, Israel, Iraq, and Jordan.[1]

This chapter represents the research and views of its authors and in no way represents the views of the United States Government.

Until 2005, al-Qaeda abstained from employing women as suicide bombers. The organization crossed this threshold on September 28, 2005, when it claimed responsibility for an attack perpetrated by an unidentified woman who detonated an explosive belt in the midst of a crowd gathered near an army recruitment center in Tal Afar, Iraq.[2] Since then, a number of other women have participated in suicide bombing attacks in Iraq; al-Qaeda has explicitly claimed responsibility for at least four of these incidents.[3] The sex of the bomber aside, there is in general limited data available on suicide bombers in Iraq. This study is limited to the documented cases between 2005 and 2007, but it is likely that women conducted more suicide attacks in Iraq during that time period and that they have committed more since then than we aware of. Press reports indicate that an element of al-Qaeda in Iraq located in the Diyala province was devoted exclusively to recruiting females for suicide bombings.[4]

All of the known attacks perpetrated by female suicide bombers during this period took place in the central and northern parts of Iraq; these areas are well known for their significant Sunni and al-Qaeda presence. Of the ten executed or attempted suicide attacks by women in Iraq during this period, almost half took place in Baghdad; others were carried out in Tal Afar, Mosul, Baqubah, and Muqdadiyah. Almost all of the female bombers targeted Iraqi police officers or police recruits. Three of the operations targeted American troops, Iraqi college students, and Shiites in line for fuel.[5] The attacks on the college students and fuel customers were significantly more lethal than the other attacks; each killed approximately forty people and wounded as many or more. The explosive belt or vest has been the weapon of choice for female suicide bombers in Iraq. With the exception of Myrium Goris, whose car bomb plot was thwarted in November 2005, all female suicide bombers have carried their explosives on their person.[6] While this trend may be a function of belts being the most cost-effective and efficient tactic for a bomber with limited operational experience, it is also possible that al-Qaeda adjusted its procedures in response to Goris's failure.

The numbers of suicide bombings involving women has not varied directly with the general level of violence in Iraq nor has it fluctuated in concert with incidents of suicide bombings in general.[7] Furthermore, although the majority of attacks in Iraq during the 2005–7 time frame targeted coalition forces, female suicide bombers have focused their attacks predominately on personnel and/or facilities associated with Iraqi security forces.[8] While there are a number of ways of explaining this targeting trend, two stand out. Most significantly, the probable rationale behind using suicide belts could apply here as well: women may be assigned "softer" targets, such as crowds of police recruits, due to their rudimentary levels of training. A second, more nuanced factor that could contribute to the kinds of targets selected for women attackers has to do with the effect that al-Qaeda leaders may hope such attacks will have on domestic Muslims. According to a Jordanian researcher and acquaintance of Abu Musab al-Zarqawi, the former head of al-Qaeda in Iraq responsible for introducing female suicide bombers as an al-Qaeda strategy, Zarqawi's intent in using women may partially have been to shame Muslim men into participating in attacks, since women are generally seen as less suited to this sort of attack, and using them in this way expresses a lack of options.[9] This theory is further corroborated by a website posting attributed to Zarqawi prior to al-Qaeda in Iraq's use of female suicide bombers. In this posting, Zarqawi stated, "Are there no men, so that we have to recruit women?" He further implied that female suicide bombers were a tactic of last resort by asking, "Isn't it a shame for the sons of my own nation that our sisters ask to conduct martyrdom operations while men are preoccupied with life?"[10]

ABU MUSAB AL-ZARQAWI AND AL-QAEDA IN IRAQ

Abu Musab al-Zarqawi was renowned for his particularly savage tactics as well as for pursuing the controversial strategy of inciting sectarian violence between the Sunni and Shiite factions in Iraq. His influence and legacy is underscored by the fact that all of the documented cases of al-Qaeda's use of women suicide bombers to date either have taken place in Iraq or have been carried out by an Iraqi. The degree to which senior al-Qaeda leadership sanctioned both his tactics and his choice of targets remains contested. Al-Qaeda's second in command, Ayman al-Zawahiri, allegedly sent al-Zarqawi a letter criticizing both his sectarian agenda and the brutality of his beheadings.[11] Al-Zawahiri was concerned that al-Zarqawi's methods would alienate the Iraqi people and jeopardize al-Qaeda's long-term goals of evicting the United States from the country to ultimately establish an Islamic caliphate. While this letter predates the first instance of female suicide bombing in Iraq and fails to address explicitly the opinion of senior al-Qaeda leadership on this topic, it establishes both a philosophical and tactical tension between al-Qaeda in Iraq and al-Qaeda's central command. It is further telling that al-Qaeda in Iraq is still the only chapter of the global movement that has employed female suicide bombers.

Intelligence sources believe that al-Zarqawi's association with al-Qaeda began in 2000 when he met with a series of Taliban and al-Qaeda officials to request funding to establish training camps in Afghanistan. During this time, he also established a group called Tawhid (meaning "unity"), which operated in Afghanistan and Pakistan. Despite al-Zarqawi's fundamentalist fervor and radical ideology, his goals during this period varied somewhat from those of al-Qaeda and its then-leader Osama bin Laden. Al-Zarqawi preferred to focus on the wrongdoings and indiscretions of Israel, Jordan, and the Jewish population rather than on those of the United States.[12]

From late 2001 until 2003, al-Zarqawi worked to establish and maintain a series of militant networks throughout the region and substantially increased his follower and financial support base.[13] Soon after Baghdad fell in 2003, al-Zarqawi and his supporters emerged as a core part of the insurgency against coalition forces. In August 2003, he founded a group called Monotheism and Jihad, which executed a series of attacks in Baghdad and Najaf.[14] The group was renamed al-Qaeda in Iraq a year later, when al-Zarqawi agreed to subordinate his organization under the al-Qaeda umbrella.[15] The relationship between the two groups was mutually beneficial; association with the greater al-Qaeda network gave al-Zarqawi's group legitimacy, and al-Qaeda received greater coverage by the media because of the large number of attacks carried out by al-Qaeda in Iraq.[16] At the same time, al-Zarqawi was a charismatic personality who had an ability to prioritize and a very specific vision of how to combat enemies near and far. The global credibility his reputation lent to an al-Qaeda organization still reeling from the consequences of Operation Enduring Freedom in Afghanistan enabled him to deviate from standard al-Qaeda operating procedures with a degree of impunity.

Until his death in June 2006, al-Zarqawi worked ceaselessly to cement his global reputation and to extend his influence through his effective manipulation of the media. His trademark element, one that assured him constant attention from the media, was his employment of particularly brutal tactics.[17] Beheadings, hostage takings, and suicide car bombings became part of daily life during al-Zarqawi's leadership of al-Qaeda in Iraq. Over time, these types of attacks became synonymous with al-Zarqawi himself; eventually the use of these tactics became tantamount to a declaration of responsibility, so that no official announcement was required. Al-Zarqawi was the face of the Iraqi insurgency working to oust coalition forces from Iraq and has been described as eager to "enhance his own legend by embracing tactics that have generated enormous publicity."[18] Taking the initiative to employ women as suicide bombers was in line with his overall strategy in Iraq. Given the rapid succession of female suicide bombers employed by al-Qaeda in Iraq following their tactical debut in September 2005, it is likely that al-Zarqawi and/or his network noted the significant media response by Western news outlets and sought to capitalize on the increased media attention. Following the first female suicide attack, al-Zarqawi cultivated his global audience by conducting an additional three attacks using female suicide bombers—two in Iraq and one in Jordan—within a six-week period.

TACTICAL ADVANTAGES

Female suicide bombers embody the very characteristics that allowed al-Zarqawi and al-Qaeda in Iraq to mount such a successful campaign against coalition forces and to destabilize the nascent Iraqi government. Among other attributes, female bombers are largely unexpected, generate a great deal of media attention, demonstrate the power and reach of al-Qaeda in Iraq by challenging cultural norms, and successfully employ asymmetric means. By incorporating women into its arsenal of suicide bombers, al-Qaeda gained a number of tactical and strategic advantages.

Of primary tactical significance—and wholly dependent on the stereotype of women as playing passive or subordinate roles in Muslim culture—is the fact that women could frequently pass more easily through security checkpoints. Female suicide bombers also provided attack flexibility and, due to their rarity, an element of surprise. Overall, suicide bombing requires very little training or preparation, and so extensive, separate training facilities and pipelines for women need not be built to use bombers. Consequently, the amount of time and resources needed to prepare women for suicide missions are manageable. Finally, the ensuing backlash from security forces often took the form of aggressive searching of women by coalition or Iraqi security forces, which was perceived negatively by most of the Iraqi population. The propaganda value of this side effect alone was tremendously valuable for al-Qaeda's media campaign.

A TACTICAL TRIUMPH: AL-QAEDA'S FIRST FEMALE SUICIDE BOMBER

The tactical utility of female suicide bombers in al-Qaeda's ongoing battle in Iraq is best illustrated by the organization's first one. The still-unidentified woman responsible for the September 28, 2005, attack at an army recruitment center in Tal Afar successfully manipulated assumptions about gender roles to pass through security checkpoints and then execute her attack. Dressed in traditional female clothing, she passed undetected through the security checkpoints near the recruitment center.[19] Both cultural sensitivities and the small number of female soldiers available to conduct such searches mean women commonly pass through checkouts without being searched. Having navigated the checkpoints, the young woman subsequently changed into men's clothing, donning a dishdasha, which is a white robe traditionally worn by men, and a kaffiya, a checkered headscarf commonly worn by Iraqi men.[20] In these clothes, she was able to gain access to the crowd of army recruits and detonate her explosives without drawing a great deal of attention to herself. According to Major Jamil Mohammed Saleh, the explosives were packed with metal balls, increasing the lethality of the explosion.[21]

Al-Zarqawi and al-Qaeda subsequently capitalized on the strategic value of using a female in a kinetic operation by highlighting the event in the global media. Several days after the bombing, a website linked to al-Zarqawi posted a statement saying, "May God accept our sister among the martyrs." The statement declared that the attack had been carried out by a "blessed sister" who had defended "her faith and her honor."[22]

STRATEGIC ADVANTAGES

Strategically, there are a number of benefits to enlisting women to carry out suicide bomb attacks. The tactic was not only an important means of multiplying the size of al-Qaeda organization forces, simultaneously doubling the size of the recruit pool, but it also diluted Western resources by expanding the attack possibilities and potential perpetrators that need to be defended against. It has been suggested by some analysts and even an alleged al-Qaeda in Iraq operative that the decision to use women kinetically was partially driven by operational necessity. In other words, in direct contrast to Palestinian Islamist terror organizations such as HAMAS, al-Qaeda in Iraq did not have sufficient numbers of male suicide bomber recruits and had to resort to using women in the absence of other options. While the motivation behind the tactical shift makes no practical difference, this hypothesis does speak volumes against the theory that the use of women in an operational capacity is a precursor to long-term social change within the fundamentalist organization.[23]

That women suicide bombers may also be seen as recruiters whose attacks work to attract both male and female militants to join the cause is suggested by Laleh Khalili, a professor in Middle Eastern studies at the School of Oriental and African Studies in London, for one. She notes that "witnessing women traditionally associated with domestic duties taking part in frontline militancy operations can have a shaming effect on the men, impelling more of them to take part."[24]

Almost all of the strategic benefits derived from female suicide bombers are fed by and dependent on media attention. Transnational groups not only benefit from global attention because it allows them to operate internationally; they also profit from such publicity because their message and power are reaching the whole world. Historically, female suicide bombers have attracted more media attention than their male counterparts. Women are traditionally viewed as nurturers and the lifeblood of the family. Thus, when they come to take part in suicide operations, the juxtaposition of a nurturer taking life elicits a great deal of shock and media attention.[25] In a world where terrorists "want a lot of people watching and a lot of people dead," women suicide bombers become an invaluable resource.[26]

STRATEGIC SUCCESS: MYRIUM GORIS

The second female suicide bombing claimed by al-Qaeda was executed on November 9, 2005, by Myrium Goris, a Belgian citizen. Goris, thirty-eight, was both the first European woman suicide bomber and the first European bomber to carry out such an attack in Iraq. The participation of a Western woman in al-Qaeda's suicide campaign in Iraq functioned as a global testament to the success of al-Qaeda's recruiting efforts. It also served as an alarming indicator to the Western world of al-Qaeda's evolving asymmetric capabilities and the degree to which counterterrorism tactics needed to be updated. The global fascination with Goris's transformation from a quiet, small-town Catholic (she was born Muriel Degauque) to a Muslim fanatic willing to kill herself for her religion also validated al-Qaeda's decision to use female bombers to advance their agenda—despite the fact that the attack was, for all intents and purposes, thwarted. Goris's attack, targeting U.S. soldiers, took place in the town of Baquba, located in the northern outskirts of Baghdad. Although one American soldier was superficially injured, Goris succeeded only in killing herself.[27]

Goris, the daughter of a factory worker, Jean Degauque, and a medical secretary, Liliane, grew up in Monceau-sur Sambre, Belgium, an industrial mining town near Charleroi.[28] At the time of her 2001 marriage, Myrium's husband, Issam Goris—a Belgian of Moroccan origin—was already known by Belgian authorities as a radical Islamist.[29] In 2002, Myrium and Issam abruptly moved to Morocco, where she learned Arabic and studied the Quran. Over time, Myrium became increasingly estranged from her family. In August or September of 2005 (sources vary on the exact month), Myrium and Issam traveled by car across Turkey and Syria into Iraq, where she tried to conduct a suicide attack.[30] Authorities discovered Myrium's passport and other personal papers with her remains after the explosion.[31] On the same day, Issam was killed by U.S. soldiers after they discovered he was carrying explosives on his body.[32]

Belgian authorities believe that Goris was recruited by Islamic extremists working for al-Zarqawi's terrorist network in Iraq. The extensive recruiting network had been monitored by the authorities for several months before the November 9, 2005, suicide bombing.[33] Several phone calls later known to have been placed by Goris from Iraq had been intercepted by the Belgian police in the weeks prior to the attack. After intercepting the calls, the police notified the American and Iraqi authorities that two Belgians were planning a suicide bombing mission in Iraq. The exact date and location of the mission and the identities of the bombers were unknown at that time.[34]

Belgian authorities continued to monitor the suspected terrorist network after the phone interceptions, hoping to gather additional information. When a French radio station broadcast that Myrium Goris had killed herself in an attempted suicide bombing in Iraq, investigators feared that members of the terrorist network would go into hiding.[35] As a result, twenty-one suspects were arrested in Belgium in a series of raids on November 30 and December 1, 2005.[36] Sixteen of the suspects were later released. The five individuals who remained in custody were charged with a series of "terrorism offenses including participating in terrorist activities and falsifying documents."[37]

EXPORTING TERROR

A final strategic development relevant to al-Qaeda in Iraq's introduction of female suicide bombers is its demonstrated ability not only to import female suicide bombers but to export them as well. It is significant that in al-Qaeda in Iraq's first attack outside of Iraq, a female was included in the cell. The vast amount of publicity the Jordan bombings conducted by Sajida Mubarak Atrous al-Rishawi received also served to further al-Zarqawi's agenda by demonstrating the power and reach of the al-Qaeda in the Iraq branch of the organization. The sophisticated level of infrastructure and planning demonstrated by the November 9, 2005, attack in Jordan demonstrated, just as Myrium Goris's pilgrimage to Iraq to participate in the jihad had done, that the Western counterterrorism community needed to significantly update its assessment of the global threat from al-Qaeda in Iraq.

In the fourth attack executed by a female suicide bomber for al-Qaeda in Iraq, Sajida Mubarak Atrous al-Rishawi, thirty-five, accompanied her husband to the Radisson SAS Hotel in Amman, Jordan, and tried to detonate her suicide vest in the middle of a wedding party. Although her husband detonated his explosives, killing at least twenty-three people, Rishawi walked away from the incident largely unscathed, carrying with her a wealth of information and an insider's perspective on suicide bombing operations. She was apprehended four days after the bombings; within hours of her capture, al-Rishawi's videotaped confession appeared on Jordanian state television:[38]

My name is Sajida Mubarak Atrous, born in the 70s. I am an Iraqi national. I reside in Ramadi. On November 5, I accompanied my husband to Jordan carrying a fake Iraqi passport. His was under the name of Ali Hussein Ali, and mine was Sajida Abdel Kader Latif. We waited in Iraq, and a white car picked us up. There was a driver and a passenger. We entered Jordan together. My husband is the one who organized everything. I don't know anything else. We rented an apartment. My husband wore an explosive belt and put one on me. He taught me how to use it. The targets were hotels in Jordan. We took a car, and we went on November 9 to a hotel. There was a wedding ceremony in the hotel. There were women, men, and children. My husband took a corner and I took another one. My husband detonated his bomb, and I tried to detonate mine but failed. People fled running, and I left running with them.[39]

Many people were shocked to see al-Rishawi's confession aired on Jordanian state television, particularly because her confession was released such a short time after her apprehension and because she appeared wearing her diffused explosive belt. According to Jordanian prime minister Marwan Muasher, al-Rishawi's confession was aired because the Jordanian government felt it was "very important for the public to know exactly what happened. I think the public was a bit relieved also to know that there were not Jordanians involved."[40] Al-Rishawi's confession was also aired across the globe through a variety of communication mediums, and the story was further sensationalized by the fact that she appeared wearing her explosives belt. Thus Jordanian authorities inadvertently aided the al-Qaeda/al-Zarqawi media campaign. It is not clear why the authorities made her put the belt on during her interrogation. She was not wearing it at the time of her arrest; it was later found among her belongings.[41]

Reports have stated that al-Rishawi attempted to detonate her explosives in the ballroom but had trouble with the primer cord. Al-Rishawi's husband was aware of her struggle with the explosive belt detonator and so as not to draw unwanted attention to the couple, he either pushed her out of the ballroom or told her to leave. He then went back into the ballroom and detonated his own explosive belt.[42] Suicide bombings also took place that day at the Grand Hyatt and Days Inn hotels. All told, fifty-nine people were killed in the three explosions, including the fathers of both the bride and the groom at the Radisson SAS Hotel wedding party.[43] Countless others were injured.

The significance of the female component to the attack was underscored by the fact that Jordanian authorities only became aware of al-Rishawi's involvement after al-Qaeda in Iraq claimed responsibility for the attack on its website, stating that four bombers, including a woman, had been involved in the attack. The posting further explained that the attack was in response to "Jordan's support for the United States and other Western powers."[44]

While the motivation behind al-Rishawi's attempted suicide bombing may never be completely understood, the death of several close relatives at the hands of American military forces in Iraq is reported to have played a role in her decision to participate in these attacks.[45] Two of her brothers and her brother-in-law were killed in the Anbar province in Iraq during U.S. military operations in 2004. Her brother, Samar Mubarak al-Rishawi, whom al-Qaeda referred to as the al-Anbar prince, was a top al-Zarqawi aide. He was killed in the American offensive in Fallujah.[46] Another brother, Thamer Atrissi al-Rishawi, was also killed in Fallujah in 2004. Her brother-in-law, Nidal Arabiyat, twenty-nine, was killed in Ramadi in 2004 and is believed to have been one of the primary bomb makers used by al-Zarqawi in insurgency operations in Iraq.[47]

Al-Rishawi's lawyer later repealed her confession, stating that it was co-erced while she was under duress. The lawyer claimed that while al-Rishawi did don two explosive belts and enter the wedding party at the Radisson SAS Hotel, she never had any intention of detonating them.[48] During her trial, an explosives expert testified that the explosive belt did not detonate because the trigger mechanism had jammed.[49] In addition, during her trial, al-Rishawi's lawyer claimed that she had been forced to participate in the bombings by her husband. A Jordanian intelligence officer stated that "her education is limited. She knows little about the Holy Koran and the various fatwas. She has been brainwashed and believes that her mission in life is to wage a war against all infidels, including Muslims who do not practice Islam according to al-Qaeda interpretations, including Shias, their avowed enemies."[50]

Furthermore, a larger, organized party with developed resources had to have planned and facilitated al-Rishawi's participation in the Amman bombings and the bombings themselves. During her trial, al-Rishawi's lawyer claimed that she had only married Shamari a few days before the attacks and that their relationship had not even been consummated.[51] It is likely that al-Rishawi's marriage to Shamari was a deception to allow her to travel legally from Iraq into Jordan, since traditionally Muslim women are not allowed to travel with-out being accompanied by a spouse or male relative. Marrying Shamari would have allowed al-Rishawi to carry out all of the preliminaries to the bomb-ing, including entering the wedding party in an unassuming manner. A single woman traveling with a group of men to whom she was unrelated would have caused a great deal of suspicion and unwanted attention.

FEMALE SUICIDE BOMBING: INDICATIVE OF A LARGER TREND IN AL-QAEDA?

Al-Qaeda's use of female suicide bombers in Iraq has garnered increased media attention for the organization, likely facilitated its recruiting, and enhanced its overall global prestige, not to mention the significant tactical and strate-gic advantages to having women in the suicide attack arsenal. However, as this book goes to press, al-Qaeda in Iraq is the only part of the al-Qaeda organization that has used women in this capacity. Female suicide bombers will certainly continue to be a presence, however minor, in Iraq, but it is unlikely that the global al-Qaeda movement will widely adopt this tactic. Not only are there certain ingrained cultural norms that would be difficult to surmount in a generation, but many of the advantages to using a female suicide bomber are contingent on the novelty associated with their use. That being said, it is entirely feasible that women may be incorporated into a cell for camouflage purposes—much like al-Rishawi was—or selected specifically to circumvent certain force protection practices. As recently as January 2010, press reports cited rumors that female suicide bombers of "non-Arab" appearance and affiliated with al-Qaeda in Yemen may be traveling to the United States.[52]

The failure of female suicide bombers to gain significant traction within the overall organization probably stems, in part, from a cultural reluctance to use women in an operational capacity. Senior al-Qaeda officials have expressed diverging views as to what role women should play in al-Qaeda and in the jihad. The rift exists among senior al-Qaeda leadership and extends across generational lines.[53] Older leaders tend to adopt a more conservative position: they wish to only recruit men and believe that a woman should only offer support to jihad as mother and wife because her primary responsibility is to the family.[54] Younger leaders within al-Qaeda, on the other hand, argue that women should be recruited and should actively participate in operations.[55] What does this mean for future operations? Farhana Qazi, an associate at RAND Institute and contributor to this volume, predicts that over the next several years, women will play a bigger role in operations but will remain in the minority and will continue to be viewed as secondary to men. She feels that the dominant view will argue that Islamic law does not permit women to become jihadi leaders or to participate in combat operations.[56]

Currently, women do play an integral role within the organization and its affiliated movements. Women presently fill largely support functions, such as mother, caregiver, and wife, providing moral support for those engaged in combat operations. These women also serve as the womb of the jihad, giving birth to future fighters and ensuring that the next generation will be ready and able to carry on the jihad. In Iraq, as in other countries such as Somalia and Afghanistan, al-Qaeda has used marriage to al-Qaeda-affiliated women as a way to gain entrance into local political or tribal power hierarchies.[57] Of course, this tactic has also sown seeds of discontent in the local communities and, according to some experts, has been one of the factors that has contributed to the growing disenchantment with the al-Qaeda organization in Iraq's Anbar province.[58]

Additionally, women associated with al-Qaeda, particularly those in Western Europe, have been known to operate in a logistic capacity for the organization. They have opened bank accounts, translated documents, and carried out book-keeping duties for the terror network.[59] Women have also been known to form sisterhoods, utilizing technology such as the Internet to "meet" in chat rooms and discussion boards.[60] Several of the wives and girlfriends of the men arrested in connection with the Toronto terror plot, which became public during the summer of 2006, had frequently communicated in an Internet chat room, freely discussing their radical viewpoints.[61]

The context in which al-Qaeda began using female suicide bombers provides significant insight into the circumstances driving this innovation and, consequently, into the tactic's probable future within the larger group. It is likely that this tactical evolution, instituted by al-Zarqawi, is the result—first and foremost—of operational necessity in Iraq's unique operating environment. In no other arena must al-Qaeda maintain the kind of tempo and attack volume that al-Qaeda in Iraq has to and in no other faction did al-Qaeda have a leader who was so willing to push the envelope to achieve strategic objectives.

The arrest in early August 2007 of a number of al-Qaeda-affiliated personnel responsible for training female suicide bombers has made it clear that al-Qaeda in Iraq remained in the business of cultivating female attackers even after al-Zarqawi's death.[62] In addition, there has been a resurgence in attacks conducted by female suicide bombers following an operational pause in 2006. There were five suicide attacks perpetrated by women attempted in 2007, almost thirty documented in 2008, and several in 2009. However, given the current sectarian dynamic in Iraq and the backlash against al-Qaeda operations in certain areas, there is less incentive to claim responsibility for some of al-Qaeda in Iraq's activities and/or for it to brand its attacks. It is also worth noting that two of the five attempted attacks in 2009 were thwarted by security forces. In one instance, a woman abandoned her suicide vest outside a courthouse after she was prevented from entering. Also in 2009, a sixty-year-old woman was detained by security forces in Baquba before she could detonate her explosives.[63] Security forces have adapted their counterterrorism practices to defend against the possibility of female bombers, though these practices are not, of course, foolproof.

While female combatants may never become a majority, or even a significant minority, within al-Qaeda or its affiliated movements, women do play an integral role in the organization as supporters, wives, and mothers of the jihad and are likely to continue to do so. The female suicide bombings executed in Iraq have demonstrated a shift in tactics and perceived roles for women participating in the jihad. While this tactic has yet to be adopted by any of the al-Qaeda factions outside of Iraq, the ability for the broader al-Qaeda organization and transnational networks to successfully utilize women in their operations has been firmly established.

NOTES

1. Clara Beyler, "Messengers of Death: Female Suicide Bombers," *International Institute for Counter-Terrorism*, February 12, 2003, www.ict.org.il/articles/articledet.cfm?articleid=470 (accessed January 15, 2006).

2. "Woman Suicide Bomber Strikes Iraq," *BBC News*, September 28, 2005, http://news.bbc.co.uk/2/hi/middle_east/4289168.stm (accessed January 10, 2005).

3. On April 3, 2003, a car driven by a man and containing two female passengers conducted a suicide attack against a patrol of U.S. service members in western Iraq. While some media outlets reported this as a female suicide bombing, it is not considered as such for purposes of this study. See Erica Solvig, "Survivor of Iraqi Bomb Tells Church of His Faith," *Cincinnati (Ohio) Enquirer*, May 26, 2003, www.enquirer.com/editions/2003/05/26/loc_patrioticservice26.html (accessed December 24, 2010).

4. Steven Lee Meyers, "Recruiter of Female Suicide Bombers Tells Her Story," *New York Times*, February 3, 2009, http://www.nytimes.com/2009/02/03/world/africa/03iht-iraq.4.19904240.html (accessed March 6, 2011).

5. Responsibility for this particular attack was claimed by Jamaat Jund al-Sahaaba, a Sunni insurgent group with no known ties to al-Qaeda.

6. A second possible exception might be an attack allegedly conducted by a husband and wife team in Mosul in October 2005. Al-Qaeda claimed that a female was involved in the attack but failed to specify the attack method.

7. See Michael E. O'Hanlon and Jason H. Campbell, *Iraq Index: Tracking Variables of Reconstruction & Security in Post-Saddam Iraq*, October 1, 2007, www.brookings.edu /fp/saban/iraq/index.pdf (accessed March 26, 2011).

8. Ibid.

9. Christopher Dickey, "Women of al-Qaeda," *Newsweek*, December 12, 2005, http:// www.newsweek.com/2005/12/11/women-of-al-qaeda.html (accessed March 22, 2011).

10. Ibid.

11. Al-Zawahiri was second in command until Osama bin Laden's 2011 death. The leadership was not clear at the time of this book's publication. Michael Scheuer, "Al-Qaeda in Iraq: Has al-Zawahiri Reined in al-Zarqawi?" *Jamestown Foundation Terrorism Focus* 3, no. 14 (2006), http://www.jamestown.org /programs/gta/single/?tx_ttnews%5Btt_news%5D=734&tx_ttnews%5BbackPid %5D=239&no_cache=1 (accessed March 10, 2011).

12. Lee Hudson Teslik, "Profile: Abu Musab al-Zarqawi," *Council on Foreign Relations Backgrounder*, June 8, 2006, www.cfr.org/publication/9866 (accessed January 1, 2007).

13. Ibid.

14. Craig Whitlock, "Al-Zarqawi's Biography," *Washington Post*, June 8, 2006, www .washingtonpost.com/wp-dyn/content/article/2006/06/08/AR2006060800299.html (accessed January 1, 2007).

15. Ibid.

16. Ibid.

17. Ibid.

18. Ibid.

19. Ibid.

20. Dickey, "Women of al-Qaeda."

21. Lee Keath, "Women Suicide Bomber Marks Possible New Insurgent Tactic in Iraq," *AP*, September 28, 2005.

22. Ibid.; Dickey, "Women of al-Qaeda."

23. Evan Kohlmann, "Interview with Foreign Fighter from the 'Islamic State of Iraq,'" *Global Terror Alert*, April 27, 2007, www.globalterroralert.com/pdf/0507 /isimaqdisi0507.pdf (accessed September 19, 2007).

24. Neil Arun, "Women Bombers Break New Ground," *BBC News*, November 15, 2005, http://news.bbc.co.uk/2/hi/middle_east/4436368.stm (accessed March 10, 2011).

25. Farhana Ali, "Muslim Female Fighters: An Emerging Trend," *Jamestown Foundation Terrorism Monitor* 3, no. 21 (2005), http://jamestown.org/terrorism/news /article.php?articleid=2369824 (accessed April 1, 2007).

26. Brigadier General (retired) Russell D. Howard, speech given at the opening ceremonies of the Jebsen Center for Counter-Terrorism Studies, Fletcher School of Law and Diplomacy, Medford, Mass., January 28, 2006.

27. Craig S. Smith, "Raised in Catholic Belgium, She Died as a Muslim Bomber," *Militant Islam Monitor*, December 6, 2005, *www.militantislammonitor.org/article/id/1353* (accessed January 14, 2006).

28. "Journey of Belgian Female 'Bomber,'" *BBC News*, December 2, 2005, http://news.bbc.co.uk/2/hi/europe/4491334.stm (accessed January 13, 2006).

29. Sebastian Rotella, "Before Martyrdom Plan, Belgian Woman's Faith Turned Radical," *Los Angeles Times*, December 2, 2005, A3.

30. Ibid.; Smith, "Raised in Catholic Belgium, She Died as a Muslim Bomber."

31. Ibid.

32. Rotella, "Before Martyrdom Plan."

33. Smith, "Raised in Catholic Belgium, She Died as a Muslim Bomber."

34. Ibid.

35. Ibid.

36. Ibid.

37. "Belgian 'Suicide Bomber' Is Named," *BBC News*, December 2, 2005, http://news.bbc.co.uk/2/hi/europe/4488642.stm (accessed January 13, 2006).

38. "Jordan 'Failed Bomber' Confesses on TV," *CNN*, November 14, 2005, www.cnn.com/2005/WORLD/meast/11/13/jordan.blasts/index.html (accessed March 10, 2011).

39. "Transcript: Confession by Accused Jordanian Bomber," *CNN*, November 13, 2005, www.cnn.com/2005/WORLD/meast/11/13/jordan.confession/index.html (accessed March 10, 2011).

40. "Bomber Confession Shocks Jordanians," *CNN*, November 14, 2005, www.cnn.com/2005/WORLD/meast/11/14/jordan.blasts/index.html (accessed April 1, 2007).

41. Ibid.

42. Rick Jervis, "Iraqi Woman Confesses on Jordanian TV," *USA Today*, November 13, 2005.

43. Jonathan Finer, "The Best Day Became the Worst," *Washington Post*, November 11, 2005.

44. Shafika Mattar, "Iraqi Anbar Woman, Sajida al-Rishawi, Confesses on Jordan TV About Hotel Bombings," *AP*, November 14, 2005.

45. Michael Slackman and Souad Mekhennet, "Jordan Says Bombing Suspect Aimed to Avenge Brothers," *New York Times*, November 15, 2005, A3.

46. Alia Shukri Hamzeh, "Would-Be Female Suicide Bomber Arrested," *Free Muslims Coalition*, November 13, 2005, www.freemuslims.org/news/article.php?article=1071 (accessed November 5, 2006).

47. "Jordanian Female Suicide Bomber 'Illiterate al-Qaeda Diehard' Who Believed Her Mission Was to Wage War against Nonbelievers," *Militant Islam Monitor*, November 14, 2005, www.militantislammonitor.org/article/id/1268 (accessed March 6, 2011).

48. Jamal Halaby, "Death Penalty for Female Would-Be Bomber," *AP*, September 21, 2006.

49. Ibid.

50. Ibid.

51. Ibid.

52. Richard Esposito, Rhonda Schwartz, and Brian Ross, "Alert: Female Suicide Bombers May Be Heading Here from Yemen," *ABC News*, January 22, 2010, http://abcnews.go.com/Blotter/female-suicide-bombers-heading-yemen/story?id=9636341 (accessed March 6, 2011).

53. Farhana Ali, "Examining the Role and Contribution of Muslim Women to the Global Jihadi Movement," International Institute for Strategic Studies, London, March 12, 2007.

54. Ibid.

55. Ibid.

56. Ibid.

57. David Kilcullen, "Anatomy of a Tribal Revolt," *Small Wars Journal* blog entry, August 29, 2007, www.smallwarsjournal.com/blog/2007/08/anatomy-of-a-tribal-revolt (accessed September 17, 2007).

58. Ibid.

59. Conversation with Katrina Von Knop, "Women and Al Qaeda" conference, Tufts University, Medford, Mass., April 2008.

60. Ibid.

61. Mark Hosenball, "Narrow Escape?" *Newsweek International*, www.msnbc.msn.com/id/13190292/site/newsweek (accessed September 17, 2007).

62. "Iraq: Woman Would-Be Suicide Bomber Blocked," *ADNKronos International*, August 7, 2007, www.adnkronos.com/AKI/English/Security/?id=1.0.1186298203 (accessed March 10, 2011).

63. Ibid.

The Neo-Orientalist Narratives of Women's Involvement in al-Qaeda

Caron E. Gentry

On February 25, 2007, after fighting with the guards, a woman in Iraq blew herself up at Mustansiriya University in Baghdad, injuring forty-six and killing forty-one students. Very little information has been found about this woman; in the weeks that followed, rumors circulated that the bomber was neither a woman nor affiliated with al-Qaeda.[1] While there have been a plethora of bombings since the Iraq War began in 2003, each February since 2007 at least one more woman has perpetrated a suicide attack. In February 2008, two women, who possibly had Down syndrome, killed seventy-three people in Baghdad. A February 5, 2009, an attack left fifteen dead, and another on February 13 left forty dead. On February 1, 2010, a large attack on pilgrims at a way station killed fifty-four. Again, however, these were not isolated attacks, and they are not the only suicide bombings carried out by women. From 2003 to 2008, there were 1,715 attacks in Iraq, 51 of them by women. Seven happened before or at the beginning of the surge of American forces; after the surge, attacks by women rose significantly, as did the media coverage of them. Those first five women received very little attention, while women from the West (the United States and Europe) with ties to al-Qaeda received an enormous amount of attention. Once the number of female self-martyrs began to rise, however, the media began to research and speculate about the reasons.

While the three groups of women with ties to al-Qaeda have all been treated differently by the press, they have been treated similarly enough to perpetuate a problematic neo-Orientalist image of Islam. When I began this research project in 2007, I expected to find investigative reports on the small numbers of women who had carried out martyrdom attacks in Iraq. Yet there was a surprising dearth of information. In part, this lack of information could be related to access, but it also has to do with media and consumer interest. Still, it's surprising because of the abundant amount of information about women with ties to al-Qaeda, including about one other female suicide bomber in Iraq. A deeper investigation revealed that the women involved with al-Qaeda who have received a disproportionate amount of attention are those with ties to the West. Even after the upsurge in female self-martyrdom attacks from 2007 through 2008, the attention given to them was small and grounded in certain gendered images of women. In all three instances, the attention works to rhetorically "veil" the women in a neo-Orientalist manner.

Across time and place in global politics, rhetoric has often been used to perpetuate certain social "truths" and norms. A speaker or author uses language to direct an audience toward a manufactured truth, one in which some information is emphasized while other information is concealed. In this way, the speaker designates certain ideas, norms, and events superior to others and ignores actions or events that might challenge them. This chapter shows how media coverage subordinates the actions of women tied to al-Qaeda with connections to the West. In light of this subordination, the "near-silence" surrounding the early Iraqi female self-martyrs in Iraq is interpreted as yet another subordination, as is the treatment of the women who acted later. This subordination, which recurred throughout the Iraqi insurgency, has Orientalist implications.

Using the narrative and rhetorical theories of Kenneth Burke and Walt Fisher, I demonstrate that this subordination is in part effected through the use of rhetoric. Both Burke's and Fisher's starting point is the question of motive. Burke's theory tries to answer what the motive is behind a person's words.

Fisher gives the rhetorician a way to evaluate the motives a consumer reads and hears. This chapter attempts to make the neo-Orientalist subordination of women who participate in suicide terrorism clearer by drawing on the theories of Fisher and Burke to uncover motives of the media and governments.

THE CHILDLESS WOMAN, THE SOCCER MOM, THE WIFE, AND THE DIVORCÉE: IMAGES OF WOMEN IN AL-QAEDA

In descriptions of the women by both the media and family members, they are portrayed as rebels, infertile outcasts, or submissive wives. These gendered accounts sensationalize their violence within a highly gendered and even racialized context.[2] Of the fifty-one women who have detonated themselves in Iraq, extensive information can be found only on Myrium Goris (born Muriel Degauque). Goris was a white, Western, Belgian woman. Outside of Iraq, the other women associated with al-Qaeda who have received Western media coverage are women with ties to the West or who participated in unprecedented acts. One is Aafia Siddiqui, who was investigated when she was living in Boston. Another, Sajida Mubarak Atrous al-Rishawi, was part of the hotel bombing campaign in Amman, the only suicide attacks ever committed in Jordan.[3]

Applying Fisher's narrative theory, one might argue that stories of these women that rely on stereotypes help the U.S. public create a narrative that coheres with its beliefs. Narrative fidelity is just one element of narrative theory. According to narrative theory, all communication is about telling a story. Narrations are words and deeds that have a sequence and a meaning for those who live, create, or interpret them. In order for a narrative to work, it needs narrative probability and narrative fidelity. Narrative probability means that the story is credible in its sequence and that it makes sense in reality.[4] Narrative fidelity means that the story matches the values and beliefs of the audience. If it does, then the audience is more likely to believe the narrative.[5] What this implies then is that if the U.S. public and/or the Western public primarily ascribe certain gender roles (mother and wife) to women, then, in order to make sense of these women's political violence, the public ascribes these roles to women, even politically violent women.

These gendered public imaginaries of Middle Eastern women who engage in terrorism echo what Edward Said calls "Orientalism." Orientalist actions and perceptions (falsely) established extreme differences between the West and the East.[6] Orientalism is multifaceted and addresses everything from mindset, to sexuality, to political activity. In 2000, Susan Akram suggested that a neo-Orientalism was emerging as a way of othering all Muslims in the world in scholarship and policies. Such othering constructed, rather absurdly, all one billion Muslims in the world as supportive of violent regimes, religiously devoid of a humanitarian ethos, and as oppressive toward women.[7] Therefore, what emerges in the narrative frames of women with ties to Iraq is a very neo-Orientalist perspective, one that is detrimental to women's agency.

The media and society create these narratives in order to maintain narrative fidelity about what it means to be a woman in the West. The Western women with ties to al-Qaeda have, according to the narratives grounded in neo-Orientalism that emerge about them, betrayed some form of Western privilege. Why would a Western woman choose Islam of all things when the West is open to them? Neo-Orientalism assumes that women in the West

- want to stay in the West, either literally or figuratively,
- do not betray (Western) religious beliefs,
- have children and want to raise their children in the West, and
- do not betray country and culture by joining and working for al-Qaeda.

Thus, in these narratives women betray their gender and their culture and so disrupt narrative fidelity. The narrative then seeks to smooth over this infidelity by representing the women as rebellious, unfulfilled, or, the fallback, controlled/oppressed—all because there is this pernicious assumption that women in the (Middle) "East" are controlled by their husbands and will act or die at their direction. "Good" women in the West do not blow themselves up or support al-Qaeda; but "good" women in the "East" do or try. When women with ties to the West do die to kill, there must be an explanation for their violence that does not implicate any Western values or traditions for why the women did what they did.

The al-Qaeda female operatives are rhetorically veiled by the narratives. Valerie Moghadam argues that "in some historical instances, representatives of modernity and national progress include the unveiled, educated, and *emancipated* modern woman, whereas the woman who is veiled signifies cultural and economic backwardness."[8] Veiling arguably also indicates that the woman is oppressed and controlled. The women's husbands in these narratives are implicitly or explicitly portrayed as manipulative and controlling. This is indicative of a neo-Orientalist narrative: Muslim husbands are all-consuming. Their wives have no ability to resist their husband's overpowering will. This is a simple extension of the "polemics" of veiling.[9] It upholds the narrative fidelity of the women as good wives but "fortunately" not as good Western wives. Instead, they are "good," controlled, and submissive Muslim wives. Even if female al-Qaeda operatives are actors in their own right, doubt is cast and agency denied because of their religious and cultural choices and/or heritages.

Goris was the fifth female suicide bomber in Iraq, carrying out her attack on September 28, 2005, in Tal Afar. She is also the most well known. The account that emerges about Goris from news articles is one rhetorically constructed in such a way as to deflect her agency.[10] She was raised in Belgium as "a good Catholic girl," meaning she was "well-dressed, well-behaved and went to Mass."[11] The image of a good Catholic girl blowing herself up as a Muslim in Iraq disrupts that narrative fidelity of what it means to be a good Catholic girl—namely, "well dressed" and "well behaved." Therefore another narrative had to be constructed to secure fidelity. There are two different treatments of Goris that accomplish this. In two sources she is portrayed as a rebellious teenager; another source undermines her "femininity."

In order to dispel the good Catholic girl image, the media dredged up Goris's wayward teenage past. There may be truth to the idea that she was rebelling, but the use of her past to deflect her agency is problematic. However good of a girl she was, she was also "spoiled."[12] As a teenager she "fell in with a gang of bikers [and] dabbled in drugs."[13] She was known to leave the house in the classically rebellious way: "in a black leather jacket on the back of a boyfriend's motorcycle."[14] Apparent experts were quoted as saying that her later embrace of radical Islamic (suicide) terrorism was strongly indicated by her teenage behavior.[15] Yet, Robert Pape, author of *Dying to Win*, argues that there is no singular profile for suicide terrorists.[16] And if even a minority of semirebellious teenagers chose to become suicide bombers, the world is headed for trouble.

The second narrative the media crafts focuses on Goris's adult life as a wife and her apparent failed attempts at motherhood. As an adult, she converted to Islam before marrying for the second (possibly third) time and changed her name to Myrium.[17] Her conversion was welcomed by her parents at the time because it helped her to quit drinking. It was her second husband who introduced her to radical Islam.[18] In the *Newsweek* article by Christopher Dickey about her there is no mention of her Catholic background or rebellious teenage years. Instead, the opening pages of the article set the scene as she approached the security forces. The explosives she carried were "strapped around her womb."[19] After referring to her failed marriages, Dickey quotes the Belgian prosecutor's office, which remarked in reference to her actions that she "couldn't have children."[20] This seems to imply that her actions stemmed from her sterility and not any political or religious beliefs.

But this is a woman who detonated herself; such a dismissal of her actions undermines her agency. The media is seemingly helping Western society make sense of why a "white, middle class," "attractive, long-haired woman" would take up the cause of radical Islam, betraying her religion and her Western "birthright" of presumed emancipated womanhood.[21] Presenting her as a troubled teen or troubled (sterile) woman is one (gendered) way of making sense of her violence.

The second woman I want to look at here is a Pakistani woman who was educated in the West and was raising her family there. In 2003, Aafia Siddiqui, an MIT graduate and mother of three, landed on the FBI's wanted list after Khalid Sheik Mohammed indicated that she was serving "as a 'facilitator for future [al-Qaeda] attacks.'"[22] She is thought to have played some role in an al-Qaeda plot to blow up gas and fuel-storage tanks in the Baltimore-D.C. area.[23] Siddiqui's name and email address were used to purchase night-vision goggles, bomb-making books, and body armor.[24] In the same year, Siddiqui, her husband, and their children disappeared. In 2008, she was arrested in Afghanistan with bomb-making materials, instructions, and a list of New York landmarks in her possession.[25] At the scene of the arrest, she managed to shoot at the agents before being shot herself. In February 2010, she was found guilty of attempted murder.[26]

When she first disappeared, an extensive public debate raged in regards to her guilt. While her extended family says Siddiqui was simply a "woman with children, wearing a hijab, [and] driving a Volvo."[27] Siddiqui's extended family maintains that her marriage was in trouble and that Siddiqui had filed for divorce in Karachi in 2001, citing abuse of her person and their children. It was her husband, her family said, who purchased the materials and used her email address to send deceptively happy emails to friends and family.[28] Staying true to the narrative fidelity of woman as wife and mother, her family maintained there was no possible way that Siddiqui was a terrorist because she was simply a Muslim-American soccer mom. Yet, the subtext also contains the elements of veiling. What if Siddiqui was not just a soccer mom, but really a woman who made these choices under the influence of her controlling (Muslim) husband?[29]

The veiling facet is present in the narrative covering Sajida Mubarak Atrous al-Rishawi as well. In its history, Jordan has suffered only three suicide bombing attacks; all three of these took place in the November 9, 2005, attack on Amman hotels. Al-Rishawi was supposed to be the fourth bomber. She tried to detonate herself at a wedding reception at the Radisson SAS; her husband, who was with her, succeeded, but her bomb failed to go off because she had left a "crucial component in the car."[30] She was arrested four days later. Although at one point al-Rishawi claimed she gave her confession after being tortured, she recanted this.[31] Her confession gave extensive details of the attack's organization and "significant intelligence into . . . Zarqawi's group, Al-Qaeda in Mesopotamia, which claimed responsibility."[32]

Al-Rishawi's motivation is depicted as stemming from the death of her brother, Mubarak Atrous al-Rishawi, and the domination of her husband. Her brother had served as one of Zarqawi's aides and was killed in Iraq.[33] With respect to her husband's control over her, much has been made of one of her statements: "He [her husband] taught me. He taught me how to pull, what to do, and how to control it."[34] Other articles portrayed her as "nervous" or even chastened owing to her "hand wringing" during her confession.[35] Thus her violence is determined by the strength of her emotional ties to her relationships, as sister and wife, and not her embrace of any political agenda.[36] This maintains the narrative fidelity to traditional gender roles and the belief that Muslim women are controlled by the men, both dead and alive, in their lives. These three women have had certain narrative fidelities imposed on them so that the public can comprehend their decision to support al-Qaeda, but other women are practically left without any narrative at all.

THE (NEARLY) SILENCED WOMEN

Kenneth Burke claims that to understand human behavior one has to understand human language. The task of the critic then is to judge the motives of the rhetor. Burke's idea of "terministic screens" is especially relevant here. These screens both reflect and deflect different realities.[37] According to Burke, "even if any given terminology is a *reflection* of reality, by its very nature as a terminology, it must be a *selection* of reality; and to this extent it must be a function as a *deflection* of reality."[38] Terministic screens are used by the rhetor to convey a certain idea or agenda to a specific audience. The screens "direct the attention" of the audience "into some channels rather than others."[39] Thus, the rhetor uses terminology that leads an audience to a specific figurative location (reflection) rather than to an unwanted place (deflection). For Burke, motive, again, is key—why is the audience guided in this direction?

Because of the attention given to Goris, Siddiqui, and al-Rishawi, I fully expected to find similar coverage of the woman who acted on February 25, 2007. Indeed I expected to find an overwhelming amount of information about her, but at the least, I thought I would find stories that included her name, her political affiliation, her age, and speculation about her rationale. I expected this not because extensive information is available with every bombing, but because women's martyrdom operations seem to receive a disproportionate amount of attention. But in reality this is not the case.[40] The women with ties to the West (or who are an anomaly) who go on suicide missions are the ones who receive the attention.[41] In the competitive media environment in the West, this is a given—people pay attention to what most directly affects or speaks to them, namely similar people or experiences. But because of whom committed act and where it took place, I wrongly expected to see more information. It was not until women's participation became more significant, however, after the surge in Iraq, that media coverage became more extensive.

THE VEIL OF SILENCE

Articles from major news sources and in databases all basically contain the same amount of information about the February bomber. The woman who detonated herself on February 25, 2007, was wearing a vest filled with ball bearings and explosive.[42] The attack took place at the predominately Shiite Mustansiriya University and killed forty-one people and injured forty-six, many of them women.[43] The event occurred in the early afternoon, just before a midterm session was set to begin. She was waiting in or trying to skirt the security line for women. For whatever reason the guards became agitated, argued with her, and she proceeded to blow herself up.[44] It is more than likely that she acted as part of the insurgency; no group has claimed her actions. Suddenly, I found myself interested in what was not being said about women's violence and the implications of this near-silence.[45]

This is not unlike the dearth of information surrounding the four previous non-Western suicide bombers in Iraq and the ones who carried out attacks before the postsurge upswing in female self-martyrs in Iraq. While these women are alluded to in other work on female suicide bombers, my own included, the details have to be actively sought out.[46] No blatant gender-based subordinating narrative of the violence emerges out of the very basic information that is publicly available. The reporting of the event remains just that, a report. In April 2003, Nusha Mujalli Munayfir al-Shammari and Walid Jamil Jasim al-Dulaymi blew themselves up in a car bombing, killing three U.S. soldiers.[47] They were awarded medals of honor by Saddam Hussein.[48] Two other nameless women detonated themselves at Baghdad's police academy on December 5, 2005, wounding thirty-five and killing twenty-seven.[49] They were presumably students at the academy.[50] On April 10, 2007, a woman in an *abaya* entered a crowd of two hundred police recruits north of Baghdad and detonated her bomb, killing twenty-two people.[51] Another woman was captured in the Green Zone wearing an explosive belt in October 2004.[52] Because there is so little information available about the women's action, speculation about motivation is noticeably absent from the reports, unlike in the reports about their contemporaries from the West.

The unsensationalized facts of these events provide just enough detail to let the article reader know what happened and very little else. In some ways, this bare-bones narrative deflects attention away from their political violence. At the time, in 2007, it seemed as if the desired reflection of the war in Iraq on the part of coalition forces was that it was going well or that any lost ground could be regained. Women blowing themselves up for the various militias and possibly al-Qaeda would indicate that the war is not going well. This was, after all, just as General Petraeus's surge was getting underway.

Furthermore, these women are primarily nameless and ageless, like the hundreds of male suicide insurgents before and after them. While there is no specifically gender-based subordinating narrative here, the lack of details, lack of sensation, and general lack of interest, creates its own subordination. Non-Western women can be virtually ignored because they do not directly challenge traditional gender roles. Under neo-Orientalism, Muslim women are nameless and faceless. This is especially noticeable when these incidences are directly contrasted with the contemporaneous coverage of the women in the West with ties to al-Qaeda. Yet this began to change as the situation in Iraq shifted with the new strategy by U.S. forces under a new leader. One indication of the effectiveness of the surge was a decrease in the number of suicide attacks in Iraq. At the same time, however, there was an increase in female self-martyrdom operations, which is often attributed to the relative ease with which women can pass through checkpoints and to the *abaya*'s ability to hide the bulk of the bomber's vest. Nonetheless, such an increase led to speculation about Iraqi women's rationale for engaging in political violence.

NARRATING THE LIVES OF THE (PRIMARILY) FACELESS AND NAMELESS

Before I examine the proposed reasons behind women's political violence in Iraq, it is important to note that the number of women who have participated is still unknown. The numbers cited in table 1 come from a variety of sources, and it is clear that the actual numbers are neither fully known nor totally accessible. While I used the RAND Database of Worldwide Terrorism Incidents to find the base number of female suicide bombings in Iraq, there were several bombings the RAND database did not record. For example, there were two female suicide bombings in Iraq in 2003 that the database did not display. A number of sources recorded eight female suicide bombings in 2007, whereas RAND only recorded five.[53] RAND is possibly reporting the number of *attacks*, not the individuals involved, which is a crucial distinction when doing a study of this nature. Further, multiple sources report approximately thirty female suicide bombings by August 2008 alone, and an article from 2009 reports a final figure of thirty-two, whereas in April 2010 RAND reports only sixteen for all of 2008.[54] Finally, the RAND data only goes through December 2008, as in fact does most aggregated data that is available online for the monthly or yearly suicide attacks in Iraq.

As table 1 demonstrates, during the first three years of the war in Iraq, there were only five female suicide bombers, out of a staggering total of 940 attacks. But a radical shift came in 2007 with retaliatory violence against the surge. As General Petraeus's surge got underway, especially toward the end of 2007, violence, especially suicide attacks, started a downward trend in Iraq. Yet suicide attacks by women were on the rise. The violence that had once been ignored was suddenly capturing Western attention. And the subordinating silence disappeared only to be replaced with some sadly recognizable frames instead. In reading through articles that were published during and after the period in the summer of 2008 when the largest number of suicide missions were perpetrated by women, one finds that the rationale the stories offer for the women's decision to engage in terrorism is often similar to those used to frame the choices and lives of Goris, Siddiqui, and al-Rishawi. Such frames serve to discredit women's agency and to subordinate their violence. In this context, they also serve to reflect the neo-Orientalist notion that any activity or any choice a Muslim woman makes is apparently outside of her control.

The othering so intrinsic to neo-Orientalism is deeply troubling because it blinds scholars, researchers, and law enforcers to any deeper realities or nuances in people's lives. The assumption that women affiliated with *any* form of Islam are incapable of making choices — such as political, nationalistic ones — is subordinating. Such subordination is clear in the statement that "it appears that women's motives for such attacks are rooted less in ideology than in histories of physical, mental, and sexual abuse within their own families. Their motives

Table 1   Suicide Attacks in Iraq, 2003–2009

YEAR	TOTAL NUMBER OF SUICIDE ATTACKS IN IRAQ	NUMBER OF FEMALE SELF-MARTYRS	PERCENTAGE OF ALL ATTACKS
2003	25	2	8
2004	140	0	0
2005	478	2	0.4
2006	297	3	1.01
2007	442	5 or 8	1.1 or 1.8
2008	257	16 or 32	6.2 or 12.5
2009	76	4	5.3
TOTAL	1,715	32 or 51	1.86 or 2.97

The online RAND Database of Worldwide Terrorism Incidences is a clearinghouse of most worldwide terrorist activity between 1968 and 2008. The search parameters that yielded some of the numbers in table 1 included an incident date between January 1, 2003, to April 4, 2010; suicide = true; country = Iraq; data aggregated by year. To sort for female perpetrators "female" was entered as the search term.

rarely involve free will, but rather blackmail or the hope of redemption for sexual indiscretions through violence and self-sacrifice."[55] The common perception of Iraqi women's motivation echoes this notion: Iraqi women are apolitical victims of exploitation and manipulation.[56]

The articles written during the height of the campaigns that involved women reported that a majority of the female self-martyrs came from the Diyala province, northeast of Baghdad, where there is a high concentration of radical Islamists and al-Qaeda in Iraq leaders. This is important to the framing of appropriate womanhood—where women in Diyala did not *make* the choice to join the jihadi resistance but are instead women living behind the veil of male oppression and abuse. Since Diyala was controlled by "extremists," it was more believable that any woman in that context was going to be oppressed by religion and then exploited and controlled by the men in her life. Multiple articles cite that women in Diyala lived in violent, isolated communities dominated by "extremists" immersed in "the" jihadi culture.[57] The women there were powerless, and it is suggested that the men they were forced to marry against their will also introduced or coerced them into the martyrdom missions.[58] Additionally, there is speculation that some women were forced into the vests and detonated by remote once they reached their targets.[59]

The despair that results from control, exploitation, and abuse is also another apparent reason for the rise of female self-martyrs in Iraq. For example, a *Los Angeles Times* article gives an even more troubling and explicit example of life in Diyala. Women were forced into marrying the al-Qaeda in Iraq leaders, known as emirs, and then passed from one to the next until they got pregnant. They were unable to determine who the father was, and the resultant "despair, hopelessness and fear" forced them into committing crimes, including, apparently, suicide attacks.[60] The loss of male relatives also caused despair and in turn drove women to suicide attacks; this is similar reasoning as is invoked to explain the self-martyrdom attacks of women in Chechnya and Sri Lanka.[61] The final rationale linked to despair stems from sexual impurity. Apparently a woman working to recruit women for al-Qaeda, Samira Ahmed Jassim (also known as "Umm al-Mumineem," or "the Mother of Believers"), was part of a scheme in which women were raped and then in their shame came to her for counseling; she would convince these "broken women" (her words) to become self-martyrs as a means of regaining honor.[62]

WOMEN, AL-QAEDA, AND THE OTHER: SOME CONCLUDING THOUGHTS

Fisher's and Burke's rhetorical theories help us understand the motives behind the narratives. For Fisher, by interpreting narratives, one uncovers the motives. For Burke, the analysis of rhetoric uncovers motives. Together these theorists provide a way of conceptualizing the polarity between who gets too much, oversensationalized attention and who does not. The narratives occupy opposite ends of a subordinating spectrum. Neo-Orientalist images and assumptions of what Muslim women "should" be undermine their political agency. The images that are instead left in the eye of the public are ones of rebellious, infertile, or controlled women. Yet, for some women, women who did not (yet) pose a threat to Western interests (the self-martyrs in the early years of the war), virtually no image exists in the public eye. They almost do not exist.

How then does this relate to women and al-Qaeda? The crux of the problem is the "us versus them" subtext in the subordination of al-Qaeda female operatives and Iraqi female suicide bombers. If the West is the norm (as portrayed by Western media), then why would someone (Goris as a Western woman and Siddiqui as non-Western in the West) want to give this status up and become part of the other, to be either a Muslim or a member of al-Qaeda? This neo-Orientalist subtext reflects a gross misunderstanding of how all women in a religion of one billion people are treated. It is also indicative of what type of women matter when it comes to examining the security threat that is "al-Qaeda." In such a context, the only women that the media cares about are women with ties to al-Qaeda or that present threats to the Western "us" and not the Middle Eastern "other."

NOTES

1. This woman was followed by an April 10, 2007, female suicide bomber who carried out an attack the day this chapter was originally given as a talk ("Iraq Female Bomber Hits Police Post," *Hobart (Tasmania) Mercury*, April 11, 2007, http://web.lexis-nexis .com/universe [accessed May 8, 2007]; Bianna Golodryga, "Deadly Day in Iraq; Female Suicide Bomber Killed at Least 22 People," *ABC News Now*, April 10, 2007, http://web .lexis-nexis.com/universe [accessed May 8, 2007]).

2. In *Mothers, Monsters, Whores: Women's Violence in Global Politics* (London: Zed, 2007), Laura Sjoberg and I examine the gender-subordinating narratives that have been promoted by the media, academics, and various governments about women's violence in global politics. There are three narratives surrounding women's violence (mother, monster, and whore) that try to explain women's violence but in fact end up denying women's agency in their politically violent actions. See also Laura Sjoberg and Caron Gentry, "Reduced to Bad Sex: Narratives of Violent Women from the Bible to the War on Terror," *International Relations* 22, no. 1 (2008): 5–23, and Caron Gentry, "Twisted Maternalism: From Peace to Violence," *International Feminist Journal of Politics*, 11, no. 2 (2009): 235–52.

3. Arguably, the reporting on the 2010 arrest of Colleen "Jihad Jane" LaRose supports this argument; however, the scope of this essay does not extend beyond 2007.

4. Walter R. Fisher, *Human Communication as Narration: Toward a Philosophy of Reason, Value, and Action* (Columbia: University of South Carolina Press,), 47.

5. Fisher, *Human Communication as Narration*, 47.

6. Edward Said, *Orientalism: Western Conceptions of the Orient* (New York: Pantheon, 1978).

7. Susan Mussarat Akram, "Orientalism Revisited in Asylum and Refugee Claims," *International Journal of Refugee Law*, 12, no.1 (2000): 10–11, 15.

8. Valerie Moghadam, introduction, in *Gender and National Identity: Women and Politics in Muslim Societies*, ed. Valerie Moghadam (London: Zed, 1994), 2–3, italics added.

9. Moghadam, introduction, 2.

10. In this instance, agency refers to the actor's ability to make decisions, political, personal, or social, in light of the power structures in place. This chapter is not using agency as defined by Burke.

11. Craig S. Smith, "Raised as Catholic in Belgium, She Died as a Muslim Bomber," *New York Times*, December 6, 2005, http://www.nytimes.com/2005/12/06/international/europe/06brussels.html?ex=1168491600&en=c9b61ab7ea879dea&ei=5070 (accessed December 6, 2005), 2; Gareth Harding, "Portrait of a Female Suicide Bomber," upi, December 7, 2005, http://web.lexis-nexis.com/universe (accessed April 1, 2007).

12. Smith, "Raised as Catholic in Belgium," 2.

13. Harding, "Portrait of a Female Suicide Bomber"

14. Smith, "Raised as Catholic in Belgium," 2.

15. Harding, "Portrait of a Female Suicide Bomber"

16. Robert Pape, *Dying to Win: The Strategic Logic of Suicide Terrorism* (New York: Random House, 2005), 200.

17. Although media reports implicate her marriages in her reasoning and actions, they

do not deal with them in a precise fashion. Christopher Dickey claims she was married three times, but Smith only accounts for two marriages (Christopher Dickey, "Women of Al Qaeda," *Newsweek*, December 4, 2005, http://www.newsweek.com/2005/12/11 /women-of-al-qaeda.html (accessed December 5, 2005); Smith, "Raised as Catholic in Belgium").

18. Dickey, "Women of Al Qaeda," 1.

19. Ibid.

20. Ibid.

21. Harding, "Portrait of a Female Suicide Bomber"; Smith, "Raised as Catholic in Belgium," 2.

22. Evan Thomas, Daniel Klaidman, Michael Isikoff, Babak Dehghanpisheh, Scott Johnson, Andrew Murr, Mark Hosenball, Tamara Lipper, Emily Flynn, and Avi Karshmer, "Enemies among Us," *Newsweek*, June 75, 2004.

23. Thomas et al., "Enemies among Us," http://www.newsweek.com/2004/06/06 /enemies-among-us.html (accessed March 7, 2011).

24. Ibid.; Chitra Ragavan, Douglas Pasternak, and Rochelle Sharpe, "Femme Fatale? Al-Qaeda's Mystery Woman," *U.S. News and World Report*, April 7, 2003, 33.

25. Alison Gendar, "'Lady Al Qaeda' Aafia Siddiqui Convicted of Attempted Murder," *New York Daily News*, February 3, 2010, http://articles.nydailynews.com/2010 -02-03/news/27055245_1_afghan-police-station-aafia-siddiqui-defense-lawyer (accessed March 7, 2010).

26. Gendar, "'Lady Al Qaeda.'" There is another narrative surrounding Siddiqui's disappearance and subsequent arrest that is outside of the scope of this chapter. The website dedicated to her claims that she was detained for four years (between 2004 and 2008) by the United States at Baghram Air Force Base as prisoner 650 and kept in isolation. Yvonne Ridley, a British journalist, describes her as "the 'grey lady' because she is almost a ghost, a spectre whose cries and screams continues to haunt those who heard her. This would never happen to a Western woman" (qtd. in "Dr. Aafia Siddiqui: A 'Missing Person with a Name," August 5, 2008, http://www.draafia.org/2008/08/05 /dr-aafia-siddiqui-a-%E2%80%98missing-person%E2%80%99-with-a-name-2 [accessed March 8, 2011]).

27. Chitra Ragavan, Douglas Pasternak, Rochelle Sharpe and Aamir Latif, "All in the Family," *U.S. News and World Report*, April 21, 2003, 50.

28. Thomas et al., "Enemies among Us"; Ragavan et al., "Femme Fatale," 33; Ragavan et al., "All in the Family," 50.

29. An interesting side note: during her trial Siddiqui was nicknamed "Lady al-Qaeda" by the press (Gendar, "'Lady Al Qaeda'").

30. Musa Hattar, "Iraqi Woman to Hang over Amman Hotel Bombings," *Agence France Presse*, September 21, 2006, http://web.lexis-nexis.com/universe (accessed April

1, 2007); "Female Suicide Bomber Motivated by Revenge," *International Herald Tribune*, November 16, 2005, 4.

31. Hattar, "Iraqi Woman to Hang."

32. Hassan M. Fattah, "Jordan Arrests Iraqi Woman in Hotel Blasts," *New York Times*, November 14, 2005, 1.

33. Stefanie Cohen, "Her Bro is Zarqawi Aide," *New York Post*, November 14, 2005, http://web.lexis-nexis.com/universe (accessed April 3, 2007), 5.

34. Hannah Allam, "Hotel Bombers Linked to Anti-U.S. Groups in Fallujah," *The Age*, November 15, 2005, http://www.theage.com.au/news/iraq/hotel-bombers-linked-to-antius-groups-in-fallujah/2005/11/14/1131951100281.html (accessed May 8, 2007); Maddy Sauer and Hoda Osman, "Female Suicide Bombers: A New Al-Qaeda Tactic?" *ABC News*, November 14, 2005, http://www.abcnews.go.com/WNT/Investigation/story?id=1312273 (accessed August 4, 2006), 1; "Would-be Bomber Confesses," *The Record*, November 14, 2005, http://web.lexis-nexis.com/universe (accessed April 3, 2007), A1.

35. Allam, "Hotel Bombers Linked"; "Would-be Bomber," A1.

36. This chapter maintains that women with ties to the West generate the most attention; therefore al-Rashiwa is an exception. Still, plausible reasons for the attention are that Jordan is a strong Arab ally of the United States and that the October plot was unprecedented in Jordan and remains a unique event.

37. John Beitler, "Constitutive Rhetoric as Rhetorical Prompt: Analyzing the Truth and Reconciliation Commission of South Africa Report," Inscription Conference, Abilene, Texas, 2006.

38. Kenneth Burke, *Language as Symbolic Action: Essays on Life, Literature, and Method* (Berkeley: University of California Press, 1966), 45.

39. Ibid.

40. Sometimes it seems as if the press thinks female martyrdom began with the Palestinians, when in reality it has historical precedence in Sri Lanka and within the Kurdish movement.

41. Arguably, in spite of the postsurge rise in female self-martyrs in Iraq, this is still true when one considers how much attention Colleen "Jihad Jane" LaRose garnered in comparison with how little attention the Iraqi female self-martyrs *still* attract.

42. Damien Cave and Wisam A. Habeeb, "Blast Kills 40 as Cleric Faults Baghdad Plan," *New York Times*, February 25, 2007, http://www.nytimes.com/2007/02/25/world/middleeast/25cnd-iraq.html?ex=1175572800&en=00e519d8badb4bd1&ei=5070 (accessed February 26, 2007).

43. Ibid; Barry Newhouse, "Suicide Bomber Kills 40 at Baghdad College," *Irbil*, February 25, 2007, http://www.globalsecurity.org/military/library/news/2007/02/mil-070225-voa01.htm (accessed March 17, 2007).

44. Cave and Habeed, "Blast Kills 40"; Newhouse, "Suicide Bomber Kills 40"; Tina Susman, "As the Shiite-Dominated Institution is Targeted Again, Sadr Calles Security Plan a Failure," *Los Angeles Times*, February 26, 2007, http://www.latimes.com/news /printedition/front/la-fg-iraq26feb26,1,5429464.story?page=1&cset=true&ctrack =1&ctrack=rss (accessed March 13, 2007).

45. There is not a complete silence around the actions because they are reported on (hence "near-silence"). This distinction is important because there is a body of work on the rhetoric of silence, which this does not apply to this situation (see Carrie Crenshaw, "Resisting Whitness' Rhetorical Silence," *Western Journal of Communication*, 61, no. 3 [1997]: 253–78).

46. See Mia Bloom, "Mother, Daughter, Sister, Bomber," *Bulletin of the Atomic Scientists*, 61, no. 6 (2005): 55–62; Sjoberg and Gentry, *Mothers, Monsters, and Whores*, 88-140.

47. Michael Howard and Ewan MacAskill, "New Tactics on Two Fronts," *Guardian International*, September 29, 2005, http://web.lexis-nexis.com/universe (accessed April 1, 2007), 13.

48. "Iraqi President Awards Medals to Two Female Suicide Bombers," *BBC Monitoring International Reports*, April 7, 2003, http://web.lexis-nexis.com/universe (accessed April 1, 2007).

49. Sameer N. Yacoub, "Female Suicide Bombers Kill Scores at Baghdad Policy Academy," *AP*, December 6, 2005, http://web.lexis-nexis.com/universe (accessed April 1, 2007).

50. Yacoub, "Female Suicide Bombers Kill Scores."

51. "Iraq Female Bomber"; Golodryga, "Deadly Day in Iraq."

52. "Female Suicide Bomber Reportedly Arrested in Iraq's Al-Najaf," *BBC Monitoring International Reports*, October 14, 2004, http://web.lexis-nexis.com/universe (accessed April 1, 2007).

53. See Qassim Abdul Abdul-Zakram and Brian Murphy, "Iraq Arrests Female Suicide Bomber Recruiter," *Huffington Post*, February 3, 2009, http://www.usnews.com /articles/news/iraq/2008/07/28/the-rising-number-of-female-suicide-bombers-in-iraq .html (accessed April 22, 2010); Alex Kingsbury, "The Rising Number of Female Suicide Bombers in Iraq," *U.S. News and World Report*, July 28, 2008, http://www.usnews.com /articles/news/iraq/2008/07/28/the-rising-number-of-female-suicide-bombers-in-iraq .html (accessed April 22, 2010); Jim Muir, "Iraq's Growing Female Bomber Fear," *BBC News*, July 29, 2008, http://news.bbc.co.uk/2/hi/middle_east/7532235.stm (accessed April 22, 2010); Steve Niva, "Behind the Surge in Iraqi Women Suicide Bombers," *Foreign Policy in Focus*, August 11, 2008, http://www.fpif.org/articles/behind_the_surge _in_iraqi_women_suicide_bombers (accessed April 22, 2010).

54. See Abdul-Zakra and Murphy, "Iraq Arrests Female Suicide"; Alissa J. Rubin, "How Baida Wanted to Die," *New York Times*, August 12, 2009, http://www.nytimes.com/2009/08/16/magazine/16suicide-t.html?_r=1 (accessed April 21, 2010); Niva, "Behind the Surge in Iraqi Women"; Alexandra Zavis, "Grooming a Female Suicide Bomber," *Los Angeles Times*, August 21, 2008, http://articles.latimes.com/2008/aug/21/world/fg-women21 (accessed April 22, 2010).

55. Judy Mandelbaum, "What Drives Female Suicide Bombers?" *Salon*, April 10, 2010, http://www.salon.com/life/broadsheet/2010/04/05/female_suicide_bombers_open2010 (accessed March 6, 2011).

56. There are some striking exceptions to this, such as Steve Niva's "Behind the Surge in Iraqi Women."

57. Rubin, "How Baida Wanted to Die"; Farhana Ali, "Female Suicide Bombers in Iraq: Why the Trend Continues," *Counterterrorism Blog*, March 23, 2008, http://counterterrorismblog.org/2008/03/female_suicide_bombers_in_iraq.php (accessed April 22, 2010); Kingsbury, "The Rising Number of Female Suicide Bombers"; Muir, "Iraq's Growing Female Bomber Fear"; Huma Yusuf, "Female Suicide Bombings in Iraq: Why the Recent Surge?" *Christian Science Monitor*, July 8, 2008, http://www.csmonitor.com/World/terrorism-security/2008/0708/p99s01-duts.html (accessed April 22, 2010); Zavis, "Grooming a Female Suicide Bomber."

58. Rubin, "How Baida Wanted to Die"; Zavis, "Grooming a Female Suicide Bomber."

59. Kingsbury, "The Rising Number of Female Suicide Bombers."

60. Zavis, "Grooming a Female Suicide Bomber."

61. Rubin, "How Baida Wanted to Die"; Ali, "Female Suicide Bombers in Iraq"; Yusuf, "Female Suicide Bombings in Iraq"; Zavis, "Grooming a Female Suicide Bomber." See Sjoberg and Gentry, *Mothers, Monsters, Whores*.

62. Abdul-Zakra and Murphy, "Iraq Arrests Female Suicide."

Blinded by the Explosion?

SECURITY AND RESISTANCE

IN MUSLIM WOMEN'S

SUICIDE TERRORISM

Katherine E. Brown

Throughout history women have participated in proscribed violence, performing strategic, supportive, and combat roles in a wide range of violent movements.[1] Statistics show that between 1981 and 2007 women carried out approximately 26 percent of all suicide attacks and that there has been a marked rise in women's participation in such attacks since 2005.[2] This empirical shift combined with the media attention given to the phenomenon has led a number of policy analysts and academics to conclude that female suicide terrorism is a growing trend.[3]

The analysis, opinions, and conclusions expressed or implied in this chapter are those of the author and do not necessarily represent the views of the U.K. Joint Services Command and Staff College, the U.K. Ministry of Defence, or any other governmental agency.

In response to the scholarly analyses addressed in the introduction to this volume that treat this "trend" in a variety of unsatisfactory ways, I argue that addressing women as agents in suicide terrorism exposes how the "gender blindness" of the mainstream of the field does not lead to gender-free or gender-neutral theories of suicide terrorism. When one examines women's engagement with suicide terrorism from their standpoint, the focus of research necessarily shifts from a public policy output to something more complex. This complexity reveals three significant challenges to orthodox thinking on suicide terrorism: that suicide terrorism (not only female suicide terrorism) is a gendered phenomenon; that agency transcends the have/have not binary; and that the power to know or represent the suicide terrorist is as important as the bomber's material power to wreak destruction.

These claims and their consequences are assessed in detail in this chapter. The chapter first reviews existing mainstream theories on suicide terrorism. Given the limitations this review exposes, the chapter then proposes an alternative framework based on resistance. This framework relies on the key steps in the *Subaltern Studies* project, which are considered in turn and applied to the case of Muslim women's suicide bombing. The chapter puts forward the conclusion that understanding Muslim women's political violence, and suicide terrorism, through the lens of resistance maintains a feminist ethic in research and overcomes the "blindness" characteristic of the mainstream of this field of study.

SUICIDE MISSIONS AND SUICIDE TERRORISM

Analysis and research on suicide terrorism is dominated by a quest to find "root causes." In poplar writings, suicide terrorism has been characterized as a "weapon of the weak" and the last recourse for those facing oppression.[4] Consequently, suicide terrorists and the organizations behind them are understood to be simply reacting to structural and externally imposed pressures in a mechanistic manner. In this framework, suicide terrorism becomes the domain of an isolated few among a largely passive, submissive, and oppressed population. Largely accepting this conceptualization of suicide terrorism, researchers have sought to explain why these particular few engage in such activities. A large body of work has established that this "unusual and unnatural form of human behavior" is attributable to individual suicide terrorists' madness, perpetrators' weak personal and social worth, their homesickness and the alienation they experience as migrants, their quest for redemption, the importance of friendship and kinship networks, and madrassa education.[5] Given the variety of factors identified by researchers, it seems that "individuals are motivated differently. There is not a single pattern."[6]

The inability and failures to effectively profile for why particular individuals engage in such violence have driven the research agenda to consider the organizations that sponsored these acts as the objects of research, as opposed to individuals. Explanations operating at the organizational level consider strategic effectiveness, political goals, organizational structures, and an opportunity to increase market share in a potentially sympathetic population as causal factors of suicide terrorism.[7] Reviewing these organizational features, Bruce Hoffman and Gordon McCormick conclude that "there are only two basic operational requirements that an organization must be able to satisfy to get into the game: a willingness to kill and a willingness to die."[8] As a result, there is little to help distinguish organizations that deploy the tactic/strategy from those that do not.

In light of this limitation of the organizational approach, analysis on suicide terrorism has followed the cultural turn in the social sciences and shifted toward a consideration of the role culture and society play in martyrdom operations. In these works a few dominant themes emerge: public support for perpetrators and their organizations; a culture of martyrdom and violence; societal humiliation; societies' marginal status in the neoliberal capitalist world order; and Islam's geography.[9] However, this move brings the research back "full circle" to the structural determinism that characterizes suicide terrorism as a "weapon of the weak" as well as risking cultural essentialism and Orientalism.[10]

Given the inability to predict or explain suicide terrorism through these models, a number of works explicitly make policy advice and damage limitation the primary purpose of research instead. This means that the research does not have to fully explain suicide terrorism in causal terms. Rather its goal is to evaluate the effectiveness and utility of known strategies and counterstrategies.[11] Such researchers consider vulnerabilities and geopractical risks of targets, what technologies, capabilities, tactics, and strategies to introduce to counter the threat, and how to amend foreign or domestic policy.[12]

Thus, despite this variety of approaches and differing "levels of analysis," in the words of one author of over thirteen books on suicide terrorism, "the concept remains imprecise, the facts are not well established, and neither explanations nor policy recommendations distinguish sufficiently between suicide and other terrorist or insurgent attacks or account for variations within the phenomenon. . . . Findings are often based on incompatible datasets, and references to cases or examples do not always fit the stated definitions of the concept."[13]

These empirical and methodological ambiguities are significant flaws, and some contend that terrorism studies has failed to progress to the level of being able to provide a mature explanatory framework of knowledge.[14] This failure is perhaps symptomatic of the "problem-solving" approach that Lee Jarvis argues characterizes terrorism studies. The mainstream, he argues, has an "overwhelming preference for an essentialist conception of terrorism as a coherent and bounded object of knowledge."[15] Claudia Brunner goes further by suggesting that this essentialist conception reinforces the "naturalness" of suicide terrorism and of existing international power relations.[16] The confusions of the mainstream hint at another oversight, namely a failure to address issues of agency and structure.[17] Thus, there is little reflection on the historical and social processes through which this identity, behavior, or threat has been constituted.

In light of these flaws, instead of relying on assumptions about rationality, strategy, security, or culture, this chapter uses a different framework to analyze suicide terrorism: resistance. This framework has a number of advantages. It allows for a complex understanding of how power works, it grants agency to actors while recognizing their constraints, and it allows the symbolic and material nature of political violence and suicide terrorism to be accounted for.

RESISTANCE

Feminist ethnography, history, sociology, and insights into international relations have been especially influential in moving the social sciences and humanities to take up the issue of resistance. Once the personal is redefined as political, and the political as personal, the everyday survival strategies of individuals can be reconstituted as subtle forms of resistance.[18]

This extension of the political into the private is important to the very public cases of female suicide terrorism because it reveals how the boundaries between the public and private are constructed and controlled through such violence at the same time that this form of violence is held up as a means of resisting the hierarchization of the public over the private. Thus, according to Michael Brown, "resistance . . . has become a central, perhaps even a dominant, theme in the study of social life."[19] One of the reasons resistance has become a dominant theme is that it is also a "diagnostic of power," turning the Foucauldian dictum "where there is power, there is resistance" upside-down to yield "where there is resistance, there is power."[20] Utilizing resistance therefore has considerable appeal; it can generate multicausal and complex explanations of political violence because it enables the researcher to focus on relationships and interfaces between different agents, events, and contexts.

But the resistance approach has not been without criticism. One of the criticisms leveled against it is that the term "resistance" suffers from conceptual elasticity, such that it is to be found everywhere and almost nowhere.[21] A second criticism of resistance as "conceptual stretching" is not just that it loses its intellectual coherence but that it is a mere academic substitute for ideological systems that have been discredited. As Brown notes, "Attention to resistance has increased as revolutionary dreams have lost their luster. When the great meta-narratives of the modern era, especially Marxism, became impossible to sustain, intellectuals shifted their focus to the political nuances of daily life."[22] Thus academic concern for the everyday and its attendant resistances tells us more about the construction of an epistemic community seeking stability through the creation of a new public ideology following the loss of the "great traditions."

Christine Sylvester takes up this charge for feminist international relations when she wonders whether when we follow the subaltern to the everyday, we simply give a megaphone to our egocentrism.[23] Other concerns have been voiced in addition to the idea that by focusing on resistance academics are cynically narrating their discipline into existence. Gaytri Spivak, for example, questions whether we narrate the complete "subject" into existence through an obsession with resistance and the everyday.[24] Postcolonial, feminist, and other cultural theories that appeal to resistance tend, critics charge, to "reduce [human subjectivity] to the . . . idea of a conscious agent-subject having both the capacity and the desire to move in a singular historical direction: that of increasing self-empowerment and decreasing pain."[25]

In an attempt to address some of these concerns and to develop a better understanding of feminist antiglobalization movements, Catherine Eschle and Bice Maiguashca explore the "nature of the subject of the politics of resistance, the conditions under which resistance emerges and how resistance is enacted and expressed."[26] They find the conceptualization of power in the form of an external opponent to be problematic because it fails to treat power relations as internal to movement politics. Second, they argue that that resistance is best understood as simultaneously a "politics of recognition" and a "politics of redistribution."[27] They insist that the political ethos or value system that motivates is not only rational but is in part characterized by "principled pragmatism" and empathetic cooperation. As a result, the nature of resistance cannot be reduced to a singular history, place, or human subjectivity. Recognizing these points in relation to Muslim women's political violence and suicide terrorism allows for an analysis of the symbolic and the material elements of the acts.

Additionally, through such awareness of resistance, the relational autonomy of victims, perpetrators, agents, and voyeurs is highlighted. Female suicide terrorists, like men, are neither "free agents" nor passive victims.[28] In other words, resistance emerges as constitutive of the power relationships it challenges. Consequently resistance may involve behavior that at times ostensibly appears fully collaborative but that does not necessarily compromise its status as resistance.[29] Importantly, resistance is not considered automatically self-empowering or, conversely, nihilistic. Conceptualizing resistance as embedded in a series of complex unending power relations means that we are not forced to seek a singular underlying principle to explain violence. "The act" itself is not to be thought of as a pure complete expression, nor are we confined to noting success and failure in terms of the (in)security of Western states.

Given the complexity of resistance, this chapter adopts the methodological approach to it as developed by subaltern studies. The purpose is not to present this one conceptualization of resistance as all-encompassing but to use it as a tool for analysis that might help recover what has been "left unsaid" about the politics of suicide terrorism and political violence. The *Subaltern Studies* project was undertaken by a group of scholars who sought to reclaim history for/of a marginalized group, namely that of the subaltern peasant of Indian colonial history. These scholars were not interested in a history that had been "bestowed" on the subaltern by the elite but rather in subaltern modes of consciousness and practices. Recovering such modes and practices, they realized, would require them to identify "the logic of the distortions in the representation of the subaltern in official or elite culture."[30]

However, the declared aim of *Subaltern Studies* was not just to identify dominant modes of representation; it was also to produce historical analyses in which the subaltern groups were viewed as the subjects of history. As Ranajit Guha put it once in the course of introducing the third volume of *Subaltern Studies*, "We are indeed opposed to much of the prevailing academic practice in historiography . . . for its failure to acknowledge the subaltern as the maker of his own destiny. This critique lies at the very heart of our project."[31]

There are three key steps in the *Subaltern Studies* project: first to make visible and fill the emptiness of colonial history; second to reclaim the subaltern as a conscious human-subject-agent who engages in practices and reasoning that are not dependent on the actions of the elite; and third to configure resistance as having decentered familiar notions of power.[32] These three steps match in Eschle and Miaguashca's focus on the "who, what and why" of resistance among antiglobalization protestors.[33] After taking each step in turn, I use this method to posit Muslim women's political violence as a vehicle for developing a more complete understanding of (male and female) political violence in the public sphere.

MAKING VISIBLE SUBALTERN AND FEMALE SUICIDE TERRORISTS

The *Subaltern Studies* project sought to reclaim history for the peasant of colonial India. It sought to install the subaltern as the subject of history rather than as a casual bystander or victim of colonial projects. In "The Prose of Counter Insurgency," Guha argues that existing histories fail to recognize the subaltern because they are blinded by the glare of "immaculate consciousness."[34]

This idea is echoed in recent feminist research into international relations, which seeks to make "the invisible visible" by "putting the spotlight on women as competent actors and understanding women as subjects rather than the objects of men."[35] Nancy Hirschmann, like other feminists, reveals how women's lives, as human lives, are written out of public discourse and are systemically eliminated from public ideologies of politics and security.[36] It is necessary to move beyond a consideration of the security of the powerful, as is characteristic of the mainstream of terrorism studies, because, as Cynthia Enloe argues, only taking the powerful into account "presumes *a priori* that margins, silences and bottom rungs are so naturally marginal, silent and far from power that exactly how they are kept there could not be of interest to the reasoning, reasonable explainer."[37]

Instead, subaltern studies, like feminisms, recognizes that the marginal provide unique insights into their condition. More than simply making the subaltern visible as part of modernity, however, and in common with feminist standpoint theory, subaltern studies stresses the self-perceptions of the subaltern. Guha suggests, for example, that the subaltern "did in fact read his contemporary world correctly."[38] As MacKinnon elaborates, when women are excluded, "the male point of view forces itself upon the world as the way of apprehending it."[39] With respect to Muslim women's suicide terrorism, making the subaltern visible helps to reclaim the subaltern from the powerful and to overcome blindness to women's resistance in the public sphere.

All research is grounded in certain conceptual assumptions and approached through certain theoretical lenses that "foreground some things, and background others."[40] Mainstream security scholars focus their attention on those powerful actors capable of directly influencing the causal chain of interstate conflict—if they focus on actors at all.[41] With relatively few exceptions the majority of terrorism/suicide terrorism scholars tie their understanding of terrorism to both the activities of nonstate actors and to the targeting of particular victims: noncombatants or "innocent civilians." Suicide terrorism is therefore structured by a conception of the object as an "unconventional form of illegitimate violence"; this automatically leads to a policy focus and state centrism.[42]

Consequently, in this mainstream view in which the principal frame of reference is the state, and in particular Western states, female suicide terrorism simply becomes a variant of an already known threat to the state. This security approach consequently leads to homogenization based on method of attack and its security impact rather than to a recognition of the politics of those involved. This means that states do not have to engage with the politics of terrorist groups but only need to respond to terrorist methods by improving physical security and engaging in detection activities so as to deny the terrorist success. Research that adopts the security approach is thus blinded by the glare of the explosion: the corporality and immediacy of the violence and state responses and state responses are overexposed at the expense of other features of the phenomenon.

The state security approach to understanding suicide terrorism also fails to see the insecurity of women, including that women are significantly more likely to die in a suicide terrorist attack than men (women make up 79 percent of all fatalities).[43] In particular this approach does not see those women as "worth saving." Cristina Masters makes this point in relation to the obsession of both the media and policy maker with Lynndie England and Abu Ghraib.[44] For Masters, the focus on Lynndie England's crimes against the U.S. Army means that the allegations of rape and sexual assault against forty-two female detainees are not investigated, that the gang rapes of Iraqi civilian women by U.S. troops are not considered, and that the fact that in 2002 30 percent of U.S. servicewomen reported rape or attempted rape while on active duty is ignored.[45]

Similarly, the insecurity of Muslims living in the West is not seen in this frame of state security. Explanations for Muslim (male and female) proscribed violence that is carried out in the context of the "war on terrorism" are often grounded in a "clash of civilizations" narrative that renders Europe's Muslim population as forever alien.[46] In Europe, Muslim communities are cast within this global framing as "apart" from rational, modern civilized Europeans and thus become objectified as security problems, because of their "unreasonable demands" to express their religious identity in the public sphere.[47] Their lives are pushed outside Europe's imagination and consequently rendered "bare"— neither worth sacrificing nor saving.[48]

Across Europe, new legislation to control Islam in the public sphere is combined with a wider moral concern, even moral panic, generating a counteridentity of Islamic radicalism and criminality that is not countenanced as European.[49] In the U.K., for example, the significantly higher percentage of Asians who are stopped and searched by police and the increased surveillance of them, the negative impact on them of new citizenship laws, and the disruptive activities carried out by law enforcement in Muslim neighborhoods reveal that the security of Muslim communities and individuals are overshadowed by state security responses.[50] In highlighting changes in law, policing, and notions of citizenship, we see that the relationship between terrorism and counterterrorism has the potential to bring about a steady securitization of social and political life in which civilian populations (some segments to a greater degree than others) become "squeezed in the middle."[51] However, in the mainstream analysis of terrorism and suicide terrorism, state security and its attempts to become more secure are in the foreground of analysis, while subaltern Muslim politics and security are obscured from view.

The overexposure of the "state-security" approach to suicide terrorism does not only mean that others are not seen, but the function of gender as constitutive of suicide terrorism is lost in the overly dark background. In mainstream analysis of terrorism, gender is read directly and unproblemati-cally from sexed bodies.[52] Helen Kinsella argues that the continual need to verify women's engagement in violence, such as is apparent in the report con-ducted under the auspices of the Security Council Resolution 1325 on Women and Peace and Armed conflict, indicates that although women are indeed combatants and perpetrators of violence, the gendered binary of protected civilian/protector combatant remains unchallenged in politics, policy, and the laws of war.[53]

Thus men's participation in political violence is assumed and taken for granted whereas women's needs proof and explanation. Indeed, women's per-petration of political violence and conflict as perpetrators has led to analy-ses that rely on the assumption that the phenomenon requires that violent women be exceptionalized, which enables gendered binaries to remain in-tact.[54] Laura Sjoberg and Caron Gentry argue that the special reasons in-voked to explain women's violence often rely on gender stereotypes of women as "mothers, monsters, and whores," while explanations of men's violence make no reference to gender.[55] This remains the case even when researchers argue that there is little difference between individual men and women in their motivation; such researchers maintain that societies where female sui-cide terrorism is a phenomenon are exceptional cases and that what accounts for the presence of female suicide terrorism in them is malfunctioning gen-der norms and hierarchies.[56] Women's political violence, it seems, needs to be explained away rather than incorporated in order to refine existing theories of violence.

Including gender in one's analysis demonstrates how the security focus on male perpetrators of political violence frames them in "hypermasculinized" models of behavior. Political violence is largely represented as a phenomenon that can be understood in terms of security or militarism. Understood this way, these activities can be firmly detached from the feminine "peaceful" and "pri-vate" spheres of human activity and turned into exemplars of politics and the public sphere. Twentieth-century nationalist movements evidence this point of view; there was little expectation that women would participate in such movements except as symbolic "mothers of the nation" whose duty was to preserve the national and cultural heritage.[57]

This public-private dichotomy is troubled in writings about jihad that draw on Orientalist stereotypes. The private sphere intrudes on representations of jihad that rely on these stereotypes via the emphasis on the sexual rewards the martyrs will receive and the sexual activities of modern-day martyrs prior to their missions.[58] Mujahideen (male jihadists) are presented as overtly sexual and therefore irrational and deviant (for example, sensational reports abound alleging that the 9/11 terrorists gambled and visited prostitutes and strip clubs in the days and weeks prior to their attacks). In accounts of jihad by jihadists, the defense of faith and politics is treated as both a personal choice and a public obligation of all believers, thereby blurring the public/private divide that underpins orthodox thinking on security and politics.

According to Farhana Qazi, researchers are blind to the role of women in political violence in Muslim groups because the idea of it runs "counter to Western stereotypes and misconceptions of male terrorists; we assume that women are second class citizens and rely on the men to run the organizations."[59] In line with these assumptions, writers and academics studying female suicide terrorism tend to focus on male handlers, husbands, and male leadership. For example, in 1987 Leonard Weinberg and William Eubank argued that there were so many married couples in terrorist organizations that the women must be drawn into it by their men.[60] More recently, in a report on three German women held in 2006 on suspicion of plotting suicide attacks, *Agence France Press* reported that "the women in their late 20s to 40s became radicalised under the influence of their Islamic extremist spouses."[61] Similarly in the case of Myrium Goris, it has frequently been reported that she was "brainwashed" by her husband.[62] CNN claimed that "she came upon a rather radical Moroccan man who managed to, apparently, talk her into becoming the first Western European to blow herself up."[63] This case is further dramatized by the fact that her husband is presented as the trigger or cause of her conversion to Islam, and although he was a Belgium citizen, he was frequently represented as North African. This threat is quantified by Mia Bloom, who notes that "Degauque's [sic] attack raises an added element of female converts, of which there are thousands in Europe, married to Muslim men and willing to make the sacrifice."[64] Here Goris's marriage and conversion become securitized and intrinsically linked to proscribed violence. In short, she is denied political agency, and her actions become the responsibility of men.[65]

The task remains to make female suicide terrorists visible independent of their alleged male handlers. Or, to put it differently, "How does the third world write its own history?"[66] A standpoint perspective reveals that it is not possible simply to add women's experiences to the dominant discourse on political life (and agency) because the men's and women's experiences are grounded in different ontological and epistemological frameworks.[67]

In addition, placing women (or the insurgent peasant) at the center of the analysis helps in pushing back against homogenization—it enables the researcher to see a variety of politics, of resistances. Putting the interlocutor at the center of the analysis stands in contrast to a common strategy in "critical terrorism studies," which seeks to avert the gaze from an exploration of terrorism per se to an exploration of representations of terrorism.[68] As with critical counterterrorism studies, this resistance approach moves away from a state-security approach; however, this method does not privilege "our" representations of terrorism in order to reveal how global politics is constructed. Instead, it foregrounds the representations and politics of the subaltern. The point is not to "trade truths about terrorism" in order to create a more accurate picture but rather to explore the interplay between different events and different contexts.[69]

This approach is not without difficulties. As Sherry Ortner argues, "Resistance studies are thin because they are ethnographically thin: thin on the internal politics of dominated groups, thin on the cultural richness of those groups, thin on the subjectivity—the intentions, desires, fears, projects—of the actors engaged in these dramas."[70] This thinness is particularly difficult to overcome in the case of female suicide terrorists because if successful they leave only their fragmented bodies behind. In the case of Myrium Goris, for example, she left behind no jihadi video, no message, and no archive. Therefore the quest must be to make visible how gender is constructed by the organizations, by women, and by men themselves, that is, to "ask what assumptions about gender . . . are necessary to make particular statements, policies and actions meaningful."[71] This can in part be achieved by considering the next stage of the *Subaltern Studies* method.

RECLAIMING SUBALTERN AND FEMALE SUICIDE TERRORIST AGENCY

A focus on agency is a necessary step because "visibility, in and of itself, does not erase a history of silence, nor does it challenge the structure of power and domination—symbolic or material—that determines what can and cannot be seen."[72] For subaltern studies, it is important not only to shed light on the history of silence but also to be "heard." To do this it is necessary to acknowledge as inherently political the agency of subaltern groups.

Extending the logic of visibility to that of agency, Ortner argues that "if we are to recognize that resistors are doing more than simply opposing domination, more than simply producing a virtually mechanical re-action, then we must go the whole way. They have their own politics."[73] Subaltern politics is not simply framed vis-à-vis the oppressor but through all of the relationships found at the local level, between men and women and elders and juniors and in battles over wealth, supremacy, and power that transpire beyond the histories and politics of the elite.

Yet this is not a plea to seek an authentic, holistic cultural frame in which jihad or any groups' resistance can be understood. Rather it is to argue that understanding how internal and external dynamics operate together can lead to better analysis. To ignore the problems that are potentially caused by subalterns' presence and participation in the modern political sphere yields only elitist histories. For, according to Guha, without taking into account such problems, it would not be possible to analyze the consciousness of the subaltern—the discourses of kinship, caste, religion, and ethnicity through which they have expressed themselves in protest—except as a "backward" consciousness trying to grapple with a changing world whose logic it could never fully comprehend.[74]

For example, the standard tendency in global historiography is to look on peasant revolts against colonial rule organized along the axes of kinship, religion, caste, and so forth, as movements exhibiting a "backward" consciousness, the kind that Eric Hobsbawm in his work on social banditry and "primitive rebellion" had called "prepolitical."[75] The subaltern in this framework is seen as a consciousness that has not quite come to terms with the institutional logic of modernity or capitalism.[76] Subaltern studies explicitly rejects the characterization of peasant consciousness as "prepolitical" and avoids revolutionary models of "consciousness," insisting that instead of being an anachronism in a modernizing colonial world the peasant was a real contemporary of colonialism and a fundamental part of the modernity that colonial rule gave rise to in India. "The peasants' consciousness was not 'backward,' a mentality left over from the past, baffled by modern political and economic institutions and yet resistant to them."[77]

Like Guha and subaltern studies, this chapter seeks to take seriously the agency of the subaltern. Explanations for terrorism and suicide terrorism are contemporary versions of the "backward" consciousness idea in that they have often tried to explain it by claiming it is caused by mental illness and trauma.[78] Critiquing these forms of explanation, Charles Ruby asks whether "terrorists are mentally deranged" and concludes that there is no evidence to suggest that those who participated in suicide terrorisms suffered from mental illness.[79]

Nevertheless, such behavior is frequently attributed to individual or societal trauma.[80] For example, it is often reported that in Palestine the entire society is traumatized by violence and that this explains the relatively high rate of suicide bombings.[81] This idea combines with contemporary constructions of suicide in the general population as a medical illness.[82] Additionally, accounts relating to female suicide terrorists seem to suggest that they are more vulnerable to trauma of conflict and change. In short, a narrative has emerged that specifies emotional irrational reasons as the cause of individual vulnerability to the terrorists' message. Despite the fact that research now shows that there is limited usefulness in considering martyrdom operations in the same vein as suicide, media reporters, academics, and policy makers continue to make this connection.[83] By doing so they are able to focus on the abhorrent, deviant individual and are able to depoliticize the act.

However, the "backward consciousness" thesis is not limited to labeling suicide bombers as insane. In addition, this approach ascribes suicide terrorism to irrational religious belief and theology. This framing of terrorism as attacks driven by a primordial identity and a rejection of modernity relies on specific narratives about Muslim-proscribed violence. Such terrorist activity is now understood as a consequence of ideology as opposed to "political causes."[84] Richard Jackson argues that it is typically asserted that "Islamic terrorism" is motivated largely by religious or sacred causes, a notion that helps build the "widely accepted 'knowledge' that certain forms of Islam are by nature violent and terroristic."[85]

The 2007 U.K. *Building on Progress* policy review follows this logic, presenting the current threat as emanating "from those who seek to cause the death and destruction in the name of a perversion of the faith of Islam."[86] As a result, Muslim violence is seen to lack any possibility of "explanation or mitigating circumstance, and [is] isolate[ed] as well, from representations of most other dysfunctions, symptoms and maladies of the contemporary world."[87] This is because it is seen to be a reaction to, rather than a consequence of, modernity and globalization. Dag Tuastad has identified this process as an instrument of "symbolic power" that sustains neocolonial interests through what he refers to as the "new barbarism thesis"—"presentations of political violence that omit political and economic interests and contexts when describing that violence, and present the violence as resulting from traits embedded in local cultures."[88]

Framed as irrational, ideological, and antimodern, Muslim violence is therefore reduced to a security problem rather than analyzed as a sociopolitical phenomenon rooted in a specific time and place. This argument can be taken one step further; according to Brunner, "The presumed irrationality, insanity, immorality and otherness of 'suicide terrorism' will sooner or later refer us back to the presumed rationality and naturalness of wars on terror, of the logic of the legitimate use of physical violence by nation states and international bodies, and of the masculinist, racist, and occidentalist nature of International (power) Relations as such."[89]

However, within security studies there are some significant voices who challenge this irrationality thesis.[90] Such research tends to foreground narrowly political determinants. Frequently these accounts are counterpoised against religious explanations; they are instead based on a rational-actor model in which suicide terrorism takes on a strategic logic.[91] Nevertheless, if actions are considered rational, then it is because the "West" devised them. For example, in orthodox explanations of Reem al-Reyashi's detonation of a suicide bomb at a border crossing in Jerusalem, Sheikh Yassin's statement that HAMAS decided to use a female attacker due to the increasing operational difficulties of getting men to their targets is widely cited. The voices and agency of male figures is given priority over Reem's actions. Alisa Stack similarly argues that women are used by organizations because it is a successful strategy but only as a matter of last resort.[92] Agency is here denied; groups are simply responding to the agency of the Western state. Women's agency is denied in a double move because they are simply responding to male commands.

In addition, such narrow definitions of the political are androcentric in that they necessarily render women's agency invisible.[93] This is because they rely on a particular construction of agency as grounded in a particular form of reason and rationality, a reasoning and rationalism that prioritizes the liberal white male subject. As Barbara Hudson notes, "Agency is only granted to those who demonstrate their possessions of the quality of the liberal subject; each subject must suppress her inherent traits of 'otherness' (the child within; the savage within) to demonstrate that she is political and thereby civilized rather than one of the barbarians."[94]

This leads to an interesting contradiction in the way suicide terrorism is approached. It denies women's agency but at the same time posits a faulty agency. The interplay between these two sets of explanations demonstrates the limitation of existing understandings of agency and reason deployed by mainstream security studies, which fail to capture the nuances and contradictions of subalternality. Indeed it demonstrates that explanations for suicide terrorism that hinge on rational reasoning (either having it or not) are based on the myth of the autonomous sovereign subject that "itself is more deeply implicated in our oppression; [therefore] the problem is not one that can be solved by a shift in emphasis[;] . . . the core idea is that a rational stance is itself a stance of oppression or domination, and accepted ideals of reason both reflect and reinforce power relations that advantage white privileged men."[95]

Brunner, for example, demonstrates how female suicide terrorists are produced in literature, academia, and the media as the irrational other of the rational enlightened Western self: "The secular cosmopolitan West is constructed in opposition to a ubiquitous, threatening and orientalized patriarchy."[96] This binary only works because of the oppositional and hierarchical view of agency and rationality. Adopting a more relational view of autonomy prevents the construction binaries of liberated/oppressed and stops us from seeking narratives of redemption from our research. Likewise Hirschmann, relying on feminist understandings of obligation, interdependency, and responsibility, argues that agency is best understood as relational.[97]

For Sjoberg, recognizing relational autonomy has three significant implications for just war theories, which can also be applied to understanding suicide terrorism.[98] First, suicide terrorists, like states, do not always have complete freedom of choice or action and instead rely in part on the choices and actions of others. The mutual interdependency of perpetrators, victims, and wider societies in constituting suicide terrorism, reveal a potential for "empathetic cooperation."[99] Second, different suicide terrorists, victims, societies, and states are situated in different positions and consequently hold different perspectives. As such no single explanation or criteria that would legitimize suicide terrorism is universally applicable. Third, since the actors in suicide terrorism (perpetrators, victims, societies, etc.) have different degrees of power and freedom, the meaning they ascribe to their suicide bombings and the justifications they offer are not on equal footing with the various explanations offered by Western analysts; instead the understandings of more powerful actors are often more powerful in determining the (il)legitimacy of the action.

Reclaiming subaltern agency from security studies therefore requires acknowledging that preexisting and ongoing politics among Muslim jihadi groups impact the actions and thought processes that lead to their agency. This means making visible a history over and above the elite politics of terrorism and acknowledging the various logics of agency/politics. For example, commonly it is understood that the traditions of the Prophet and the holy texts forbid women from participating in violence as jihad. Traditionally, women have been encouraged to view undertaking a pilgrimage to Mecca (hajj), which was seen to be a very dangerous trip, as their jihad.[100]

Although classical authorities did not envisage women participating in violent forms of jihad, they allowed that there could be exceptional and extraordinary circumstances that required it, and as such the ulema did not forbid it.[101] As a result, contemporary movements have reclassified what constitutes extraordinary circumstances, thereby making it possible for women to participate in the battlefield or in martyrdom operations. It is this logic of "accepting of women where necessary" that leads some to argue that better security measures in the West have led to the rise of female suicide terrorists. While strategic and tactical decisions are part of developments in jihadist movements, the limitations on how women may carry out suicide missions indicate that even where it is tactically useful to use women, normative constraints exist.

Those seeking to limit women's participation in violent jihad do not refer to Western logics or the war on terror; rather they appeal to internal gender codes of modesty and authority. For example, on January 31, 2002, Sheik Yassin declared to *al-Sharq al-Awast* that women should be allowed to carry out suicide terrorism but only if they are chaperoned by a man. On February 2, 2002, in the same newspaper, he granted a woman the right to launch such an attack alone only if it would not take her more than twenty-four hours to carry it out and so long as she had permission from her family (parents or husband). And it was another two years before Reem al-Reyashi carried out an attack on behalf of HAMAS, which was the first time the organization used women in martyrdom operations.[102]

Another argument used to limit women's participation is the need to maintain strict gender segregation. In some classical treatises, it is argued that women distract men from performing jihad as they tempt them away from glory. *al-Sharq al-Awsat* published an interview with an alleged leader of the female *mujahidaat* of al-Qaeda, a women's only section, that challenged this notion. In this article, she argued "Our organization is open to all Muslim women wanting to the serve the [Islamic] nation[,] . . . particularly in this very critical phase."[103] She noted that technology enabled gender segregation to be maintained while performing jihad.

Yet another argument put forward to limit women's participation in jihad and particularly in suicide terrorism has to do with the imperative of preserving women's modesty. There is a practical fear that as a woman blows herself up, her body will literally be revealed, and if she fails in her mission then she will be "paraded by the State," thereby violating her modesty on two accounts. These hesitations are expressed even though women are reported to be "more deadly than the male" and garner more media coverage than a male attacker.[104]

Nevertheless, to date, six recognized fatwa have been issued that allow women to participate in martyrdom operations. Those that seek to justify *shaheedas* (female suicide terrorists) draw on a history of jurisprudence and engage in a debate that moves beyond the issue "tactical necessity." Muhammad Khayr Haykal argues when jihad is *fard ayn*, that is, the obligation of every individual within a community (as opposed to a collective duty that can be fulfilled by some members of a community on behalf of the entire community), then women too may carry out their duties in combat.[105] This notion is based on a logic of spiritual equality between the sexes that entails equal obligations to the *ummah* (global Muslim community). Al-ʿAyyiri asserts that performing hajj is not as important as fulfilling jihad because even the poor are not exempt from jihad (as they are from hajj) — thereby denying the equivalency that some classical scholars sought to establish.[106]

There is also an internal discourse that seeks to create a historical justification for women's participation that would alleviate fears that this phenomenon is a new and alarming "innovation." Such fears are allayed by appeals to the *shahada*, that is, the bearing of witness to the essence of being Muslim, an essence that reaches back to human origins both biographically (in God's giving breath to each individual) and historically (to the original covenant between God and human kind), which sees women performing jihad during the lifetime of the Prophet and that of his immediate successors. This is not to claim that Muslim women carry out suicide bombings because Islam demands it or that suicide terrorism is an inherent feature of Islam. Rather it is to suggest that Islamic discourses can be deployed to grant authority, legitimacy, and authenticity to a particular political causes and acts. In other words, these internal discourses "serve as heuristic devices or templates that outline the path to salvation" that are distinct from the histories of the West.[107] However, although they offer "paths to salvation" it is worth remembering that the relational autonomy of individuals (and consequently these discourses) means that no one engages in "pure acts" of resistance.

REEVALUATING SUBALTERN ACTIONS AND FEMALE SUICIDE TERRORISM

In reclaiming agency, Guha and others working in the field of subaltern studies also seek to avoid writing "politically redemptive narratives based on liberation from an evil oppressor."[108] Instead, many within the group have explored minute contradictions in power relations and have traced the various and sometimes internally conflictual strategies developed by subaltern peoples.[109] Therefore, the final strategy of the *Subaltern Studies* project is to reevaluate peasant activities in terms of resistance. This aspect of the project relies on the argument that power is organized differently in different times and places and that politics is not just about systems of control but also about systems of meaning.[110] Our theories of resistance thus must reflect not only a concern with the effects of politics and culture but also with the interpretations and evaluations that surround them.[111] Subaltern studies has consequently focused on resistance in its broadest sense by breaking down the separation between the instrumental and symbolic and by considering resistance as additionally the "systemic breach of authoritative culture codes."[112] Resistance is characterized by the *Subaltern Studies* project as a "fight for prestige which was at the heart of insurgency. Inversion was its principal modality. It was a political struggle in which the rebel appropriated and/or destroyed the insignia of his enemy's power and hoped thus to abolish the marks of his own subalternity."[113] This matches the realization often documented in feminist writings in international relations that resistance is about the politics of representation and reproduction.[114] If suicide terrorism is only approached through a security lens that is focused on "winning/losing" a war, then the symbolic is overshadowed by a concern for the instrumental and rational. A more complex understanding of power calls for looking at the challenges to dominant culture codes that female suicide terrorism engenders.

The relationship between power, knowledge, and resistance is important not just to understanding the act of suicide terrorism. The postcolonial, postmodern, and feminist canon reveals a growing awareness of the issues raised by European representations of non-European others, issues having to do with the control of discourses, the production of professional canons for the presentation of truth about the other, and the epistemological and ethical ambiguities that the position of the researcher gives rise to.[115] This critical concern demands not just cultural empathy but also a "fundamental exploration of the epistemological constitution of non-European and colonial societies as objects of knowledge within the disciplines of Western social science."[116]

The existence of a unified universal and sovereign "rational human agent" that grounds writings on the Middle East and suicide terrorism has been challenged through a series of deconstructive turns. This critique was initially launched by Edward Said, who argued against the production of knowledge in which the "one human history" uniting humanity was written from the vantage point of Europe.[117] Because the mainstream research on this political phenomenon relies on the security lens, it mimics the "one human history" approach. In it, the agency and politics of the *mujihadaat* and *shadeeda* are decontextualized by the search for the global identikit female terrorist. This profile is bestowed on female suicide bombers by the security elites, and the act is framed in terms of the "war on terror."[118] In addition, this security approach deploys gender myths in particular ways, myths that according to Sjoberg and Gentry deny "women's agency in their violence" and imply that the cause of a woman's desire to engage in violence is a problem with her femininity.[119]

Within security studies, the majority of research on *shaheedas* focuses on individual life histories, which brings to the fore the emotional and private sphere.[120] In a review of academic and media reporting on women terrorists, Rhiannon Talbot examines some of the gendered myths that have been established as a means of "containing" their challenge to the accepted gender order.[121] She argues that "the construction of a 'terrorist' is a strongly masculine one, whereas the perception of femininity excludes use of indiscriminate violence. Not surprisingly, when a woman terrorist is represented her culpability as an empowered female employing traditionally masculine means to achieve her goals very rarely emerges. She is seldom the highly reasoned, non-emotive, political animal that is the picture of her male counterpart; in short, she rarely escapes her sex."[122]

According to Karen Jacques and Paul Taylor's archival research, female suicide terrorism is associated with significantly fewer religious/nationalistic motivations and significantly more personal motivations compared to male suicide terrorism. In addition, women were significantly more likely to carry out suicide attacks as a means of revenge than men.[123] Barbara Victor, Mia Bloom, Yoram Schweitzer, and Adam Dolnik all focus on personal motives for women's engagement in terrorism generally.[124] This type of analysis denies women political agency and creates a binary divide between the private and the public. Consequently, recognizing women's agency as extending beyond the private sphere challenges many of our inherited gender images as well as the dichotomy of women as "beautiful souls" and men as "just warriors."[125] Recognizing women's agency also challenges the gender order, which deems women inferior owing to their supposed emotional and physical weaknesses.[126]

However, this feminizing or sexing of the act is also deployed by Muslim resistance groups, operating as a rejection, and, paradoxically, simultaneously as an appropriation of Western ideals of femininity. Femininity is deployed as symbolic capital that problematizes Western assumptions about equality.[127] According to an editorial in *al-Sha'ab*, "It is a woman who today teaches you, o Muslim women, the meaning of true liberation, with which the women's rights activists have tempted you. . . . It is a woman who has now proven that the meaning of [women's] liberation is the liberation of the body from the trials and tribulations of this world . . . and the acceptance of death with a powerful, courageous embrace."[128] In another Middle Eastern newspaper, *al-Akhbar*, a columnist claimed that "women will not settle for being mothers of martyrs anymore."[129] The Hofstad cell serves as an example; it is alleged that women in this group have played an especially assertive role in planning attacks. The cell is described as "an extremist network whose wives watched videos of female suicide terrorists and posed for photos holding guns."[130] One woman linked to the group, Soumaya Sahla, a twenty-one-year-old nursing student, helped coordinate the attempted assassination of former Dutch legislator Ayaan Hirsi Ali, an outspoken feminist. She worked out the logistics of the attack and accompanied her husband, Nouredin al Fahtni, as he set out with a machine gun to conduct the attack. Ayaan Hirsi Ali, reflecting on the prominent role women played in the Hofstad cell, said that "Western Muslims, whether they like it or not, have grown up with the idea of women being equal."[131]

Other participants focus on female social roles and modify them to generate legitimizing discourses. Gender consequently becomes one of the chief organizing principles of resistance. For example, one reference to Wafa Idris's suicide terrorism draws on religious motifs: "From Mary's womb issued a child who eliminated oppression, while the body of Wafa became shrapnel that eliminated despair and aroused hope."[132] In August 2004, *al-Khansaa*, on online magazine, issued a call for women to participate in jihad in a variety of ways.[133] The magazine distinguished between women's roles in the family (where she is a mother, daughter, and wife) and roles in society (where she is an educator, propagator, preacher of Islam, and female jihadi warrior). Narratives that celebrate women's femininity and cite their private roles as political agency in this way stand in contrast to the narratives articulated in the majority of contemporary "state-security studies" approaches. In the words of Salman Rushdie, here "the Empire writes back."[134]

BLINDED BY THE EXPLOSION NO MORE?

This chapter has argued that mainstream work on suicide terrorism is currently blinded by the myth of security. As a result, it adopts a narrow definition of power (as power over), it relies on rationality as the mode of agency, and it presumes the state is the primary subject of concern. At the same time, much contemporary work on female suicide terrorists ignores critical and postmodern feminist studies of the Middle East, Islam, and Muslim politics. However, the chapter has sought to do more than deconstruct security approaches to suicide terrorism. By deploying the concept of resistance as extrapolated by the *Subaltern Studies* project, it has also explicitly sought to undo the epistemic violence that Brunner perceives to be occurring in academia.[135] The resistance model locates the interlocutor at the center of the analysis, recognizes diverse forms of agency and politics, and decenters traditional conceptions of power. This analysis corresponds with a feminist ethic located at the periphery of history and international relations that aims to restore suppressed politics and agency.[136]

In addressing female suicide terrorists by reference to their own particular forms of subjectivity, experience, and agency (which are at present subjugated by the universalizing modes of analysis of mainstream approaches), this chapter has tried to reconstitute them as subaltern and restored them to politics. Ultimately, this chapter has hoped to have demonstrated that analysis on female suicide terrorism need no longer be blinded by the explosion.

NOTES

1. Cindy Ness, "In the Name of the Cause: Women's Work in Secular and Religious Terrorism," *Studies in Conflict and Terrorism* 28 (2005): 353–73; Karla J. Cunningham, "Cross-Regional Trends in Female Terrorism," *Studies in Conflict and Terrorism* 26 (2003): 171–95.

2. The term "suicide terrorism" is not uncontested, and it is not widely used in the Middle East, where the term "martyrdom operation" is preferred. However, given the intended readership of this book, I used the more common phrase "suicide terrorism" throughout. See Jerrold Post, Ehud Sprinzak, and Laurita Denny, "The Terrorists in Their Own Words: Interviews with 35 Incarcerated Middle Eastern Terrorists," *Terrorism and Political Violence* 15, no. 1 (2003): 171–84; Lindsey A. O'Rourke, "What's Special about Female Suicide Terrorism?" *Security Studies* 18, no. 4 (2009), 681–718; Mia Bloom, "Death Becomes Her: Women, Occupation, and Terrorist Mobilization," *PS: Political Science and Politics* 43, no. 3 (2010): 445–50. Statistics from Chicago Project on Security and Terrorism, http://cpost.uchicago.edu/search_results.php (accessed October 2, 2010).

3. Farhana Ali, "Muslim Female Fighters: An Emerging Trend," *Terrorism Monitor* 21, no. 3 (2005): 9–11; Mia Bloom, "Female Suicide Bombers: A Growing Trend," *Daedalus* 136, no. 1 (2007): 94–103; Rosemarie Skaine, *Female Suicide Bombers* (Jefferson, N.C.: McFarland, 2006).

4. Robert Pape, *Dying to Win: The Strategic Logic of Suicide Terrorism* (New York: Random House, 2005), 93.

5. Hilal Khashan, "Collective Palestinian Frustration and Suicide Bombings," *Third World Quarterly* 24, no.6 (2003): 1049–67; Andrew Silke, "Cheshire-Cat Logic: The Recurring Theme of Terrorist Abnormality in Psychological Research," *Psychology, Crime and Law*, 4, no. 1 (1998): 51–69; Harvey Gordon, "The Suicide Bomber: Is it a Psychiatric Problem?" *Psychiatric Bulletin* 26 (2002): 285–87; Ami Pedahzur, *Suicide Terrorism* (Cambridge, U.K.: Polity Press, 2005), 125; Farhad Khosrokhavar, *Suicide Bombers: Allah's Martyrs*, trans. David Macey (London: Pluto, 2005), 149–223; Anne Speckhard, "Understanding Suicide Terrorism: Countering Human Bombs and Their Senders," in *Topics in Terrorism: Towards a Transatlantic Consensus on the Nature of the Threat*, vol. 1, ed. Jason S. Purcell and Joshua D. Weintraub (Washington, D.C.: Atlantic Council of the United States, 2004); Speckhard, "Understanding Suicide Terrorism"; Scott Atran, "The Moral Logic and Growth of Suicide Terrorism," *Washington Quarterly* 29, no. 2 (2006): 127–47; Robert S. Leiken, "Europe's Angry Muslims," *Foreign Affairs* 84, no. 4 (2005): 120–35; Oliver Roy, *Globalized Islam: The Search for a New Umma* (New York: Columbia University Press, 2004); Mohammed M. Hafez, "Dying to Be Martyrs: The Symbolic Dimension of Suicide Terrorism," in *Root Causes of Suicide Terrorism: The Globalisation of Martyrdom*, ed. Ami Pedahzur (Oxford, U.K.: Routledge, 2006), 54–80; Marc Sageman, *Understanding Terror Networks* (Philadelphia: University of Pennsylvania Press, 2004); 9/11 Commission, *9/11 Commission Report* (Washington, D.C.: GPO, 2004), http://www.9-11commission.gov (accessed March 27, 2010).

6. Martha Crenshaw, "Explaining Suicide Terrorism: A Review Essay," *Security Studies* 16, no. 1 (2007): 157.

7. Robert Pape, "The Strategic Logic of Suicide Terrorism," *American Political Science Review* 97, no. 3 (2003): 1–19; Bruce Hoffman and Gordon H. McCormick, "Terrorism, Signalling, and Suicide Attack," *Studies in Conflict and Terrorism* 27, no. 4 (2004): 243–81; Pape, "The Strategic Logic of Suicide Terrorism"; Karla Cunningham, "Countering Female Terrorism," *Studies in Conflict and Terrorism* 30, no.2 (2007): 113–29; Mia Bloom, *Dying to Kill: The Allure of Suicide Terror* (New York: Columbia University Press, 2005); Atran, "The Moral Logic and Growth of Suicide Terrorism"; Brian Jenkins, "The Organization Men: Anatomy of a Terrorist Attack," in *How Did This Happen? Terrorism and the New War*, ed. James Hoge and Gideon Rose (New York: Public Affairs, 2001), 13.

8. Hoffman and McCormick, "Terrorism, Signalling, and Suicide Attack," 272.

9. Hafez, "Dying to Be Martyrs"; Mohammed M. Hafez, "Rationality, Culture, and Structure in the Making of Suicide Bombers: A Preliminary Theoretical Synthesis and Illustrative Case Study," *Studies in Conflict and Terrorism* 29, no.2 (2006), 165–85; Mark Jurgensmeyer, *Terror in the Mind of God: The Global Rise of Religious Violence* (Berkeley: University of California Press, 2003); Jessica Stern, "Beneath Bombast and Bombs, a Caldron of Humiliation," *Los Angeles Times*, June 6, 2004, M1; Colin Flint and Steven M. Radil, "Terrorism and Counter-Terrorism: Situating al-Qaeda and the Global War on Terror within Geopolitical Trends and Structures," *Eurasian Geography and Economics* 50, no.2 (2009): 150–71; Samuel P. Huntington, "The Clash of Civilizations?" *Foreign Affairs* 72, no. 3 (1993): 22–49; Walter Laqueur, *No End to War: Terrorism in the Twenty-First Century* (London: Continuum, 2003); Benjamin R. Barber, *Jihad vs. McWorld: Terrorism's Challenge to Democracy* (London: Corgi, 2003).

10. Claudia Brunner, "Female Suicide Bombers—Male Suicide Bombing? Looking for Gender in Reporting the Suicide Bombings of the Israeli-Palestinian Conflict," *Global Society* 19, no. 1 (2005): 29–48.

11. Lee Jarvis, "The Spaces and Faces of Critical Terrorism Studies," *Security Dialogue* 40, no. 1 (2009): 12.

12. Scott Atran, "Genesis of Suicide Terrorism," *Social Science Review* 299 (2003): 1534; Cunningham, "Countering Female Terrorism"; Daniel Jacobson, "Suicide Bombings and Targeted Killings in (Counter-)Terror Games," *Journal of Conflict Resolution* 51, no. 5 (2007): 772–92; Melissa Bull and Mark Craig, "The Problem of Terrorism: Balancing Risk between State and Civil Responsibilities," *Current Issues in Criminal Justice* 18, no. 2 (2006): 202; Debra Zedalis, *Female Suicide Bombers* (Carlisle, Penn.: Strategic Studies Institute, 2004), http://www.strategicstudiesinstitute.army.mil/pdffiles/PUB408.pdf (accessed March 8, 2011); Hillel Frisch, "Motivation or Capabilities? Israeli Counterterrorism against Palestinian Suicide Bombings and Violence," *Journal of Strategic Studies* 29, no. 5 (2006): 843–69.

13. Crenshaw, "Explaining Suicide Terrorism," 134.

14. Andrew Silke, "An Introduction to Terrorism Research," in *Research into Terrorism: Trends, Achievements and Failures*, ed. Andrew Silke (London: Routledge, 2004), 1–29.

15. Jarvis, "The Spaces and Faces of Critical Terrorism Studies," 14.

16. Claudia Brunner, "Occidentalism Meets the Female Suicide Bomber: A Critical Reflection on Recent Terrorism Debates: A Review Essay," *Signs* 32, no. 4 (2007): 957–72; Claudia Brunner, "Discourse—Occidentalism—Intersectionality: Approaching Knowledge on Suicide Bombing," *Political Perspectives* 1, no. 2 (2007): 1–25.

17. Hafez, "Rationality, Culture, and Structure in the Making of Suicide Bombers";

Paul Gill, "A Multi-Dimensional Approach to Suicide Bombing," *International Journal of Conflict and Violence* 1, no. 2 (2007): 142–59.

18. Cynthia Enloe, *Bananas, Beaches and Bases: Making Feminist Sense of International Politics* (Berkeley: University of California Press, 1989); Rose Weitz, "Women and Their Hair: Seeking Power through Resistance and Accommodation," *Gender and Society* 15, no. 5 (2001): 667–86; Arlene Elowe MacLeod, "Hegemonic Relations and Gender Resistance: The New Veiling as Accommodating Protest in Cairo," *Signs* 17, no. 3 (2001): 533–57; Lila Abu-Lughod, "The Romance of Resistance: Tracing Transformations of Power through Bedouin Women," *American Ethnologist* 17, no. 1 (1990): 41–55.

19. Michael F. Brown, "On Resisting Resistance," *American Anthropologist* 98, no. 4 (1996): 729–35.

20. Abu-Lughod, "The Romance of Resistance," 42.

21. Weitz, "Women and Their Hair," 669.

22. Brown, "On Resisting Resistance," 729.

23. Christine Sylvester, "The Contributions of Feminist Theory to International Relations," in *International Theory: Positivism and Beyond*, ed. Steve Smith, Ken Booth, and Marysia Zalewski (Cambridge: Cambridge University Press, 1996), 264.

24. Gayatri Chakravorty Spivak, "Can the Subaltern Speak?" in *Marxism and the Interpretation of Culture*, ed. Cary Nelson and Lawrence Grossberg (Urbana: University of Illinois Press, 1988), 271–313.

25. Talal Assad, *Formations of the Secular: Christianity, Islam, Modernity* (Stanford, Calif.: Stanford University Press, 2003), 79.

26. Catherine Eschle and Bice Maiguashca, "Rethinking Globalised Resistance: Feminist Activism and Critical Theorising in IR," *British Journal of Politics and International Relations* 9, no. 2 (2007): 286.

27. Nancy Fraser, *Justice Interruptus: Critical Reflections on the "Postsocialist" Condition* (New York: Routledge, 1997), 6, qtd. in Eschle and Maiguashca, "Rethinking Globalised Resistance," 296.

28. Nancy J. Hirschmann, "Freedom, Recognition and Obligation: A Feminist Approach to Political Theory," *American Political Science Review* 83, no. 4 (1989): 1227–44.

29. Peter Fleming and Graham Sewell, "Looking for the Good Soldier, Švejk: Alternative Modalities of Resistance in the Contemporary Workplace," *Sociology* 36, no. 4 (2002): 857–73.

30. Latin American Subaltern Studies Group, "Founding Statement," *boundary 2* 20, no. 3 (1993): 111.

31. Ranajit Guha, introduction, *Subaltern Studies: Writings on South Asian History and Society*, vol. 3, ed. Ranajit Guha (Delhi: Oxford University Press, 1984), vii. There is an irony here in using subaltern studies to examine female suicide terrorism, because subaltern studies has been criticized for a failure to incorporate gender into its analysis. See Rosalind O'Hanlon, "Recovering the Subject: Subaltern Studies and Histories of Resistance in Colonial South Asia," *Modern Asian Studies* 22 (1988): 189–224, and Karnala Visweswaran, "Small Speeches, Subaltern Gender: Nationalist Ideology and Its Historiography," in *Subaltern Studies: Writings on South Asian History and Society*, vol. 9, ed. Shahid Amin and Dipesh Chakrabarty (Delhi: Oxford University Press, 1996), 83–125; Florencia E. Mallon, "The Promise and Dilemma of Subaltern Studies: Perspectives from Latin American History," *American Historical Review* 99, no. 5 (1994): 1509. However, in his "Chandra's Death," Guha does attempt to bring gender into his analysis; in the end he concludes that neither traditional nor colonial laws necessarily grant women freedom, although women might find autonomy in the fissures between the two systems of rule (*Subaltern Studies: Writings on South Asian History and Society*, vol. 5, ed. Ranajit Guha [Delhi: Oxford University Press, 1987], 135–65).

32. O'Hanlon, "Recovering the Subject."

33. Eschle and Maiguashca, "Rethinking Globalised Resistance."

34. Ranajit Guha, "The Prose of Counter-Insurgency," in Ranajit Guha, ed., *Subaltern Studies: Writings on South Asian History and Society*, vol. 2 (Delhi: Oxford University Press, 1983), 40.

35. Shulamit Reinharz, *Feminist Methods in Social Research* (Oxford: Oxford University Press, 1992), 248.

36. Hirschmann, "Freedom, Recognition and Obligation."

37. Cynthia Enloe, "Margins, Silences and Bottom Rungs: How to Overcome the Underestimation of Power in International Relations," in *International Theory*, 188.

38. Dipesh Chakrabarty, "Subaltern Studies and Postcolonial Historiography," *Nepantla: Views from South* 1, no. 1 (2000): 17.

39. Catherine MacKinnon, *Toward a Feminist Theory of the State* (Cambridge, Mass.: Harvard University Press, 1989), 114.

40. V. Spike Peterson and Anne Sisson Runyan, *Global Gender Issues* (Boulder, Colo.: Westview Press, 1999), 21.

41. Laura Sjoberg, "Introduction to Security Studies: Feminist Contributions," *Security Studies* 18, no. 2 (2009): 201.

42. Jarvis, "The Spaces and Faces of Critical Terrorism Studies," 15.

43. Chicago Project on Security and Terrorism, http://cpost.uchicago.edu/search _results.php.

44. Cristina Masters, "Femina Sacra: The 'War on/of Terror,' Women and the Feminine," *Security Dialogue* 4, no. 1: 29–49. See also "The Taguba Report" (www.npr .org/iraq/2004/prison_abuse_report.pdf). However an enquiry into the alleged rape and torture of women has been dropped (Suzanne Goldenberg, "U.S. Soldiers Accused of Sex Assaults," *Guardian*, May 8, 2005, http://www.guardian.co.uk/world/2005/mar/08 /iraq.suzannegoldenberg [accessed April 2, 2010]).

45. Jane Hoppen, "Women in the Military: Who's Got Your Back?" *Off Our Backs: The Feminist News Journal* 36, no. 2 (2006): 14–16, http://www.offourbacks.org /WomMilBack.htm (accessed April 2, 2010).

46. Huntington, "The Clash of Civilizations?"; Richard Jackson, "Constructing Enemies: Islamic Terrorism in Political and Academic Discourse," *Government and Opposition* 42, no. 3 (2007), 394–426; Katherine Brown, "Contesting the Securitization of British Muslims: Citizenship and Resistance," *Interventions: International Journal of Post-Colonial Studies* 12, no. 2 (2010): 171–82.

47. Liz Fekete, "Anti-Muslim Racism and the European Security State" *Race and Class* 46, no. 1 (2004): 3–29; Annelies Moors and Birgit Meyer, *Religion, Media, and the Public Sphere* (Bloomington: Indiana University Press, 2006), 5.

48. Masters, "Femina Sacra," 35.

49. David Campbell, *Writing Security: United States Foreign Policy and the Politics of Identity* (Minneapolis: University of Minnesota Press, 1998); Peter Van der Veer and Shoma Munshi, eds., *Media, War and Terrorism: Responses from the Middle East and Asia* (London: Routledge, 2003); Pnina Werbner, "Veiled Interventions in Pure Space," *Theory, Culture and Society* 24, no. 2 (2007): 161–86.

50. Brown, "Contesting the Securitisation of British Muslims," 174–76.

51. Fiona Adamson and Adam D. Grossman, "Framing 'Security' in a Post-9/11 Context," Social Science Research Council, Program on Global Security and Cooperation, 2004, http://programs.ssrc.org/gsc/publications/gsc_activities/migration /adamsongrossman.pdf (accessed February 2, 2009).

52. Laura Shepherd, "Victims, Perpetrators and Actors Revisited: Exploring the Potential for a Feminist Reconceptualisation of (International) Security and (Gender) Violence," *British Journal of Politics and International Relations* 9, no. 2 (2007): 239–56.

53. Helen M. Kinsella, "Securing the Civilian: Sex and Gender in the Laws of War," in *Power in Global Governance*, ed. Michael Barnett and Bud Duvall (Cambridge: Cambridge University Press, 2005), 249–72.

54. Laura Sjoberg and Caron Gentry, *Mothers, Monsters, and Whores: Women's Violence in Global Politics* (London: Zed, 2007), 1–27.

55. Ibid.

56. Speckhard, "Understanding Suicide Terrorism," 13–17; Bloom, *Dying to Kill*, 142–65.

57. Nira Yuval-Davis, *Gender and Nation* (London: Sage, 1997), 39–66.

58. Jackson, "Constructing Enemies," 412.

59. Farhana Ali, "Muslim Female Fighters: An Emerging Trend," *Terrorism Monitor* 21, no. 3 (2005): 9–11.

60. Leonard Weinberg and William L. Eubank, "Italian Women Terrorists," *Terrorism: An International Journal* 9, no. 3 (1987): 255.

61. "Three German Women Suspected of Plotting Suicide Attacks," *Agence France Press*, May 31, 2006, http://www.dawn.com/2006/05/31/rss.htm#27 (accessed March 28, 2010).

62. Stephen Castle, "Girl Next Door Who Became a Suicide Bomber," *Independent* December 2, 2005; Raf Casert, "Marriage Made a Radical of Belgian," *Washington Post*, December 2, 2005.

63. "Vice President Cheney Makes Case for War in Iraq; Saddam Hussein Trial; The Rise of Women Terrorists," CNN, December 6, 2005 (transcript 120601CN.V 10).

64. Bloom, "Female Suicide Bombers," 8.

65. This was further confirmed in later reporting on the trial of six men who are alleged to have been her "handlers" (Claire Soares, "Gangs Accused of Recruiting Europe's First Female Suicide Bomber Go on Trial," *Independent*, October 16, 2007, http://www.independent.co.uk/news/world/europe/gang-accused-of-recruiting-europes-first-female-suicide-bomber-go-on-trial-396974.html [accessed March 27, 2010]).

66. Gyan Prakash, "Writing Post-Orientalist Histories of the Third World: Perspectives from Indian Historiography," *Comparative Studies in Society and History* 32, no. 2 (1990), 383–408.

67. Hirschmann, "Freedom, Recognition and Obligation," 1229–32.

68. Jarvis, "The Spaces and Faces of Critical Terrorism Studies," 18–21.

69. Ibid., 21.

70. Sherry B. Ortner, "Resistance and the Problem of Ethnographic Refusal," *Comparative Studies in Society and History* 37, no. 1 (1995): 190.

71. Sjoberg "Introduction to Security Studies: Feminist Contributions," 9.

72. Evelyn Hammond, "Toward a Genealogy of Black Female Sexuality," in *Feminist Genealogies, Colonial Legacies, Democratic Futures*, ed. M. Jaquie Alexander and Chandra Talpade Mohanty (London: Routledge, 1997), 179.

73. Ortner, "Resistance and the Problem of Ethnographic Refusal," 176–77.

74. Guha, "The Prose of Counter-Insurgency," 45–47.

75. Eric J. Hobsbawm, *Primitive Rebels: Studies in Archaic Forms of Social Movement in the Nineteenth and Twentieth Centuries* (Manchester, UK: Manchester University Press, 1978), 2.

76. Ibid.

77. Chakrabarty, "Subaltern Studies and Postcolonial Historiography," 17.

78. Silke, "Cheshire-Cat Logic"; Andrew Silke, "Holy Warriors: Exploring the Psychological Processes of Jihadi Radicalization," *European Journal of Criminology* 5, no. 1 (2008): 99–123.

79. Charles L. Ruby, "The Definition of Terrorism," *Analysis of Social Issues and Public Policy* 2, no. 1 (2002): 15–26.

80. Silke, "Cheshire-Cat Logic"; Jeff Victoroff, "The Mind of the Terrorist," *Journal of Conflict Resolution* 49, no. 1 (2005): 3–42.

81. Yoram Schweitzer, "Palestinian Female Suicide Bombers: Reality vs. Myth," in *Female Suicide Bombers: Dying for Equality?*, ed. Yoram Schweitzer (Jerusalem: Jaffee Centre for Strategic Studies, 2006), 25–41, http://www.gees.org/documentos/Documen-01398.pdf (accessed March 23, 2010).

82. Andrew Silke, "The Role of Suicide in Politics, Conflict and Terrorism," *Terrorism and Political Violence* 18, no. 1 (2006): 36.

83. Ibid., 44–45.

84. Ruby, "The Definition of Terrorism"; Mark Jurgensmeyer, *Terror in the Mind of God: The Global Rise of Religious Violence* (Berkeley: University of California Press, 2003).

85. Jackson, "Constructing Enemies," 405.

86. Her Majesty's Cabinet Office, *Building on Progress*, March 2007, http://webarchive.nationalarchives.gov.uk/20091112165722/http://archive.cabinetoffice.gov.uk/policy_review/documents/building_on_progress.pdf (accessed March 8, 2011), 8.

87. Edward Said, *Orientalism* (London: Penguin, 1988), 47.

88. Dag Tuastad, "Neo-Orientalism and the New Barbarism Thesis: Aspects of Symbolic Violence in the Middle East Conflict(s)," *Third World Quarterly* 24, no. 4 (2003): 595.

89. Brunner, "Discourse—Occidentalism—Intersectionality," 18.

90. Quintan Wiktorowicz and Karl Kaltenthaler, "The Rationality of Radical Islam," *Political Science Quarterly* 121, no. 2 (2006): 295–319.

91. Pape, "The Strategic Logic of Suicide Terrorism," 2–5.

92. Alisa Stack, "Lions, Tigers, and Freedom Birds: How and Why the Liberation Tigers of Tamil Eelam Employs Women," *Terrorism and Political Violence* 19, no. 1 (2007): 43–63.

93. V. Spike Peterson, "Transgressing Boundaries: Theories of Knowledge, Gender and International Relations," *Millennium* 21, no. 2 (1992): 192.

94. Barbara Hudson, "Beyond White Man's Justice," *Theoretical Criminology* 10, no. 1 (2006): 33.

95. Sally Haslanger, "On Being Objective and Objectified," in *A Mind of One's Own:*

Feminist Articles in Reason and Objectivity, ed. Louis M. Anthony and Charlotte Witt (Boulder, Colo.: Westview Press, 2002), 209–53.

96. Brunner, "Occidentalism Meets the Female Suicide Bomber," 958, 969.

97. Hirschmann, "Freedom, Recognition, and Obligation," 1237.

98. Laura Sjoberg, "Agency, Militarized Femininity and Enemy Others: Observations from the War in Iraq," *International Feminist Journal of Politics*, 9, no. 1 (2007): 82–101.

99. Ibid.; Christine Sylvester, *Feminist International Relations: An Unfinished Journey* (Cambridge: Cambridge University Press, 2002).

100. Al-Bukhari, *Sahih* 3:264 (no. 2784); David Cook, "Women Fighting in Jihad?" *Studies in Conflict and Terrorism* 28, no. 5 (2005): 376.

101. Ibid., 375.

102. Dareen Abu Aisheh, however, is reported to have gone first to HAMAS to volunteer but was apparently turned down (*Jerusalem Post*, March 1, 2002).

103. "Bin Laden Has Set up Female Suicide Squads: Report," *Arab News*, March 13, 2003, qtd. in Bloom, "Female Suicide Bombers: A Global Trend," 5.

104. Cynthia Enloe, *The Morning After: Sexual Politics at the End of the Cold War* (Berkeley: University of California Press, 1993), 202.

105. Muhammad Khayr Haykal, *al-Jihad wa-l-qital fi al-siyasa al-shara'iyya* (Beirut: Dar al-Barayiq, 1993), 2:995–97.

106. Yousef al-'Ayyiri, qtd. in Cook, "Women Fighting in Jihad?" 380; Yusuf al-Qaradawi, qtd. in Middle East Media Research Institute, "Islamic Clerics Explain the Rationale," *MEMRI Inquiry and Analysis*, no. 82, February 7, 2002, http://www.memri.org/report/en/0/0/0/0/0/0/605.htm (accessed March 9, 2011); Middle East Media Research Institute, "Wafa Idris: The Celebration of the First Female Palestinian Suicide Bomber," *MEMRI Inquiry and Analysis*, nos. 83–84, pts. 1–2, February 12–13, 2002, http://www.memri.org/report/en/0/0/0/0/0/0/610.htm (accessed March 23, 2010).

107. Wiktorowicz and Kaltenthaler, "The Rationality of Radical Islam," 295.

108. Florencia E. Mallon, "The Promise and Dilemma of Subaltern Studies: Perspectives from Latin American History," *American Historical Review* 99, no. 5 (1994): 1543.

109. Ibid.

110. Clifford Geertz, *After the Fact: Two Countries, Four Decades, One Anthropologist* (Cambridge, Mass.: Harvard University Press, 1996), 43.

111. Sherry B. Ortner, "Thick Resistance: Death and the Cultural Construction of Agency in Himalayan Mountaineering," *Representations* 59 (1997): 135–62.

112. Jean Comaroff, *Body of Power, Spirit of Resistance* (Chicago: University of Chicago Press, 1985), 196.

113. Ranajit Guha, *Elementary Aspects of Peasant Insurgency in Colonial India* (Delhi: Oxford University Press, 1983), 75.

114. Eschle and Maiguashca, "Rethinking Globalised Resistance," 286–88, 297–98.

115. Brunner, "Occidentalism Meets the Female Suicide Bomber," 970.

116. Rosalind O'Hanlon, "Recovering the Subject: Subaltern Studies and Histories of Resistance in Colonial South Asia," *Modern Asian Studies* 22, no. 1 (1988): 189.

117. Edward Said, "Orientalism Reconsidered," *Race and Class* 27, no. 1 (1985): 1–15.

118. Brunner, "Occidentalism Meets the Female Suicide Bomber," 968–70.

119. Sjoberg and Gentry, *Mothers, Monsters, and Whores*, 30.

120. Avi Issacharoff, "The Palestinian and Israeli Media on Female Suicide Terrorists," in *Female Suicide Bombers*, 43–50.

121. Rhiannon Talbot, "Myths in the Representation of Women Terrorists," *Eire-Ireland* 35, no. 3 (2000): 165–86.

122. Ibid., 165.

123. Karen Jacques and Paul J. Taylor, "Male and Female Suicide Bombers: Different Sexes, Different Reasons?" *Studies in Conflict and Terrorism* 31, no. 4 (2008): 304–26.

124. Barbara Victor, *Army of Roses* (London: Constable and Robinson, 2006); Bloom, *Dying to Kill*; Schweitzer, "Palestinian Female Suicide Bombers"; Adam Dolnik, "Critical Commentary on 'Who are the Palestinian Suicide Bombers?'" *Terrorism and Political Violence* 16, no. 4 (2004): 845–48.

125. Enloe, *Bananas, Beaches and Bases*; Jean Bethke Elshtain, *Public Man, Private Woman* (Princeton, N.J.: Princeton University Press, 1993); J. Ann Tickner, *Gendering World Politics* (New York: Columbia University Press, 2001).

126. Talbot, "Myths in the Representation of Women Terrorists"; Jill Steans, *Gender and International Relations* (London: Polity, 2006); Sjoberg and Gentry, *Mothers, Monsters, Whores*.

127. Here I draw on Michael Kimmel's work on masculinity in terrorist movements. He argues that groups deploy masculinity as an ideological resource for the following reasons: "(1) to understand and explicate their plight; (2) as a rhetorical device to problematize the identities of those against whom they believe themselves fighting, and (3) as a recruitment device" ("Globalisation and Its Mal(e)contents: The Gendered Moral and Political Economy of Terrorism," *International Sociology* 18, no. 3 [2003]: 605).

128. Ibrahim Nafi', qtd. in Middle East Media Research Institute, "Wafa Idris," pt. 2.

129. Samiya Sa'ad al-Din, qtd. in Middle East Media Research Institute, "Wafa Idris," pt. 2, http://www.memri.org/report/en/0/0/0/0/0/0/610.htm.

130. Peter Bergen and Paul Cruikshank, "Lady Killer: Terrorism Is No Longer a

Male-Only Preserve," Center on Law and Security, New York University, 2006, http://www.lawandsecurity.org/get_article/?id=54 (accessed March 22, 2010).

131. Qtd. in Bergen and Cruikshank, "Lady Killer."

132. Adel Sadeq, hadith al-Medina, February 5, 2002, qtd. in *al-Quds al-Arabi*, February 6, 2002.

133. Middle East Media Research Institute, "Al-Qaʻida Women's Magazine: Women Must Participate in Jihad," MEMRI South Asia Studies Project special dispatch no. 779, September 7, 2004, http://memri.org/bin/articles.cgi?Page=subjects&Area=jihad&ID=SP77904 (accessed March 25, 2010). See also http://www.al-ghoul.com/al_khansa.htm.

134. Salman Rushdie, "The Empire Writes Back with a Vengeance," *(London) Times*, July 3, 1982, 8.

135. Brunner, "Occidentalism Meets the Female Suicide Bomber," 968.

136. Joyce McCarl Nielsen, ed., *Feminist Research Methods: Exemplary Readings in the Social Sciences* (Boulder, Colo.: Westview Press, 1990), 26; J. Ann Tickner "What Is Your Research Program? Some Feminist Answers to International Relations Methodological Questions," *International Studies Quarterly* 49, no. 1(2005): 1–22.

> Two women blew themselves up in the Moscow metro last month, killing 40 and injuring dozens more. . . . Both bombs could have been set off by a mobile phone. There have been cases where women were forced to be part of the operation or groomed for it.
> — *Russia Now*, April 29, 2010

Conclusion

THE STUDY OF WOMEN, GENDER, AND TERRORISM

Laura Sjoberg

This is just one of several stories about women engaged in terrorism that strongly imply that women are incapable of participating in terrorist attacks and draw a distinction between femininity and violence. The chapters in this book recount similar understandings of women involved in terrorism and insurgency across different times, cultures, and contexts. They provide more complicated accounts of women, gender, and terrorism.

This book shows that it is important to look at both women's participation in terrorist organizations and those organizations more generally through gendered lenses. This chapter draws out a number of crucial themes across the diverse chapters in this volume, particularly as they have implications both for the study of women's participation in terrorism and for the study of terrorism (and even global security) generally. It focuses on three such themes: questions of gender and agency in global politics, explorations of the interdependence of gender and discursive representations of terrorism, and potentially productive directions for theorizing terrorism and counterterrorism in gender-inclusive and gender-sensitive ways. If, as the chapters in this book have demonstrated, it is no longer possible to ignore women as participants in the study of terrorism, this conclusion suggests ways forward into exploring those connections based on the empirical and theoretical work of the volume's contributors.

SEEING WOMEN AND GENDER IN TERRORISM

While women's terrorism is as old as terrorism itself, women's participation in terrorism generally might be increasing, and women's engagement in suicide bombings has gone from virtually unheard of twenty years ago to somewhat commonplace in the current global political arena. And not only has women's involvement grown but it has become more visible in media coverage and scholarly work.

Still, the continued discursive power of gender stereotypes means that the very idea that "women" may be violent seems outlandish, despite the empirical reality. Though women have entered into many political and economic positions previously reserved exclusively for men, expectations associated with femininity remain seriously constraining not only on what women can do but also on how women's actions are interpreted by scholars and policy makers. A woman who engages in terrorism violates stereotypical expectations of women, and many analyses of women terrorists are perplexed by this apparent contradiction. The chapters in this book have dealt with the complexities of women's inclusion in terrorist organizations and the multiple dimensions of gender equality that attend that inclusion.

While there are few experts in this area and even fewer empirical trends, the chapters in this book provide a unique combination of firsthand empirical research and theoretical evaluation. Farhana Qazi traces the history of female warriors in Islamic cultures, while Caron E. Gentry and Laura Sjoberg show that women's involvement in terrorism and insurgent violence has a long history outside the Islamic world as well.

Part 2 takes up women's involvement in contemporary conflicts. Alisa Stack addresses women's participation in the Chechen insurgency against Russia, noting that the salience of narratives about "black widows" and "zombies" in that conflict rests in gendered assumptions about women's intents, capabilities, and essential characteristics and that the "facts" about women involved in terrorism are much more nuanced than the stories that media reports about the Chechen insurgents would have readers believe. Swati Parashar observes gendered narratives in play in the conflict in Kashmir, as burqa-clad women are often denied agency. Parashar observes that women's participation does not fit the victim profile, however, and explains that, in reality, it is women's support and leadership on which the fortunes of the Kashmiri nationalist movement turn. Caron E. Gentry's chapter about Leila Khaled recounts Khaled's justifications for her actions in her own words, distinguishing Khaled's thoughtful political account of her involvement in the Palestinian resistance movement from stories that characterize her as weak, sexual but apolitical, or moved by purely personal motivations in her political decisions. Miranda Alison gives a similarly complex account of women's involvement in the Liberation Tamil Tigers of Eelam, a formally feminist organization in which a number of women participated in political and paramilitary planning and execution on behalf of a potential Tamil state. Alison shows the benefits of women's membership in the organization but also discusses the problems inherent in gendered characterizations of women insurgents, gender-based double standards in the organization, and tensions between nationalist and feminist aspirations.

Part 3 focuses on a particular organization that has been the subject of much discussion about gender and terrorism in recent years, al-Qaeda. Jennie Stone and Katherine Pattillo critically examine the organizational reasons al-Qaeda recruits women, as well as the number of different roles those women involved with the organization ultimately play. Caron E. Gentry identifies a neo-Orientalist subtext in Western coverage and discussion of women associated with al-Qaeda, noting that women insurgents and terrorists who threaten the West are often represented as (gendered) threats but that no attention is paid to the complexities of their lives or accounts of those women who are not seen as directly threatening to Western lives and/or in Western eyes. Katherine Brown argues that the gendered Orientalism in traditional accounts of women's suicide terrorism is not their only problem; they also have a narrow understanding of the subject and object of the study of (women's and all) terrorism. Deploying subaltern studies' ideas about resistance, Brown presents ideas about experience and agency that characterize women in al-Qaeda not as manipulated pawns but as actors in complex relations.

Individually, these chapters impart a great deal of information about women's participation in a number of conflicts and provide a number of different theoretical perspectives on this participation, all interested in one way or another in gender emancipation. In this regard, a clear lesson in these chapters is that gender equality is more than a matter of women being "added" as members of institutions; it is about changing the institutions such that standards of what it means to be "a man" or "a woman" do not dictate either participation or how it is received or interpreted.

AGENCY

The chapters of this book tell a much more complicated story about how women get involved in terrorist and insurgent movements than one finds in earlier work on women's terrorism. Caron E. Gentry shows that Leila Khaled's motivations for her involvement in the Popular Front for the Liberation of Palestine are largely political and that she has a clear vision of what's at stake in her actions, both for her and for the movement more generally. Miranda Alison's interviews demonstrate that women in the Liberation Tamil Tigers of Eelam participated for a variety of reasons, much like men in that organization, including their belief in the political ideology of the organization, economic and educational opportunity, personal safety, family connections, and ethnic identification, which serves to question the gendered personal/political divide. Swati Parashar notes that women in the Kashmiri militant movement characterize themselves as fighting for the rights conferred on them by Islam as well as on behalf of the greater cause of militant groups in the Kashmiri valley, referencing political and religious goals though clearly living lives impacted by the constant conflict.

Katherine Brown notes that sociopolitical context and individual lives are important in reevaluating both al-Qaeda's inclusion of women and women's decisions to be a part of the organization's structure and attacks. Alisa Stack demonstrates that Chechen women terrorists are at once framed as controlled by others and as the victims of Russian aggression, when, in reality, women participants in the resistance consistently frame their participation as a furtherance of their own person or political causes. Jennie Stone and Katherine Pattillo discuss al-Qaeda's recruitment of women but also note that women are recruiters, supporters, and participants in al-Qaeda.

Previous work has suggested both that it is necessary to reevaluate the (masculine-biased) status quo in the literature as to why (male and female) terrorists engage in terrorist action in reaction to the (belated) recognition that women are terrorists too. It will not to do leave static theories of why terrorists act in place, theories that start with the assumption that all terrorists are men and then add sex-specific ideas about why women engage in terrorist acts. Instead, evaluating women's terrorism invites us to rethink the partial, biased, and often oversimplified theorizations of what motivates terrorists to act and the degree of agency they have in their actions.

No longer can we rely on pure rationality theories of individual terrorism or theories that rely on Oedipal psychology, male sexual deprivation, or other ideas implicitly or explicitly sex-specific to men.[1] And no longer can we think of terrorist organizations as men's clubs, state-like strategic calculators, or a combination of apolitical and deranged nutcases. Yet there is a reason the characterizations of women terrorists as emotionally unstable, motivated purely by personal attachment or trauma, or enslaved and sexually depraved have largely not bled over into the "mainstream" literature explaining either individual (male) terrorism or the formation and tactics of terrorist groups. If it does not make sense to frame all (male) terrorists as rational, cold, strategic actors motivated only by religious or political goals, it also does not make sense to frame either women terrorists or all terrorists as irrational, emotional, disturbed actors motivated (if at all) by purely personal reasons.

Feminist work up until this point has suggested some possible directions for retheorizing agency in terrorism to reflect accurately what motivates individuals (both women and men) to engage in terrorism. One suggestion is to think about agency in global politics generally and terrorism specifically in terms of relational autonomy.[2]

If "autonomy" as traditionally used means complete independence in decision making and individual identity, feminists have suggested that it is unrepresentative of most humans' decision-making processes most of the time. Feminists have suggested that some obligations are imposed on some people (often women) without their consent or negotiation, and that their autonomy is therefore incomplete. Feminists have suggested, instead, that people do not stand independent of their relationships with each other and the power dynamics inherent in those relationships. Feminist scholars have framed autonomy as *relational*; they characterize people as having agency and independent identity but claim that the choices that people make are constrained by their relationships with others.

Many of the chapters in this book suggest that terrorists are relationally autonomous — that they make decisions but that they do so within the social, political, and economic constraints of their relationships with other people, states, and nations. Swati Parashar suggests that women militants in Kashmir affect and are affected by their social status and the political status of Kashmir. Caron E. Gentry notes that Leila Khaled's personal and political commitments have been interdependent with her career in the Popular Front for the Liberation of Palestine throughout its development. Farhana Qazi suggests that a complicated combination of history and culture weigh into women's decisions to be a part of terrorist organizations but that women still have choices to make both in terms of whether or not they will be involved and the level and type of their involvement. Miranda Alison suggests that women made decisions to join the Liberation Tamil Tigers of Eelam but that those decisions were influenced by a whole host of structural factors in Tamil society.

Some would argue that it is just women's decisions that are constrained and just women's autonomy that is relational. Feminist theorists, however, have argued that people are never entirely independent of social and political circumstance or relations with other people. Seeing terrorists as relationally autonomous means there is no simple or single explanation for each person's (or each woman's) decision to engage in terrorism but instead a complex set of factors that both constrain and influence people's decisions. People (men and women) maintain agency in (most if not all) political decisions, including politically violent ones.

Still, the realization that terrorists' agency and autonomy is relational is not in itself enough to reconceptualize thinking about why terrorists do what they do. A second feminist suggestion has been to refocus thinking about international relations generally to account for its actors (including terrorists) differently, particularly questioning the gendered tendency to divide the "personal" and "political" spheres in the subjects and objects of political decision making.

The personal/political divide is inherent in (gendered) traditional theories of terrorism and in many of the initial responses to women's involvement in terrorism. These accounts (with some variation) tell a story of the political realm as separable from and outside of personal life. As such, (male) terrorists are strategic actors and terrorism is a political phenomena. The woman terrorist is an internally contradictory idea: femininity belongs in the private sphere, so women's violence must be personal. Even if theories allow for the possibility that individual terrorists make violent (particularly martyrdom) choices based on complex psychological configurations that include "personal" reasons, terrorist organizations as a whole are characterized as politically motivated rational actors, immune from the influences of emotion.

In this understanding, the "private" sphere is different, mysterious, random, irrational, and largely irrelevant; it's the "public/political" sphere that is the location of theoretical interest. The personal motivations of terrorists are individual and apolitical — worth studying by psychologists but not by "us" political scientists, because the political sphere of government, religion, and war is delineable and separable from the private sphere.

Feminist theories in sociology, psychology, political science, international relations, and law have critiqued the idea that the personal and political are separable realms. They have argued that it makes the lives of people at the margins of global politics invisible to students of international relations. Feminists have also recognized that there are some rights that are hard to get recognized by governments because they have been dismissed as a part of the private sphere. The division between political and private is not value neutral; it prioritizes those things understood as political while marginalizing those things understood as personal.

Instead, feminists have argued that "to the extent that personal gender identities constitute a 'core' sense of 'self,' they fundamentally condition our self-esteem and psychological security."[3] In international relations, this means that "the personal is international and the international is personal."[4] Feminist theorizing has characterized the margins of global politics as important in their own right as well as essential to understanding what is going on at the center. Feminists have described the relationship between the personal and political as hybridized and complex rather than simple and independent. Gendered lenses see people as actors, and the system as a complex interlacing of multiple hierarchies with multiple relations, where "multi-locational perspectives on patriarchal forces ... to recognize that the public/private social and spatial constructions are, in certain senses, mobilized and reconfigured in this globalizing world."[5]

This interpretation suggests that there are both a broader range of actors in global politics than traditional theories suggest and that these actors are motivated not just by personal problems (women) or political goals (men) but a combination of both. The empirical work in the chapters of this book suggests that this interpretation reflects individuals' (including women's) experiences in terrorist organizations. The stories about women in the Chechen resistance movement, al-Qaeda, the Liberation Tamil Tigers of Eelam, the Weather Underground, the Shining Path, the Palestinian resistance movement, the Baader-Meinhof gang, and the Kashmiri militant movement all include accounts that suggest that both personal and political influences are at work in the decision to join insurgent and terrorist movements and to act as members of those organizations. In some sense, this is an intuitive understanding, since political actors are people with politics. On the other hand, gendered characterizations of terrorists have steered so far away from this understanding of terrorists and their decision making that it is an important theoretical contribution of the chapters in this book and other recent work on women terrorists. As Christine Sylvester and Swati Parashar have recently argued, "A new dramaturgy [of terrorism] is required, with new actors and new scripts that can bring fresh insights about political violence," particularly as relates to agency in terrorism.[6]

The chapters in this book suggest that a crucial component of retheorizing agency in terrorism is critical consideration of both the politics of marginality and the representations of those politics as they relate to terrorism. Such a consideration would draw on the insights of religious and cultural theory, as well as on critical, poststructuralist, and postcolonial international relations theorizing. Several chapters in this book use these theoretical tools to read not just women's terrorism but also representations of that terrorism. Caron E. Gentry's chapter uses postcolonial theorizing, particularly insights from Edward Said's work on Orientalism, to understand the differential news coverage and political attention given to different women involved in al-Qaeda's attacks. Katherine Brown's chapter uses the work of the subaltern studies project to evaluate the meaning of resistance in terrorism and insurgency, accounting for and acknowledging women's participation. Each of these approaches suggests positive directions for retheorizing agency in terrorism as complex, contingent, contextual, and relational.

A caveat about these retheorizations seems appropriate here—the chapters in this book do critically interrogate both the assumption that women do not have agency in their terrorism or relationships with terrorist/insurgent organizations and that women's motivations are (personal and) fundamentally different from men's. But that does not mean the chapters in this book (or its editors) take the potential "next" step and argue that gender is irrelevant to analyzing agency in terrorism or the causes and consequences of terrorism more generally. The remainder of this section addresses gender in terrorist agency and the remainder of this chapter addresses gender in and the gendering of terrorism and terrorism studies more generally.

Farhana Qazi explores the influence of gender dynamics on women's participation in Islamic militant organizations. Caron E. Gentry and I address the silent operation of gender in the Baader-Meinhof gang and controversies about gender dynamics and gender rights in the Weather Underground and the Shining Path. Alisa Stack discusses the importance of gender dynamics in the lives of Chechen women terrorist—both in the ways that they participate in terrorist activity and in the ways the Russian government receives, re-presents, and reacts to their participation. Swati Parashar talks about the importance of gendered representations of women-as-nation in the successes and failures of Kashmiri militant groups more generally. Leila Khaled and Caron E. Gentry's conversation visits the ways her life affected and was affected by gender stereotypes on several occasions. The Liberation Tamil Tigers of Eelam's complicated political understandings of gender and even more complicated internal gender dynamics show that gender, far from being irrelevant to explaining the organization, is a key part of its legitimation and perpetration discourses. Jennie Stone and Katherine Pattillo explain the ways that gender perceptions led al-Qaeda to include women and the ways that those same perceptions make women's perpetration of terrorism strategically efficient. Caron E. Gentry explains the importance of the intersection of gender stereotypes and national pride in the al-Qaeda's attacks on its Western enemies and their retaliation. Katherine Brown explains how gender is a key part of understanding resistance in terrorist organizations generally and by women specifically.

Each of these chapters suggest that, far from being irrelevant, gender is crucial to understanding agency in terrorism—women (and men) terrorists live in a gendered world. But sex itself is not an explanatory variable—women and men do not do terrorism differently based on their biological makeup. Instead, terrorists live in and terrorism occurs in gendered worlds. Because of this, feminists have suggested that terrorism itself is gendered.

THE DISCURSIVE INTERDEPENDENCE OF GENDER AND TERRORISM

The chapters in this book show that there is more to the question of the relation between gender and terrorism than just that (men and women) terrorists make their decisions in a gendered world. Terrorism and insurgency also take place in a gendered world and are themselves gendered. Women participate in terrorism, they are impacted by terrorism, they fight terrorism, and they are represented in discussions of terrorism—but all of that takes place in the context of the gendered nature of terrorism, counterterrorism, and the study and representation of terrorism and terrorists. Gender analysis is "neither just about women, nor about the addition of women to male-stream constructions" but "is about transforming ways of being and knowing."[7]

There are several dimensions of this gendering of terrorism evident in the chapters of this book. The two that I highlight here are the gendered nature of representations of and responses to terrorism and the gendered nature of what counts as "terror" as a product of the gendered nature of what counts as security.

If understandings of women's involvement in terrorism are gendered, so are perceptions of and relationships with people understood as terrorists. A number of the chapters in this book show that gender plays a key role in discussions of what a terrorist is, whether it is H. H. A Cooper's understanding of women terrorists as erotomaniacs (in chapter 3), media portrayals of Leila Khaled as a beauty queen and celebrity (in chapter 6), or gendered representations of women terrorists as silent and submissive (chapters 9 and 10). Women terrorists are represented often not only as without agency but as personal and political aberrations, as disturbed, as corrupting femininity, or in other gendered and gender-derogatory terms.

What counts as "terror" is itself a gendered problem. Often states do not count as terrorists even when they do the same things as nonstate actors. Terror is often represented as the product of the fears and problems of a small (often masculine) elite part of the population. Feminists have also argued that domestic violence is a means of inculcating fear so as to coerce compliance, a common definition of terrorism. The gender biases in the definition of terrorism can be traced to the gender biases in what counts as security in global politics. For example, gender-based analyses have questioned the unitary nature of "state" security by arguing that states often secure themselves by making their most vulnerable citizens insecure.

Inspired by the knowledge that secure states often are sources of insecurity for women, feminists suggest that terrorism is not limited to nonstate actors who threaten states; instead, that limited interpretation of terrorism betrays many of the same gender biases as traditional (limited) theorizations of security. If feminists see security broadly, in multidimensional and multilevel terms, and are critical of the patriarchal and exclusionary story of security as the purview of (masculine) states, then gender lenses might also see terrorism broadly as the inculcation of fear to coerce not only on the part of nonstate actors who threaten states but also on the part of state actors and nonstate actors who threaten people and other nonstate actors. The chapters in this book suggest that "terror" cannot be construed as a simple, unidirectional relationship in which "terrorist organizations" terrorize states and their civilians. Terrorism is also characterized by the use of tactics to breed fear in other arenas of global social and political life. If such an understanding were adopted on a wide scale, it might make terrorism studies both less gender biased and more intellectually coherent.

THEORIZING TERRORISM THROUGH GENDERED LENSES

Lessons about women and terrorism and the gendered nature of the theory and practice of terrorism like those offered in this book are just a start to the process of retheorizing terrorism. This book concludes by mentioning some potentially productive directions for theorizing contemporary terrorism through gendered lenses.

We have already been over some of those directions. Rethinking agency in terrorist decision making is one of them. Thinking about terrorism is a second. Rethinking who and what counts as a terrorist is a third. Finally, there is rethinking the theoretical frames we use to deal with terrorism.

A number of chapters in this book individually suggest important theoretical frames. Katherine Brown's chapter shows that focusing on theoretical blind spots by drawing on subaltern studies is a productive approach. Caron E. Gentry's chapter on al-Qaeda shows the benefit of postcolonial studies approaches, particularly the lens of Orientalism. Jennie Stone and Katherine Pattillo use strategic and tactical theorizing to think about al-Qaeda's use of women terrorists. Miranda Alison uses social movement theory to analyze women and gender in the Liberation Tamil Tigers of Eelam, while Swati Parashar theorizes women Kashmiri militants by focusing on power and Alisa Stack uses the lenses of propaganda and speech acts to analyze women's terrorism in Chechnya. Farhana Qazi shows the utility of analyzing culture and religion, and Caron E. Gentry and I critically interrogate psychological approaches to the study of terrorism.

Though these chapters add different elements to gendered lenses, they share those lenses as an overarching approach. It is important to see women in studying terrorism. But seeing women leads us to see gender, which inspires thinking differently about terrorism. Across chapters, this begins to construct, from the ground up, tools to theorize contemporary terrorism through gendered lenses. These tools include relationality (particularly interdependence and constraint) and empathy (especially the attempt to identify with those understood as other or opponent). Complexity and contingency (both in causes and consequences) of terrorism are important things to take account of in terrorist studies. Along with those, it is important to analyze partiality and intersubjectivity in looking at the subjects of terrorism, male or female. Studying terrorists and terrorism is about people, about organizations, and about states, but it is also about their interaction, intersubjectivity, and inseparability.

NOTES

1. Bradley A. Thayer and Valerie M. Hudson, "Sex and the Shaheed: Insights from the Life Sciences on Islamic Suicide Terrorism," *International Security* 34, no. 4 (2010): 37–62.

2. Nancy Hirschmann, "Freedom, Recognition, and Obligation: A Feminist Approach to Political Theory," *American Political Science Review* 83, no. 4 (1989): 1177–1244.

3. V. Spike Peterson, "Sexing Political Identities/Nationalism as Heterosexism," *International Feminist Journal of Politics* 1, no. 1 (1999): 37.

4. Cynthia Enloe, *Bananas, Beaches, and Bases: Making Feminist Sense of International Politics* (Berkeley: University of California Press, 1993), 145.

5. Joshua S. Goldstein, *War and Gender: How Gender Shapes the War System and Vice Versa* (Cambridge: Cambridge University Press, 2001), 53; Gillian Youngs, "Breaking Patriarchal Bonds: Demythologizing the Public/Private," in *Gender and Global Restructuring: Sightings, Sites, and Resistances,* ed. Marianne Marchand and Anne Sisson-Runyan (London: Routledge, 2000), 56.

6. Christine Sylvester and Swati Parashar, "The Contemporary 'Mahabarata' and the Many 'Draupadis': Bringing Gender to Critical Terrorism Studies," in *Critical Terrorism Studies: A New Research Agenda,* ed. Richard Jackson, Marie Breen Smyth, and Jeroen Gunning (New York: Taylor and Francis, 2009), 178–93.

7. V. Spike Peterson, "Transgressing Boundaries: Theories of Knowledge, Gender and International Relations," *Millennium* 21, no. 2 (1992): 205.

MIRANDA ALISON is associate professor of politics and international studies at the University of Warwick. She is author of *Women and Political Violence* (Routledge, 2008) as well as a number of book chapters and journal articles that gender security through an examination of women as agents in political violence. She is module director for ethnic conflict and political violence studies and qualitative research methods. She holds a BA and MA from Auckland University and a PhD from Queen's University in Belfast.

KATHERINE E. BROWN is a lecturer in political science in the Defence Studies Department at King's College, London. She holds a BA from the University of Lancaster and an MSc and PhD from the University of Southampton. Her research has focused on the role of British Muslim women in security politics/policies as well as Muslim women's participation in political violence. Her work has been published in a number of journals, including *Women's Studies International Forum*, the *British Journal of Politics and International Relations*, and the *European Journal of Cultural Studies*.

GRACE D. COOKE has worked as a writer and editor for a variety of news organizations and several defense and security businesses. She has a master's degree in global studies from the University of Denver's Korbel School of International Studies and a master's in diplomacy from the University of Birmingham in the United Kingdom. When she isn't writing you can find her in the Rocky Mountains of Colorado.

CARON E. GENTRY (BA, Mount Holyoke College; PhD, University of St. Andrews) is associate professor of political science at Abilene Christian University. Her research interests revolve around security studies with a focus on terrorism, specifically women engaged in political violence. In 2007, she coauthored with Laura Sjoberg *Mothers, Monsters, Whores: Women's Violence in Global Politics* (Zed Books). Her second book, *Offering Hospitality: Unraveling*

Hegemonic Christian Approaches to War, is slated to be published in 2011 by the University of Notre Dame Press. Additionally, she is coediting a volume with Amy Eckert entitled *Critical Perspectives on Just War* for the University of Georgia Press. Her future work will bring hospitality, ethics, and counterterrorism together.

STACY REITER NEAL is associate director of the Center for Emerging Market Enterprises (CEME) at the Fletcher School, Tufts University. Prior to joining CEME, she was associate director of external affairs at the Jebsen Center for Counter-Terrorism Studies, also at Tufts University. She holds a BA from Boston College, and an MA in law and diplomacy from the Fletcher School, where she was a senior editor of the *Fletcher Forum of World Affairs*. Neal's published research focuses on understanding cross-sector relationships as counterterrorism tools.

SWATI PARASHAR (PhD, Lancaster University) is lecturer in feminist international relations and development at the University of Limerick, Ireland. Her work focuses on gender, "terrorisms," conflicts, and development issues in South Asia. She is the editor of *Maritime Counter-Terrorism: A Pan Asian Perspective* (Pearson, 2007) and coeditor with Wilson John of *Terrorism in South Asia: Implications for South Asia* (Pearson, 2005). She is the author of "Feminist IR and Women Militants: Case Studies from South Asia" and "Women in Militant Movements: The (Un)comfortable Silences and Discursive Strategies" and coauthor with Christine Sylvester of "The Contemporary Mahabharata and the Many Draupadis: Bringing Gender to Critical Terrorism Studies."

KATHERINE PATTILLO is a former intelligence officer in the U.S. Navy and a recent graduate of the Fletcher School of Law and Diplomacy at Tufts University.

FARHANA QAZI (formerly Farhana Ali) is a senior fellow at the Center for Advanced Study on Terrorism, and a senior instructor for the AFPAK team at Booz Allen Hamilton. A graduate of the Security Policy Studies Program at George Washington University, her research has focused on women's activism in mass sociopolitical movements and terrorist networks. Qazi has worked as an international policy analyst with the RAND corporation and for the U.S. government. She regularly appears in diverse media outlets, including BBC, CNN, Al-Jazeera, Voice of America, and NPR.

LAURA SJOBERG (BA, University of Chicago; PhD, University of Southern California; JD Boston College) is an assistant professor of political science at the University of Florida and research fellow in the Women and Public Policy Program at the Kennedy School of Government at Harvard. Her work has been published in more than a dozen political science and international relations journals, and she is author of *Gender, Justice, and the Wars in Iraq* (Lexington, 2006) and with Caron Gentry of *Mothers, Monsters, Whores: Women's Violence in Global Politics* (Zed, 2007). She is editor or coeditor of numerous volumes. She is currently president of the International Studies Association–Northeast.

ALISA STACK is the foreign relations and defense policy manager of the Office of the Assistant Secretary of Defense, special operations/low intensity conflict, and interdependent capabilities. She holds an MS from the Naval War College, an MA in international affairs from Columbia University, and a BA from the University of Washington. Her research findings have been published in *Joint Force Quarterly* and *Terrorism and Political Violence*.

JENNIE STONE received an undergraduate degree from the College of the Holy Cross and a graduate degree from the Fletcher School of Law and Diplomacy at Tufts University. She is currently serving on active duty with the U.S. Navy in Southeast Asia.

CPSIA information can be obtained
at www.ICGtesting.com
Printed in the USA
LVHW030134301221
707525LV00005B/546